ALSO BY ROBERT TIMBERG

John McCain: An American Odyssey

The Nightingale's Song

State *of* Grace

A MEMOIR OF TWILIGHT TIME

Robert Timberg

FREE PRESS
New York   London   Toronto   Sydney

FREE PRESS
A Division of Simon & Schuster, Inc.
1230 Avenue of the Americas
New York, NY 10020

FREE PRESS and colophon are trademarks
of Simon & Schuster, Inc.

For information about special discounts for bulk purchases,
please contact Simon & Schuster Special Sales:
1-800-456-6798 or business@simonandschuster.com

Designed by ISPN Publishing

Manufactured in the United States of America

10   9   8   7   6   5   4   3   2   1

Library of Congress Control Number: 2004053264

ISBN 978-0-684-85562-2

To my sisters,

Pat and Rosemarie,

and my children and their spouses, Scott and Sara,

Craig and Ruey, Amanda and Matt,

and Sam

LYNVET'S SENIOR FOOBA
WINNER'S OF ANNUAL F
FATHER LAURENCE·E·LY

The Lynvets, 1959. Inset: Larry Kelly.

Contents

Maybe you limp a little at times and you don't look as pretty when you dance, but think of the good times you had. Think of the bars you closed.
Mike Ditka, 1990

Heavenly shades of night are falling
It's Twilight Time
The Platters, 1958

Introduction

*A*t the 69th Regiment Armory on 26th Street and Lexington Avenue, in a glass display case just off the lobby, sits a World War II infantryman's helmet. The helmet is intact except for a ragged tear on the right side, about where the temple would be. The card below explains that the helmet belonged to a Redemptorist priest killed in April 1945 while administering last rites to a soldier during the fighting on Okinawa, the final land battle of the war in the Pacific.

The priest was raised on Eldert Lane in City Line, a working-class section of Brooklyn that bumps up against Queens just north of Jamaica Bay. A dozen years later, the priest's gallantry would be extolled in a book by Daisy Amoury called *Father Cyclone*. On a smaller stage, he gained recognition sooner. Less than a year after his death, the local chapter of the Catholic War Veterans renamed itself the Reverend Lawrence E. Lynch Post.

In 1950, a group of boys from City Line barely into their teens, prodded by an unmarried appliance salesman for the Brooklyn Union Gas Company, decided to start a football team to play in a new sandlot league that had sprung up in Brooklyn and Queens. The team held its organizational meetings at the Lynch post, which occupied the second floor above a fruit-and-vegetable stand at Liberty Avenue and Eldert Lane, in the shadow of the Liberty Avenue El. At one of those early gatherings, the boys realized they needed a name for their team. They tried on a few. Crusaders and Knights were popular choices, but they were already overbooked. In fact, with the proliferation of teams, there were few good names left. Finally, someone with a better sense of place than most thought about where they were: a veterans' hall named for Father Lynch. "Let's call ourselves the Lynvets," he said. Some credit the name to Bob Lulley, the team's first quarterback, others to the baby-faced wide receiver Tommy McCabe. Whoever it was, he never suspected that he had just christened an organization that would become a living memorial to the fallen chaplain.

The Lynvets were winners from the start. By the late 1950s and early 1960s, the years on which this book focuses, they were at the top of their game—sure of themselves, unquestioning of their values, imbued with a relentless if shortsighted optimism.

Much like the nation itself. It was the twilight of innocence, or what passed for innocence if you didn't look too closely. America was at peace, looking confidently to the future, when it should have been holding its breath for what lay ahead.

I played for the Lynvets after graduating from high school in 1958 and before the adult world snatched me up two years later. Though it never occurred to me then, time was running out on the Lynvets as the Fifties drew to a close. The team was balanced on a knife edge and would in a few years time tumble into a future far less hospitable to the values they embodied—and to many of the teammates who left such a lasting imprint on me.

What I didn't sense, could never begin to contemplate, were the changes that would soon sweep the nation, making the Lynvets and the things they came to stand for in my mind—courage, toughness, unflinching patriotism, and an unremitting self-reliance—little more than loutish if exotic anachronisms to the generation that was about to reshape America.

Change was surely on the way, though few of the Lynvets heard it coming. Ultimately, that change would be so powerful that it would transform the nation almost as dramatically as did the Civil War a century earlier. It now seems clear that the strains within American society that converged with such fury in the mid-1960s started making themselves felt a decade earlier. And as the Fifties faded, the clues were there, if your lens was ground just right.

In February 1960, a sit-in at a lunch counter at an F. W. Woolworth store in Greensboro, North Carolina, set off a wave of similar demonstrations throughout the South as the nonviolent drive for civil rights gained fresh momentum. In May of that same year, the first birth control pill, Enovid, went on the market. In November, the youth movement, building since the advent of rock and roll early in the previous decade, surged into national politics as a telegenic Irish-Catholic senator was elected president, succeeding a World War II general two decades his senior. And in January 1961, Hibbing, Minnesota, native Robert Allen Zimmerman moved to New York and began singing his antiestablishment folk songs at Café Wha? and other Greenwich Village coffeehouses under the name Bob Dylan.

And there was more. Over the course of the year 1961, the new president, John Kennedy, quietly made decisions that moved the nation further down the path toward a distant war. Equally as important, a generation conceived in the flush of victory by men and women who had survived the rigors of the Great Depression and the travails of World War II was closing fast on the Lynvets. By the late 1960s, the baby boomers, at least many of the more affluent and better educated among them, had rewritten the social contract in ways that few of the Lynvets would ever decipher. Along the way, they hijacked the culture, employing it to celebrate themselves, to exalt their lifestyle, and to ridicule and otherwise diminish those who weren't them and didn't want to be.

My two years with the Lynvets, a trying and uncertain time in which off-the-field issues threatened to corrode whatever prospects I had, embedded in me values that helped define my future. Even today, looking back over a daunting expanse of years, I see that at critical moments in my life I have measured my actions against what I believed my fellow Lynvets would expect of me. My coach was an often-unemployed football genius named Larry Kelly, who I now realize was one of the most influential figures in my life. What would he think of how I handled this situation or that one? What about my teammates—Hughie Mulligan, crazy Peter Connor, Kenny Rudzewick, the great Ferriola? I feel heartened when I sense their approval, uneasy when the answer comes back, as it does all too frequently, We're not with you on this one, Bob.

In my mind, and in the minds of my teammates, Larry Kelly and the Lynvets have long since been interchangeable. But in that summer of 1958, when I arrived on the scene from alien territory, the Kew Gardens section of Queens, the entwined legend of coach and team was just beginning to build. By then, the Lynvets were fielding teams in all four divisions of the Pop Warner Football Conference. The year before, Kelly had helped coach the Lynvet Juniors to a second straight championship. Now he had taken over the Seniors, the organization's marquee team, but an underachieving one during the previous two seasons. The players ranged in age from eighteen to twenty-one, and everyone was out of high school, one way or another. Some were married. There were a handful of guys like me going to local colleges—Hofstra, St. John's, Queens College, Fordham, Manhattan—but we were the exception. Most had already joined the workforce in a variety of jobs much like those held by their fathers—construction workers, city employees, laborers at nearby Idlewild Airport. Several worked for the Fire Department, or soon would. There were perceptible variations in educational level, economic strata, sophistication, professional promise. What we shared, and this transcended all the differences,

Glenn's baseball

was an unadulterated love of the game. That and a desire to be the best so fierce that it must have been tied to something deeper, more complex, perhaps the sense that our youth was slipping away and soon we would be like most of our older friends—good guys, nothing special.

Over the next four years, the Lynvet senior team was indeed special, piling up victories at a staggering rate. Like the New York Yankees in major league baseball, the Lynvets became the team to beat in sandlot football. Opponents could dream of winning a championship, but even in their dreams they knew they would have to take down the Lynvets first. Larry Kelly was the brains of the team, the center of gravity, a great coach and a complicated man. For three of those four years, he was blessed with a gifted quarterback in Bob Ferriola—tall, elegant, a commanding presence in the huddle, his passes impossibly tight spirals that defied you to drop them. Add to Ferriola a corps of racehorse running backs led by the graceful Marine Tommy Vaughan and a sweet-natured kid named Joe Aragona who lived in Rego Park with his older sister and widowed mother. In that fourth year, because of the league's age limit, Kelly had to turn to others, among them the talented but troubled Tommy Wall and an angry kid not long removed from an Army stockade, Mike Montore. But the heart and soul of those teams were blue-collar players like Peter Connor, the Faulkner brothers, Chipper Dombo, Jackie Meyer, and Kenny Rudzewick. Rudzewick was the oddball in the group, the normal one. A bank teller during the day, a college student at night, a fiery defensive tackle in his off-hours, he would become the president of a bank and a pillar of society in the years ahead. The others led lives in varying degrees of disarray. Together, though, they played with such intensity and abandon that at times their own teammates feared being on the same field with them.

I will recount their tales in this book, and also my own, not because any of us are particularly special but because we shared the same transforming experience with a special team, one that flew below radar in the outback of the world's most cosmopolitan city. I also hope to pay homage to a time, for me and the nation, when the path to an honorable future seemed as straightforward as playing hard, hitting clean, and not fumbling the ball.

The Lynvets of those days were not without blemish. Heavy drinking, at team parties but not only then, would in the years ahead diminish more than a few in ways no opponent ever could. Petty thievery was rare, but not unknown. The Lynvets, after all, were educated on the same streets that schooled John Gotti and his crew of mobsters-in-waiting. Many more were stunted by limited ambitions, often arising from the near poverty of their youth, that would cripple their promise as they entered full-fledged adulthood.

In the end, though, their transgressions were small ones. Today, as a nation unsure of its identity finds itself struggling into a new century, the virtues that the Lynvets embodied shine that much more brightly. And the years during which they ruled football on the sandlots of Queens and Brooklyn seem frozen in time— nothing less than that condition of fragile innocence between confession and the next big sin known to the faithful as a state of grace.

1

The Lynvets

On a mild December day in 1959, Tommy Wall was leading the Woodside Chiefs to a lopsided victory over St. Vincent's Home for Boys, a team from an orphanage in Brooklyn. At five foot eight, 155 pounds, Tommy was small for a quarterback, but he was quick and smooth, a sure if not spectacular passer. More to the point, he took charge. The Chiefs always fielded a talented team in the Pop Warner league's Junior Division, which consisted mostly of high school kids from the many city schools that did not have football, but they had a reputation as undisciplined and poorly coached. Tommy, at seventeen a tough Irish kid out of Woodside's coldwater Mathews Flats, not only knew the game but kept his rowdy teammates in line. He was slick, too. On one play, he faked to his fullback as he dove into the line, faked a second time to a flanker coming around behind him, dropped the ball to his hip, and drifted untouched into the end zone. The officials lost the ball, clustered over a pile of St. Vincent's players who had tackled the flanker. "Yo, ref, over here," shouted Tommy, holding the pigskin aloft.

Near the end of the game a guy named Sal DiFiglia, whom

Wall knew from sandlot football circles, stopped by the bench. "Tommy Wall," said DiFiglia, his tone laughingly formal, "Larry Kelly, the head coach of the Lynvet Seniors, is up in the stands. He'd like to see you after the game." Typical of Kelly to send a messenger rather than coming down himself, Tommy later thought.

But not then. At the moment DiFiglia delivered Kelly's summons, Tommy felt a stab of excitement. The game over, Sal hurried him, still in uniform, into the stands. His cleats clattering on the cement steps, Wall saw Kelly in a maroon Lynvet parka at the center of a clump of Lynvet players he knew, if only by reputation: Chipper Dombo. Tommy Vaughan. The one everyone said was nuts, Peter Connor.

Kelly was younger than Wall expected, twenty-five at the most, and more Ivy League in dress and demeanor than seemed plausible for someone with roots in City Line. Wall noticed that Kelly wore white bucks. In Woodside, Tommy reflected, only fags wore white bucks, fag being his all-purpose word for anyone who went to school regularly, stayed out of the bars, or lived in a detached single-family house. Kelly greeted Tommy cordially, if not effusively, congratulating him on a nice game. Then, with studied nonchalance, Kelly said, "We'd like you to come out for the Lynvet Seniors next year. Bring Ted Horoshak and John McCann and Buster Fiore and anybody else on your team you think can play for us."

Wall, whose mind was as nimble as his personal life was chaotic, quickly processed Kelly's words. During the course of that one game Kelly had singled out the three best players on the Chiefs other than Tommy himself. That was part of Kelly's growing reputation, an unerring eye for talent. Most important, Kelly—facing the loss of his All-League quarterback—was at the game primarily to scout him, Tommy Wall. Kelly asked him for his address and phone number, said he'd be in touch, then, as Tommy recalled it, "basically dismissed me," as if he were a kid who had been called to the principal's office.

In the years to come, Kelly's occasionally off-putting manner would strike Tommy as curious, as if the coach felt compelled to discourage familiarity between himself and his players, at least those who weren't his close drinking buddies. After all, this wasn't the big time, not college, not the pros. This was sandlot football, for Christ's sake. But as Tommy thought more about the day he met Kelly, he realized that it had been a big deal. That day, sure, but in the years that followed, too. Larry Kelly and the Lynvets wanted him. Yes, a very big deal. It would be too strong to say that Tommy Wall, during that brief conversation in the stands, felt touched by God. But it was close.

It didn't feel anything like that to me when I decided to go out for the Lynvets the previous year. I was just a month out of high school that summer of 1958 when I saw a small announcement in the sports section of the *Long Island Daily Press*, which was not exactly the *New York Times* but covered the smaller movements of ordinary lives like mine in Queens, a world away from the glamour of the city, which meant Manhattan. The notice said the Lynvet Seniors, whoever they were, would be holding tryouts the following Saturday at some place called Cross Bay Oval, wherever that was. I was preparing to enter St. John's University, a few miles from where I lived in Kew Gardens, but St. John's did not have a football team and I wanted to play football—it didn't much matter where. I called the number in the paper, spoke briefly to somebody named Larry Kelly, telling him who I was and of my experience as a running back at Stuyvesant High School.

"Come down to practice—we'll see what you can do. Bring your equipment," said Kelly, his tone maddeningly neutral.

True, I hadn't actually played my senior year at Stuyvesant, but I had been slated to be a starting halfback and, after a season-ending injury, had been replaced by a kid who was probably going to make All-City that fall. See what I can do? A sandlot team was going to see what I could do? How about, "Great, glad you called, anything we can do for you, need a ride to practice?"

Bruised pride and all, I went to practice. Cross Bay Oval turned out to be in Woodhaven, which was accessible from the apartment building in Kew Gardens where I lived with my mother and two younger sisters only by catching the bus at Union Turnpike and

Queens Boulevard, then transferring twice, about an hour trip—
assuming you didn't have a car, which we didn't. If you had a car,
something that practically no one I knew had, Cross Bay Oval was
fifteen minutes away.

Riding the bus to the field, I wondered what I was getting into.
Two years of high school football, though injury-plagued, had
given me a sense of how a good football team should practice and
play. I worried that I was about to throw in with a bunch of guys
with guts hanging over their belts who played something that
barely resembled the game that Murl Thrush, the Stuyvesant
coach, had taught us. Yes, I wanted to play football, but I didn't
want to screw around. I decided before I made it to the field that if
the Lynvets fell short of my expectations, which were not all that
high, but high enough, I would look for another team.

I found the field, was surprised to see players already in uniform. I located Kelly and introduced myself. He was friendly, if
reserved. "Get dressed," he said, pointing to a bar called McLaughlin's across the eight lanes of traffic on Cross Bay Boulevard. "We're
gonna get started in about ten minutes." The bartender was deep in
conversation with a handful of Saturday-morning customers as I
walked in. He looked up and gestured toward the back stairs,
which led to a musty basement room complete with an out-
of-order jukebox and scarred linoleum flooring, presumably the
Lynvet locker room. Grumpily I changed into my pads and uniform and jogged back to the field, dodging the southbound traffic
streaming toward the Rockaway beaches. Kelly had already gathered the team together.

"The latecomer is Bob Timberg," he said. "He goes to St.
John's. He played at Stuyvesant. Sort of. He wants to be a Lynvet.
He didn't know that when we call practice for ten, we mean suited
up by ten. Now he knows."

I glanced around, saw two dozen pairs of eyes looking me over,
all friendly enough, none obviously impressed. Also a few grins. At
the time, I thought my prospective teammates had detected my
consternation and were privately enjoying it. I would soon learn

that the grins were nothing more than recognition that I was getting my first taste of Larry Kelly and Lynvet football.

As we broke up into backs and linemen, a swarthy, smiling kid a little bigger than me came over, stuck his hand out, and said, "Hey, I'm Joe Aragona. You went to Stuyvesant? That's some school—you must be one smart guy. And you're going to St. John's? Wow!"

To me, St. John's didn't exactly rate a "wow," not in those days anyway, but I agreed that, yes, those things were true.

"And you played ball at Stuyvesant? Wow! Did you start?"

Reluctant to explain my checkered history as a high school player, I mumbled something that seemed to meet Joe's need for an answer. By then, he was on to something else, about how the Lynvets were really lucky to have me and how he was a halfback, too, but he had just moved up from the Junior team and probably wouldn't play all that much this season because the team was loaded with running backs, but he had played for Kelly the year before and he was a terrific coach and I was going to love playing for the Lynvets.

As Joe prattled on—that first day he rarely took a breath and talked in transitions—I looked over the field. Cross Bay Oval was not an oval at all, but a pie-shaped public athletic field surrounded by a ten-foot-high chain-link fence at the intersection of Cross Bay Boulevard and North Conduit Avenue, the service road for the Belt Parkway. Howard Beach was just across the parkway, Idlewild Airport, gateway to exotic worlds, about two miles away.

Kelly, I quickly found out, was a no-nonsense coach. Practice was crisp, businesslike, and demanding. There was very little standing around, but several of my presumptive teammates took time to wander over and introduce themselves. I met others, thanks to Joe Aragona, who squired me from group to group between drills. "Kenny, Kenny, meet Bob Timberg, he played for Stuyvesant." Other than Joe, no one seemed to care about my credentials, but each made me feel welcome. More than one used the phrase, "Kelly's a ballbuster," but with an odd twist, as if to say, don't take the coach's comments at the beginning of practice seriously, but take Kelly seriously.

Within half an hour, I knew the Lynvets were the team I was looking for. In an hour, I was marveling at my good fortune at having idly plucked Larry Kelly's phone number out of the paper. I knew nothing about my teammates, but I felt good being with them. Whatever else they might be, they came across as guys who loved the game as much as I did. More than that, they carried themselves like winners. Many of them were. Joe Aragona was just one of a half dozen players who had moved up from the previous year's Lynvet Junior team that Kelly had helped coach to the Pop Warner championship. Joe himself—though it was not at all evident from his earnest, self-deprecating demeanor—had been named the league's Outstanding Back. Bob Ferriola, the quarterback, had been the junior league's MVP two years before, though I gathered that something had not gone well last year, his first as a member of the Senior team. Kenny Rudzewick, a big, blond, sunny defensive tackle, had never played on a championship team in his two years with the Lynvet Seniors, but he had winner written all over him. By the time practice ended that day, I could tell I had stumbled onto something out of the ordinary.

I knew nothing of Lynvet tradition that first day. But as we drilled and scrimmaged, I knew that the Lynvets would not be a flabby, ragtag bunch of football frauds who would swill beer on the sidelines and disgrace themselves on the field. I did well in the scrimmage, breaking loose a couple of times, but I noticed the precision of the blocks that cleared the way for me and the sureness of the tackles that brought me down. These were not my Stuyvesant teammates, who almost to a man were heading for elite colleges and universities all across the country. But the Lynvets were at least as tough and easily as skilled. My first impression, which was accurate, was that many of them were the kind of kids who had dominated the schoolyard or the street corner in the days before we started sorting ourselves out through education, socioeconomic standing, and career choices. They dominated not through intellectual candlepower and rarely through physical intimidation, but by virtue of who they were, their unvarnished selves, the force and magnetism of their personalities, their personal presence.

I headed home after practice that first day thinking that at least one thing in my life was settled. I wanted to be a Lynvet. Everything else was in play.

2

Necessary Roughness

*F*ootball madness coincided with the onset of puberty. Girls were part of the reason. For a painfully long time, the best we could hope for was holding hands with a girl or casually draping an arm around one in a darkened movie theater, a Pyrrhic achievement as more often than not the back of the seat cut off the flow of blood to the extremities and our fingers went numb. But whatever we wanted from girls, it seemed to many of us that our prospects were best advanced by being football players.

From the time football first grabbed our imaginations, we also sensed that the game existed within an ether of sexuality, an intoxicating earthiness that we didn't quite understand, but without which the sport would have mattered less to us.

John Updike understands. "Do you remember a fragrance girls acquire in autumn?" he begins his 1961 short story "In Football Season." The evocative, richly textured opening concludes, "This fragrance, so faint and flirtatious on those afternoon walks through the dry leaves, would be banked a thousandfold on the dark slopes of the stadium when, Friday nights, we played football in the city."

In truth, for many of us football as the key to a girl's heart turned out to be pretty much a fool's errand.

"I hoped through football to become a ladies' man," said Tommy Wall. "I thought, for some twisted reason, that women would be attracted to good football players. As a matter of fact, do you know how much I believed in this? I used to be embarrassed for guys who didn't get in the games who would bring their girlfriends. I'd think, 'How the hell could he bring that foxy-looking girl, and he doesn't even play?' I never realized she didn't even know who was playing—or care."

But there was more to it for me and, I suspect, for many of my football friends. By the time I was thirteen I had come to think of my first love, baseball, as a childish diversion, not something that went to the heart of who I was, or hoped to be. And what was that? Who knows? A hero, I guess, and by my youthful definition a hero had to accomplish great things, but he had to do so in the face of danger. Years later, I learned an expression that summed it up: No guts, no glory.

Guts were more important than glory. Courage—and back in the 1950s that meant physical courage—was crucial. Did you have it or did you not? If you didn't have it, how could you get it? Baseball did not provide the answer to these questions, not for me. Football did. Years before I ever put on a uniform, I knew that the gridiron was going to be my youthful testing ground, the place where I would find out if I had it. Not the only place, but the first place.

In those days, the issue was important. My friends and I had lived through World War II even though we were small children during the war years. The postwar jubilation had lasted barely five years before the nation found itself at war again, this time for reasons that lacked the resonance of the epic showdown with the Germans and the Japanese. From 1950, when I turned ten, to 1953, Korea was with us every day. We pored over maps on the front page of the daily papers, following the movement of the battle lines. The early withdrawal of Allied troops into the Pusan Perimeter, the daring Marine landing at Inchon, MacArthur's invasion of the

North, the Communist Chinese sweep across the Yalu, and the First Marine Division's bloody retreat from the Chosin Reservoir through a blizzard and at least seven Chinese divisions. Young men we knew went, and some of them died.

Tommy Wall recalled the screams in his heavily Irish Woodside neighborhood the day that Mrs. Silk tried to throw herself out the window of her third-floor shotgun apartment. She had just gotten the news that her youngest son, eighteen-year-old Jimmy, had been killed in Korea. And there was Mrs. Reese. She left her flat every afternoon at three o'clock sharp when the *Long Island Star-Journal* arrived at the newsstand, only to return sobbing a short time later, having learned that once again her son, Richie, missing in action, had not turned up on the latest prisoner exchange list.

By the mid-1950s, as we were coming of age, the Cold War was raging and the draft hung over all of us. Veterans of World War II and Korea were awe-inspiring figures in our neighborhoods, especially the ones who had distinguished themselves in combat. Though there was no armed conflict at the moment, we sensed that battlefield challenges awaited many of us as well. We needed to be ready to meet them, and back then, when the game still had a regular-guy scale to it, football seemed a good way to prepare. In those days, I refused to wear gloves even on the most frigid days. I wanted my hands to get used to the cold so that I could catch passes in the icy weather late in the season. And I wanted to be ready for the Red Chinese hordes when they came charging through the snow in subzero cold, bugles blaring, burp guns belching—just as they had at the horribly outnumbered Marines at the Frozen Chosin.

Compared to baseball, football had the feel of war—at least it did to teenage boys too naive to know better. We marched up and down the field, hurled bombs, launched aerial attacks. And we hit people. The goal wasn't to maim, but hurting and getting hurt were part of the game, not some aberration. And while baseball rewarded concentration and finesse, football was about passion and courage, things that we prized, wanted for ourselves.

No one I knew wanted to go to war. Years later, in the heat of the Vietnam era, some of those opposed to the war tried to paint those who fought in it as deluded products of books and movies that they claimed glorified combat. Perhaps to an extent they were right. Certainly movies like *Sands of Iowa Jima* and such books as *Battle Cry*, Leon Uris's tribute to the Marines, had an impact on us. When *Battle Cry* was made into a movie, Marine recruiters in dress-blue uniforms stationed themselves in the lobbies of neighborhood theaters all across the city, pens and enlistment papers at the ready. But those of us growing up in the 1950s were not dolts. We knew that thirty-six thousand Americans, most of them not much older than us, had died in Korea and not long before that four hundred thousand men barely old enough to be our fathers had been killed in World War II. Many more had been maimed, and we saw them all over, legless men, men with hooks for hands, blind men. Some wearing their wounds as badges of honor, others gamely trying to fashion normal lives for themselves as if their afflictions were unremarkable, still others selling pencils on street corners, their pedigree—Disabled WWII Vet or some variation—scribbled on torn pieces of corrugated cardboard dangling from their necks on fraying pieces of discolored string.

When it was being fought, World War I was described as the war to end all wars. By the late 1950s, in the wake of World War II, most of us believed, as Douglas MacArthur would put it in a West Point speech a few years later, that "only the dead have seen the end of war." We did not live in fear of war or see it as irrevocably in our future, though we expected to be drafted and to spend a couple of years in the service. There was always the chance that we'd be lucky and do our service time in a period of peace, assuming of course that we could resist the impulse to reenlist when war inevitably broke out and our younger comrades were summoned to arms.

War, or the prospect of it, did not bleed into our everyday lives. Rather, it traipsed along the edges of our consciousness, rarely in focus, but never fully obscured. When the Korean War ended in stalemate in 1953, we just let it go. We were glad it was over and the troops could come home, but we were not terribly exercised by the ambiguous outcome. Ike was elected president in 1952 after he promised to go to Korea. We understood that to mean he was going to settle the war, not come up with a master plan for victory. And, of course, we didn't lose that war, we just didn't win it. And South Korea, the country we fought the war to save, was still there, its borders unchanged. As a nation, though, America was again drenched in blood, exhausted by war, and wary of any new overseas adventures.

Oddly enough, the greater threat of a devastating nuclear exchange, one that would obliterate the great cities of the East and West, played into our lives far less than the possibility of conventional war. We had antinuke drills in school and buildings sprouted Fallout Shelter signs, but beyond that there seemed little anyone could do to prepare. It didn't even make sense to pray that it didn't happen because if it did the question of whether or not God existed would be settled once and for all.

The fresh memory of Korea made the prospect of another war, one that might involve us, more than a figment of our imagination. It did not immobilize us or cause us to view the future less confidently, but it lent an edginess to our lives, an existential quality that was beginning to mount a challenge to the precepts of religion and conventional morality that still restrained our behavior. But when Elvis burst on the scene a couple of years later, we were primed for him. My sisters, Pat and Rosemarie, and I turned on the Dorsey Brothers' show that Saturday night in January 1956 to kill time until Jackie Gleason came on a half hour later. Suddenly there was Elvis, in a black shirt, a white tie, and pants with a shiny stripe on them. We had no idea who he was, only that we had never seen anything like him. He was on Dorsey every week for the next five weeks. The third week, he sang "Blue Suede Shoes" and "Heartbreak Hotel." Pat was eleven and suddenly she was screaming and madly ripping the curlers out of her hair. As the Elvis craze mushroomed, the world felt different. His popularity was far greater among girls than it was with guys, though the guys were more than willing to harvest the emotions his music stirred. The bobby-soxers

that jammed Frank Sinatra concerts now seemed to belong to another, gentler time. Sinatra was about holding hands at midnight.
Elvis was about getting laid. It would take another few years and
the arrival of the Pill for us as a nation to fully come to grips with
what that portended.

3

Living with Lenny Rochester

*I*f Larry Kelly seemed skeptical of my football credentials during our first conversation, he was simply displaying the shrewd coaching instincts of which he was justifiably, if immodestly, proud. In truth, by the time I showed up for that first Lynvet practice, my life had not been going smoothly for some time, either on the gridiron or outside the lines.

By then, two of my major illusions had collided with reality, the notion of a happy family and the belief that I might, just might, be one of the smartest kids in the world. The first fell victim to my powers of observation. At a certain point, I could see that my parents were not made for each other. That collision took place in slow motion, a grinding, extended experience. The second occurred on my first day at Stuyvesant High School, an all-boys public school in lower Manhattan that specialized in science and math and drew many of the brightest kids in New York. I had taken the test and decided on Stuyvesant not because it was arguably the best school in the city, but mostly because it had a football team and my local high school in Queens did not. I had been to twelve schools by the time I stepped into the clunky, five-story white-brick building on 15th Street between First and Second Avenues and had excelled, in my way, at all of them. I may not have always stood at the top of my class, but I always knew I could if I really wanted to.

Until Stuyvesant. That first day was like walking in on the middle of a conversation, much of it conducted in a language I barely recognized. It wasn't that the words were foreign, I just had no idea what they meant. Molecule. Covalent compounds. Metternich. Relativity. And these were the kids talking, not the teachers, and not just in class. I panicked, and for a time I struggled. Eventually I righted myself and did okay at Stuyvesant, but by then I had a much more accurate sense of where I fit in the intellectual firmament. I was smart. I was not brilliant, as were scores of my classmates.

As late as my junior year at Stuyvesant, the first year we could play football because of split sessions, I still had one illusion left. I believed, contrary to most of the available evidence, that I could be the best running back in the city. Granted, I was small, about five foot seven, 135 pounds, but that was not so small in those days. And I figured, incorrectly as it turned out, that I still had a lot of growing to do. I was fast, but I was not that fast. Stuyvesant's two starting halfbacks, Jim Norman and Chris Pendarvis, both seniors, were track stars who weighed 185 pounds and 170 pounds, respectively. Even so, I was quick and elusive, had good instincts, and could catch any pass I touched, enough at that point to keep my ridiculous conceit alive. It helped that I was hurt early in the year, a season-long injury, so I never had to compete with Jim and Chris or, for that matter, Dennis Margaris, a fellow junior who I now realize was better than I was, too. Injured, I rode the bench, biding my time, waiting for next year, when I'd be healthy again and could show the coach, Murl Thrush, what I could do.

The dream died during the last game of that season against our archival, Dewitt Clinton, a high school in the Bronx. Clinton had an All-City halfback named Lenny Rochester, a black kid whom Coach Thrush told us we had to stop if we were to have any chance of winning. Of course, every team had someone. Lenny Rochester sounded like just the latest in a string of opposing players the coach had warned us about during the course of the season.

I have never seen a performance equal to Lenny Rochester's that Saturday in the late fall of 1956. From my seat on the bench, I watched Lenny Rochester take Stuyvesant apart. He was untouchable, literally. Stuyvesant had a good defense, but I don't remember anyone on our team even touching him. He ran through and around our line for touchdowns, returned kicks for touchdowns, caught passes for touchdowns. There was something else, no doubt an optical illusion or the product of an overheated imagination. Whenever Lenny Rochester put a move on one of the Stuyvesant players, his belt buckle seemed to emit shimmering rays of light, a phenomenon all the more remarkable in that he didn't even have a belt buckle—no one did. But that's what I saw that day, Lenny Rochester swiveling his hips as he was about to be tackled, his belt buckle flashing, and Stuyvesant guys falling on their faces as Lenny left them for dead. Late in the game, Peter Cobrin, one of our defensive linemen, leveled him deep in the end zone as he slowed down after still another touchdown. "I just wanted to see what it was like to tackle him," Peter said afterward.

Depression doesn't begin to describe my emotions during that game. I never thought of Jim Norman or Chris Pendarvis, as good as they were, as threats to my private dream. They were different kinds of backs. Lenny Rochester ran just like me. He cut like me, he faked like me, he ran pass patterns like me. Except he did all those things—and more—so much better than I did that there could be no denying that on my best day, if and when it ever came, I didn't belong on the same field with him. Lenny Rochester was not me in my wildest imagination, he was beyond my imagination.

That night, I lay in my bed trying to come to grips with what I had seen that afternoon. I understood what it meant. I would never be the same. Lenny Rochester was the first person that I had ever encountered who was better than I was at something I wanted to be the best at. Never again would I be able to think of myself as unique, one of a kind. Now I was like everyone else. For the rest of my days, I knew, I would have to live with Lenny Rochester. In my experience, football was the only sport that allowed a young man to see so deeply into his own soul, however shallow it might be.

There was life, it turned out, after Lenny Rochester. Dennis Margaris and I were slated to be the starting Stuyvesant halfbacks in our senior year. During the spring and summer leading into that season I worked at gaining weight and strength through a system of my own devising. My friend Larry Sifert and I would go to the YMCA in Jamaica three times a week and lift weights. I hated it, felt uncomfortable being around guys working on their pecs and lats, whatever they were, but I was on a mission. After lifting, even though I felt dehydrated, I would not drink any water. I had gotten it into my mind that all the lifting, and particularly the sweating, had opened the cells of my body and made them unusually receptive to weight-inducing substances. So after showering, Larry and I would sit at the counter of the drugstore on the corner of Sutphin Boulevard and Hillside Avenue and I would consume my version of androstenedione—tuna-fish sandwiches and vanilla milkshakes. Never gained a pound. Not aware that I got any stronger. My pecs and lats were looking pretty good, but all that did was make me feel self-conscious. I wanted to play football, not hang around gyms and pose in front of floor-to-ceiling mirrors.

At summer practice, in a drill without pads, I dove for a pass, caught it, landed on my left shoulder, and broke my collarbone.

My mother had told me the year before that I was going to get hurt playing football. I insisted that she was being overly protective. After I was injured in my junior year, I told her that it was a freak accident. A year later I was back where I started, this time in a sling. I hid in the closet of my bedroom when I heard her come home from work. She called to me.

"I'm in here, Mom," I shouted back.

She walked into the bedroom. I wasn't exactly there. "Bobby?" she said.

I said, "I'm looking for some stuff in the closet."

A walk-in closet would have made my explanation more credible. This one was about three feet deep. Also, to keep my mother in the dark, I would have had to stay in it at least two months, long enough for my collarbone to heal.

Stuyvesant was to play eight games that season. Fortunately for the team, a junior named Joe Lamonte moved seamlessly into my spot in the backfield. But I was determined to return to the team before the season was over, even though my doctor, a quack caught up in the spurious concept of responsible medicine, told me my collarbone would not heal in time for me to play that year.

I came up with my own rehab plan. The issue here was not strength or weight or talent. I just needed my collarbone—which, according to possibly doctored X-rays, was in two distinct pieces— to grow together. I had to make it happen. I asked my mother what would make bones heal. She didn't know, but she took a stab at it. "Milk," she said, "and maybe Knox Gelatin." I was willing to try anything. Even though I hated it, milk made sense. Calcium. Builds strong bones. Knox Gelatin, a glue-like substance, sounded so bad that I knew it had to help.

This became my regimen. Each night I would take a quart of milk to bed and drink it, suppressing as best I could the gag instinct. Also, I would pour a packet of unflavored Knox gelatin into a pan of boiling water, wait till it cooled, then drink it. It was like drinking raw egg whites—or a phlegm ball, as one of Gilda Radner's characters said of oysters. But I did it. Every night. Also, because I was a Catholic then, I would go to Mass every morning on the way to school and pray for my collarbone. Each week I would demand my mother take me to the doctor for an X-ray. Week after week he'd come in with the print and a self-satisfied smirk, put it up on his display board, click on the light, and show me that there was still a darkened slash between what he insisted were the two halves of my collarbone. At Week Eight, six weeks into the season, I saw what seemed like a milky membrane connecting the two halves. "I don't see what you're talking about," the doctor said.

The next day I told the coach I was ready to go. Made it through practice. Late in the third quarter of Saturday's game, the coach put me in. I took a pitchout and gained about a yard. A play or two later, the quarterback called a dive play, a handoff into the line. I brought my arms into position so he could slip the ball in and collapsed, so great was the pain. My season was over. Dennis Margaris made second team All-City. The next year, Joe Lamonte made first team All-City. It was as if I had never been there.

I didn't know it then, but my real gridiron career, the one in which I actually played in games instead of sitting on the bench and bemoaning my injuries, would finally take shape on a series of neighborhood football fields that bore little resemblance to the stadium on Randall's Island where two years earlier Lenny Rochester had demolished the Peglegs—yes, that was, and still is, Stuyvesant's nickname. Though I was barely aware of it, the working-class neighborhoods of Queens and Brooklyn were awash in football teams that clashed on fall weekends in the public parks of the two also-ran New York City boroughs. They were called sandlot teams, though by the time the Lynvets emerged in 1950 it had been years since anything besides pickup games had been played on actual sandlots. The teams received lavish press coverage in community papers—bylined stories, player profiles, scene setters before big games, multicolumn headlines for the games themselves. Local pride and large, close-knit families accounted for remarkably ardent followings whose passions animated the games even if they occasionally boiled over into violent sideline free-for-alls.

Names tell part of the story. Greenpoint Crusaders. Flushing Aces. Sunnyside Colts. Baisley Park Bombers. Rockaway Knights. Corona Condors. Auburndale Shamrocks. College Point Klowns. Brooklyn Cavaliers. Thirty-seventh Avenue Boys. Marine Park Uniques. Astoria had three teams—the Regalmen (sponsored by Regal Shoes), the Willows, and the Spartans. Woodside had at least four—the Chiefs, the Redskins, the Rangers, and the Mickwoppers, the last made up mostly of Irish and Italian kids (at some point, in an early bow to commercialism and political correctness, they changed their name to the Pace Olds Whippets). Ozone Park and South Ozone Park contributed three teams to the nine-team Warner conference in 1950—the Apaches, the Red Devils, and the Panthers, though before the season was over the last named became the Nat Paterson Panthers, after their sponsor, a Cross Bay Boulevard DeSoto-Plymouth dealer.

For the fans, sandlot football teams, especially the older squads, offered exciting and well-played games at a time when television was still in its infancy, and even later, when it provided only limited coverage of college and professional teams. The third nationally televised title game, but the one that really put pro football on the map, was the 1958 National Football League championship between the New York Giants and the Baltimore Colts, the famous "sudden death" game in which the gritty Johnny Unitas in his high-topped cleats led the Colts to victory in overtime.

As for the players, school district boundaries—rigidly adhered to in those days—dictated who could and could not play high school football since most New York City secondary schools, both public and parochial, did not field teams. Stuyvesant, in fact, could claim the Manhattan championship every year because it was the only public school with a team in a borough of nearly 2 million people. Attesting to the lure of the sandlot game, many high school players, usually in defiance of orders from their coaches, also suited up for their neighborhood teams. Even so, many fine athletes had no outlet for their talent and their desire to play other than the sandlots. These players were not scouted by colleges, nor did they expect to be, though some entertained vague notions that someone with connections would notice them and a football scholarship might materialize. By the time they reached the senior ranks, though, most sandlot players had long since made peace with their place in the sports universe. For them, whether or not they had played in high school, high school was over. They played because they loved the game and enjoyed the macho camaraderie that went with it.

For some of these same young men, and I was soon to be one of them, sandlot football also provided a refuge from ragged lives that seemed to be leading nowhere terribly exciting. Many others sensed that the world was rigged so that people like them would be left behind, even though, constitutionally incapable of seeing themselves as victims, they never truly came to grips with that issue. For all of us, the sandlot teams conferred a sense of belonging to something that mattered as we were being propelled into the uncertainties of adulthood.

In some ways, the season never ended. There were team parties, dances, and beer blasts that doubled as fund-raisers. Players often went to the beach together in the summer, usually Rockaway or Jones Beach, where in their brightly colored team jerseys they ran into players and cheerleaders from other teams similarly attired. These encounters—on the boardwalk or at the Irish bars like McGuire's, the Sligo House, and the White House that lined Rockaway Boulevard from Beach 103rd to Beach 108th Streets—were usually times of boozy good fellowship and braggadocio, the players akin to warriors from rival tribes in a period of uneasy peace. "Hey, you're the quarterback, right? We've got this new halfback, played for Adams, faster than hell. Big, too. We're gonna kill you guys this year." As coach of the Lynvet Senior team, Larry Kelly, beer in hand, would hold court on the boardwalk in Rockaway as if he were the lord mayor of Dublin mingling with the commoners.

Not all the off-season activities were so harmless. For some, those blowouts at the beach were part of an inexorable slide into alcoholism. And, as Tommy Wall once said of his pre-Lynvet days with the Woodside Chiefs, "In the off-season, we were a gang."

As I learned more about this colorful subculture, I realized that within the melange of teams, the Lynvets stood out, both for the caliber of its players and coaches and for its stability as an organization. Many teams were formed one year and disbanded the next. Some of the best players drifted from team to team, never finding one on which they felt at home. In the mid-to-late 1950s, Woodside's John Hourican was one of the two best quarterbacks roving the sandlots. Over an eight-year period he played for seven different teams, the Woodside Junior Rangers, the Whippets, the 37th Avenue Boys, the Woodside Redskins, the Brooklyn Cavaliers, the

Greenpoint Crusaders, and the Rockaway Knights. By contrast, his sole rival for quarterbacking preeminence, Bob Ferriola of City Line, played his entire sandlot career, ten years, for one team, the Lynvets.

For me, the Lynvets would become my salvation in ways I could not have begun to explain during the years I played for them. And I was not alone. As Lynvets, Larry Kelly, Tommy Wall, halfback Mike Montore, and others found a toehold on their better selves during troubled times in their lives. Those snatches of pride and courage and strength we shared eventually grew within us, becoming the core of a decent manhood that might have easily eluded any one of us in other circumstances. And there were times, for each of us, when it was all we had.

4

Father Cyclone

*T*he Lynvets were born on a street corner in City Line across from St. Sylvester's Catholic Church in the summer of 1950, around the time the North Korean Army swept across the Thirty-eighth parallel. The day before, as kids were bowling duckpins and playing basketball in the basement of the old wood church, Charlie Fitzgerald, an older guy from the neighborhood, passed the word that there would be a meeting after Mass the next day for anyone who wanted to play football. About twenty-five boys showed up, assembling under a street sign that marked the intersection of Grant Avenue and McKinley Street. Charlie, a standout guard at John Adams High School in Jamaica a decade earlier, told them he was starting a team for kids eleven to fifteen that would compete in the new Pop Warner Conference, which had begun play in Brooklyn and Queens the year before.

Larry Kelly was one of the kids there that day. So was Bob Lulley, destined to become the great quarterback of the first generation of Lynvet champions. One of the younger kids, Tommy Vaughan, would later become a storied Lynvet running back, but his mother decided that at 90 pounds he was too small for a league with a 135-pound weight limit and players four years older than he was.

Vaughan, later my Lynvet backfield mate for one glorious season, had to wait till 1951 to get his mother's permission. But he joined the other kids the next several weekends in collecting newspapers, piling them in a truck, and hauling them to the junkie to raise money for uniforms and equipment. The church kicked in a few bucks, as did the Father Lynch post a few blocks away on Liberty Avenue, and the kids sold raffle tickets at ten cents apiece for a chance at a Teletone radio. A few weeks before the first game, Charlie Fitzgerald took a few of the players to a sports wholesaler on Canal Street on the Lower East Side to pick out uniforms.

On Saturday, September 15, the Lynvets paraded under the lights onto Sherwood Oval in Springfield Gardens in Queens to kick off the 1950 Pop Warner season. They wore white jerseys with maroon numbers and maroon pants, establishing the team's colors, the same as Fordham, the Jesuit college in the Bronx. Their opponents, the South Ozone Park Apaches, were not nearly as well turned out. Some wore dungarees, others shorts. The Lynvets, dressed for success decades before the term gained currency, rolled to an easy victory. After the game, Art Cwergel, the conference president and the man who brought Pop Warner football to Brooklyn and Queens, told the team, "I feel you guys are going to be the Notre Dame of this league."

They did not win the title that year, beaten out by the defending champion Ozone Park Red Devils, but that first Lynvet team displayed the intensity and football skills that would soon become their hallmark. The papers began referring to the Lynvet quarterback as "Passin' Bob Lulley" and more than once the *Long Island Daily Press* noted that Lulley and receiver Larry Kelly formed "a dangerous aerial combination."

In 1951, the Lynvets' second year in the league, they won their first championship, turning the tables on the Red Devils as halfback Artie Donelon swept left end for the game's only touchdown. Along with a detailed story on the contest, the *Daily Press* carried a picture of Lulley, who had completed fourteen of twenty passes,

high in the air throwing a jump pass. The caption read, "Warner Aerial Artist."

The newspaper coverage gave the teams added cachet. Reporters and photographers were dispatched to big games, though lesser matchups seemed heavily dependent on coaches or someone else assigned by the team to call in the results, which were whipped into story form by overworked rewrite men. This made for some amusing confusion. Lulley played several games under the name Bobby Larue, lifting the last name from his girlfriend, a Lynvet cheerleader. He did so because he was also playing for his high school, St. John's Prep, and his Prep coach, wary of injuries, ordered his players to stay off the sandlots. But no one could quite keep it straight. As a result, the papers one week would talk about the fine play of Bob Lulley, the Lynvet quarterback, and the next week extol the performance of Bobby Larue, the Lynvet quarterback. A week or so later, old Passin' Bob would be back in the headlines.

A similar thing happened with Dick Petrarca, a powerhouse runner nicknamed the Bull, who played as Billy Smith because he was a few months overage. In some stories the exploits of fullback Dick "The Bull" Petrarca would be chronicled; in others the Lynvets scoring machine would be led by fullback Billy "The Bull" Smith. No one seemed to question a team having two fullbacks with the same nickname, one of whom seemed to disappear from print whenever the other was playing, or why, like Larue and Lulley, they were never seen together.

From the start the Lynvets were a talented team with a seemingly bright future, but one that might easily have fallen apart, as so many other promising squads had done, were it not for the enthusiasm and organizational smarts of Charlie Fitzgerald. Over the next half dozen years, Charlie would coach not only the original Lynvets but also a younger Lynvet team that he started in 1951. By then, the fledgling Pop Warner Conference had reorganized itself into two tiers, a Senior Division, into which Lulley, Kelly and most of the first Lynvet team moved, and a Junior Division for the younger kids.

Charlie was short and heavyset, his chubby face set off by horn-rimmed glasses. As a coach, he had his shortcomings. He was not an X's and O's guy, leaving that part of the game to his wraithlike adviser, Paul Frey, who stayed in the background as he designed offensive and defensive schemes for Charlie and the coaches who came after him. But Charlie was a motivator, a man who lived to win and communicated that desire to the kids.

Charlie was more than a rah-rah guy. He built an organization that made parents, neighbors, and local businesses part of the team's impressive support structure. He ran raffles, put on dances and beer busts, and filled programs for those events with a remarkable number of ads, most of which he sold himself. In 1953 he presided over the Lynvets' assimilation of the rival Ozone Park Red Devils, greatly strengthening the team as players like Kenny Mueller, Jimmy Sims, and Kevin Glynn became Lynvets. Over the years, many men and women contributed to the success of the Lynvets, but it is safe to say that only Charlie Fitzgerald was indispensable.

At the end of the 1955 season, having led the Seniors to four championships in six years and the Junior team to a fifth, Charlie decided to close out his coaching career. He told Bob Bushman, who played for Charlie's Senior team in 1954 and 1955, "Bob, I just can't put in the seven-days-a-week and all the nights that this team needs if we're gonna win, and if we're not gonna win, I don't want to be part of it."

There followed the Wilderness Years. In both 1956 and 1957, the Lynvet Seniors fell short of the title, in the latter season losing their final game 20–0 to the fourth-place squad. Part of the reason for the uneven performance of the Seniors was the Marine Corps. In February 1956, three important players—Tommy Vaughan, Chipper Dombo, and Hughie Mulligan—decided they hated their jobs in Manhattan, wandered over to the Marine recruiting station in Times Square, and enlisted for two years. A fourth player, John Delahunty, did the same the next day. Suddenly, players at the heart of the Lynvets were on their way to Parris Island.

That same year, though still playing for the Seniors, Larry Kelly, who had already done a hitch in the Marines, signed on as assistant coach for the Lynvet Junior team. He quickly became the brains of the operation. With Bob Ferriola at quarterback, the team won the division championship. The following year, Ferriola moved up to the Seniors and, to his dismay, was switched to end as the older team continued to struggle. The Juniors, meanwhile, repeated as champions, this time with a host of talented players whom Kelly groomed and in some cases recruited. At the end of the 1957 season, the inevitable happened. The coaches of the Senior team were ousted and Kelly, who no doubt helped engineer the purge, became head coach.

In the beginning, Charlie Fitzgerald launched the Lynvets and led them to an amazing string of championships. Later in the decade, as the Lynvet era seemed to be fading, Larry Kelly seized the reins, determined to reinvigorate the organization and lead it back to greatness. But from the start there was Father Lynch, whose tale gave the team a special dimension.

Larry Lynch, the oldest of twelve, was a child of City Line, his family's home at 415 Eldert Lane, a couple of blocks from St. Sylvester's. One story has it that he nearly died in childbirth but quickly achieved robust good health after the doctor ordered a daily bath in brandy. Ordained in 1932 at the Redemptorist Seminary north of the city, he spent the early years of his priesthood as a missionary in Brazil. When World War II broke out, he joined the Army's chaplain corps. By 1943, he was on the South Pacific island of New Caledonia, serving with the "Fighting Sixty-Ninth," as Robert E. Lee dubbed the heavily Irish regiment after tangling with it at Antietam, Fredericksburg, and Gettysburg.

Father Lynch was an unconventional priest. He moved with a street-savvy swagger and spoke at times in the brash, wise-guy argot of the neighborhood where he grew up. He introduced himself to the troops by saying, "I am Father Lawrence Lynch—and I'm from Brooklyn. I'm God's gift to the Army—and to you guys." Said one of the soldiers who served with him, "He's as Brooklyn as a pop bottle thrown at an umpire." He smoked, was known to enjoy a beer with the troops, and slipped off from time to time for a game of poker with some Marines stationed nearby. Three times a week he disappeared for hours at a time. He refused to tell his superiors where he was going, which drove them crazy, perhaps because they suspected that his destination was off limits. It was—a church-run leper colony outside the capital city of Noumea that, it turned out, was also the recipient of his poker winnings.

On April 1, 1945, Easter Sunday, Army and Marine divisions hit the beach of a narrow, rocky island called Okinawa that lay just 350 miles from Japan. The Fighting Sixty-Ninth landed ten days later as part of the Army's Twenty-seventh Division. Father Lynch, living up to his nickname, Father Cyclone, scuttled between belea-guered companies and platoons to hear confessions and celebrate Mass, the hood of a jeep his altar, the troops kneeling around him on the muddy, cratered ground.

On April 24, the Sixty-Ninth came under a relentless mortar attack. A lieutenant colonel directing the defense from an exposed position suddenly noticed that Father Lynch was standing beside him. Angrily, he told the priest, "There's the aid station, right behind you. Go to it and stay there." Father Lynch moved away, but not back to the aid station. Fearlessly, almost recklessly, he roamed the killing ground, racing from foxhole to foxhole, quickly blessing the soldiers huddled within. As he was giving last rites to a dying soldier, a mortar round exploded nearby. A piece of shrapnel tore into his back, a second fragment ripped through his helmet. A year later, on the anniversary of his death, fifty chaplains gathered around his grave on Okinawa and said fifty Masses in unison on the hoods of fifty jeeps.

5

Think Pink

*M*y parents were show-business people and New Yorkers, about all they had in common if you don't count my belief that they never stopped loving each other. My mother, born Rosemarie Sinnott, grew up in Flatbush, the oldest of seven children in a devout Irish-Catholic family. Actually, there were thirteen children, but six died in childbirth or shortly thereafter. Her father was a blacksmith. She was beautiful—blond hair, green eyes, a heart-shaped face, exquisite features—making the first of several appearances on the cover of *McCall's* magazine before she reached her teens. At thirteen, her father's ability to work sapped by illness, she became the sole support of her family. A cover girl well into her twenties, she was also a featured dancer and actress, playing major supporting roles in Broadway musicals, including several produced by Florenz Ziegfeld. Ziegfeld discovered her performing on a stage set up on the sand at Atlantic City when she was fourteen. In those days, to keep the authorities at bay (she was no longer going to school), she called herself Collette Ayres. Proud to be a Ziegfeld Girl, she nevertheless was always quick to point out, in the haughty tone on which actresses of that era hold the patent, that she was never in the chorus.

She moved on the fringe of some fast company, though she never seemed bedazzled or overly attracted by it. Or perhaps her responsibilities to her family left her little time for fun. Neysa McMein, the artist who painted her as a girl and a young woman for a succession of *McCall's* covers, was a regular at the Algonquin Round Table, the fabled collection of writers, journalists, and artists who gathered daily for lunch at the Algonquin Hotel on West 44th Street. Through Neysa, a flamboyant woman who seemed to know everyone, my mother while still in her teens found herself on the dais with Charles Lindbergh and Amelia Earhart at an airshow at Roosevelt Field on Long Island. They were promoting a new aircraft, the Ford Trimotor, a six-seater billed as the first "modern" passenger plane.

"Hey, kid, want to go for a ride?" asked Lindy.

It never occurred to my mother not to take him up on his offer. Lindbergh handled the controls; Earhart sat in the copilot's seat. Another time, my mother spent a weekend with Neysa at her home in the Hamptons. The other houseguests were actresses Helen Hayes and Tallulah Bankhead and the wickedly witty writer Dorothy Parker.

My father, Sammy Timberg, was the youngest of six children. He was born on Houston Street in Lower Manhattan. His parents were Austrian Jews, his father a barber back in the days when barbers applied leeches and otherwise practiced medicine without a license. By the time my father came along in 1903, his brother Herman was already a headliner on the vaudeville stage, a comedian with a rapid-fire delivery who wore thick glasses and used his violin as a prop. My dad's sister Hattie was also a fixture in vaudeville, performing under the name Hattie Darling, which Herman had given her to dispel the aroma of nepotism since she often worked with him.

My father was training as a concert pianist with Rubin Goldmark, Aaron Copland's and George Gershwin's mentor, when for reasons probably involving money he was drafted in his teens to join Herman and Hattie on the vaudeville circuit. Herman at about that time was writing and directing an act for a zany comedy team on the brink of stardom called the Marx Brothers. Hattie, whose boyfriend was the great Jewish prizefighter Benny Leonard, then lightweight champion of the world, was managing the act and appearing onstage with them. Leonard, who bankrolled the show, called *On the Mezzanine,* wanted to marry Hattie, but my grandparents refused to let her wed a boxer.

My father, at age eighteen, led the orchestra for *On the Mezzanine,* wrote music for many of Herman's other shows, and performed in some of them as Herman's straight man. Herman called him Fancy Pants, a name that caught on with the young women in the audience. On the road, he often roomed with one or more of the Marx Brothers, which may explain a lot. That, and perhaps the birth-order factor.

My mother was in a vaudeville review around 1930 when she met my father. They courted for the next seven or eight years, a period in which their mothers decried the religious differences and took turns threatening, and occasionally feigning, suicide. My mother's mother, a daughter of the Emerald Isle, was sweet and smart and reacted to everything from a stubbed toe to a death in the family with a breathless "Jesus, Mary, and Joseph" and a fluttery sign of the Cross. I remember my paternal grandmother as an imposing, not especially warm woman to whom my father was devoted. As a young woman, she was said to be an indefatigable stage mother and party-giver who entertained Enrico Caruso at least once in the family's apartment on the Lower East Side.

Oddly enough, neither of my parents seemed concerned about the religion problem except to the extent that it drove their mothers crazy. During their extended courtship, Walter Winchell and other tabloid columnists occasionally chronicled their on-again, off-again romance. Man-about-Town Sammy Timberg Heads for Hollywood; Showgal Rosemarie Sinnott to Follow, that kind of thing. In 1938, my mother was set to sail to Europe as part of a dance troupe aboard the *Île de France,* the sleek French luxury liner, when my father raced to the dock and begged her not to leave.

They were married that July in a civil ceremony at the Franconia Hotel on 72nd Street near Central Park West, once the home of Arnold Rothstein, thought to be the man who fixed the 1919 World Series. Under a caption that read "Musical Director Weds Ex-Dancer," the *Daily Mirror* ran a picture of the happy couple, my father kissing my mother, who looked captivating in a broad-brimmed summer hat. Both their fathers were dead by then. Neither mother attended the wedding. He was thirty-five, she had turned twenty-six three days earlier. They honeymooned in Atlantic City. I have a black-and-white picture of them strolling arm in arm along the boardwalk, my mother slim and radiant in a clingy summer dress, my father in striped pants with pleats and white shoes, a look of invincible confidence on his face, something I rarely if ever witnessed in real life.

By then, vaudeville was in its death throes and my father was working as musical director at Fleischer Studios, the domain of Max Fleischer, who through the 1930s was viewed as at least the equal of Walt Disney in the highly creative and competitive world of movie cartoons. Popeye, Olive Oyl, the racy Betty Boop, Superman, Casper the Friendly Ghost, Little Lulu—they were all Fleischer characters, and my father and his colleagues composed the music that breathed life into them.

My mother gave up the stage when she married. She never missed it. She had gone into show business to support her family. Given a choice, she would have skipped the glamour and stayed in school, which she had to leave in the eighth grade to go to work. A new wife and, with my birth a couple of years later, a mother, she was happy to be a homemaker, especially since she considered my father a musical genius destined for great achievements.

She did many things for me. When I was young, she read to me every night. During my early years in school, she held me to high standards, gently but firmly prodding me to start all over if I had to cross out something in my homework. A gifted artist, she drew the cover of every book report I ever wrote. She listened endlessly when I had to memorize a poem or make a presentation in class.

God, how many times did she sit through "Trees" or "The Village Smithy" or "The Midnight Ride of Paul Revere"?

My mother's assessment of my father's talent was widely shared. It seemed only a matter of time before he would be hailed as another Richard Rodgers or Cole Porter, perhaps the next Gershwin. It didn't happen, and no one—least of all my sisters and me—knows precisely why. And, if the love between my mother and father never died, the storybook romance crumbled. Opposites may attract, but they don't necessarily live happily ever after. My mother, her delicate good looks notwithstanding, was the toughest person I've ever met, totally incapable of backing down from any-one. She was also a fiercely proud woman. My father was different. He was handsome, witty, generous, and kind beyond reason. He was almost always fun, too. Pat was his favorite, but I didn't be-grudge her that. I was my mother's favorite, which would prove more burden than blessing.

My dad and I went to Yankee games together. He took me to the Turf Restaurant on Broadway, which had these great steak sandwiches that they sliced right before your eyes, and better cheesecake than Lindy's. The Turf was in the Brill Building, the center of the music publishing industry, and my father's composer friends like Don George, Frank Loesser, and Sammy Lerner and old vaudeville pals like Milton Berle and Phil Silvers would often stop by our table to say hello. "What are you up to, Sammy?" they'd always ask. His answers were invariably upbeat, broadly hinting that big things were just around the corner.

For all his charm and kindness, I detected a pernicious weak-ness in my father, a congenital fearfulness that made it difficult for him to advance on his own in the cutthroat world of pop music. He lost his father at a young age, and his brother Herman filled a pa-ternal role for many years, years in which my father prospered. But Herman died young, too, stripping my dad of the one person other than his mother—she died a few years before Herman—who had given direction to his life. With Herman out of the picture, my fa-ther floundered professionally. Opportunity occasionally knocked, but—deathly afraid to fail—he rarely answered the door. He had much to be proud of, but unlike my mother, he wasn't proud.

At some point my father, having left Fleischer studios, started to borrow money, usually from friends and family who, he insisted, did not care if he repaid them, and to shy away from chances to redeem his talent. My mother started to drink. To this day, I don't know which came first. She never acknowledged a drinking problem, though she freely admitted that she took a drink now and then. She did so partly because a glass of beer or a martini relaxed her, she said, but mostly because the alcohol eased the pain of my father's failure to do the things she thought he should to achieve the popular and financial success that always seemed to just elude him. My father confessed to an unfocused fearfulness, which he persisted in trying to explain rather than overcome, while insisting that my mother's drinking seriously aggravated his problems.

This I do remember. Over the years, my father had occasionally taken jobs in and around the city, playing piano either in bars or with small combos that he put together. Sometime in 1955, he was offered a job playing the piano at a new supper club in Scranton, in northeastern Pennsylvania's coal-mining region. The money was good, and he needed it. But he was afraid. He had been on the road a lot years before, but always with Herman. And he was a New York guy, someone who viewed anywhere else either as the sticks or somehow threatening, as if desperadoes armed to the teeth lurked behind every rock. He agreed to take the job, but in the weeks leading up to his departure for Scranton he got cold feet and said he was going to cancel the engagement. Though my parents were divorced by then, my father turned to my mother for counsel. She encouraged him to go, built up his confidence, told him how good he was and how he needed to get back in the action. On the day he left, she went with him to Port Authority and put him on the bus.

My father was a smash. Sleepy Scranton, it seemed, was ready for someone like him. The Europa Lounge, the club where he performed, was packed every night and extended his two-week contract indefinitely. He was the perfect supper club performer. Sitting at the piano, he ruled the room, one minute kidding with the audience, the next silencing them with his piano artistry. He did patter and shtick and even sang, often his own stuff, invariably introducing a song by saying, "I'm not a sing-guh, so you'll have to forgive my voice," then selling the tune with phrasing that anyone this side of Sinatra would die for.

He called every day, telling us he loved Scranton and, in a disbelieving tone, that he was the toast of the town, that people stopped him on the street to tell him how much they enjoyed his performance. He even wrote a song about the city. It began:

Stand up and shout about Scranton,
Our friendly town.
Lift your voice and sing a happy song,
Scranton, Scranton, that's where I belong.

We were happy for him, all of us, my mother, my sisters, and me. We didn't know what it meant, but maybe something good.

We were all shocked when my father called several months later to say that he had remarried. (Emblematic of how chaotic our lives had become, Pat, Rosemarie, and I didn't question until decades later why were were informed of the marriage only after the fact.) His new wife was a kind, generous, somewhat older Greek woman from Scranton, the widow of a candy magnate. My mother insisted that he had married her for her money, of which there is some evidence, including his efforts to frame a convincing denial even though neither my sisters nor I ever raised the issue. He was fifty-two at the time. Not long after, he quit the Europa and, after a few months in Scranton, he and his wife moved back to New York, to a splendid eleventh-floor suite in the Mayflower Hotel overlooking Central Park. He never held a regular job again, though he worked doggedly to get his music published. There is also evidence that he loved his second wife very much, especially as the years went by, although the marriage seemed to lack the passion that he and my mother had felt for one another. I think my mother always thought that she and my father would get back together someday, even after the divorce. Now, with his remarriage, her drinking got really bad.

⬭

As my parents' marriage collapsed, Pat, Rosemarie, and I suffered what today might be called collateral damage. Our family broke up for the first time while we were living on 79th Street and West End Avenue in Manhattan. It was February 1950. I was nine, Pat five, Rosemarie about seven months. My mother and father made at least one, possibly two attempts at reconciliation. Over the next six years, my sisters and I—at times together, other times separately—lived with a lot of different people in Manhattan, Brooklyn, and Queens. Sometimes one or more of us lived with one of our parents. Once I lived for several weeks with my mother in the Martha Washington Hotel for Women in Manhattan, the only male ever permitted above the lobby, or so my mother claimed. She was working as a hatcheck girl at a gay bar under the Third Avenue El called The Blue Parrot. She felt safe there, she said, since no one made passes at her. Not yet forty, she looked twenty-five. The drinking had not taken a toll on her features—in fact nothing ever did.

The pace of the odyssey that took me to a dozen schools before Stuyvesant now picked up. Twice I went to three schools in a single year. Once I went to the same school twice, about six months apart. Sports were my salvation. I was a good athlete, not as talented as I thought, but good enough to quickly make friends and fit easily into each new school. Shortstop, my favorite position, was usually taken by the time I touched down, but teams always needed a third baseman and I could play the hot corner. It was harder for my sisters. In those days, boys had teams, girls had cliques.

My parents' first try at reconciliation came a year or so after they had separated. For a few months, we all moved in with my mother's mother in a new apartment development in Brooklyn called Beach Haven, between Ocean Parkway and McDonald Avenue, not far from Coney Island. That must have been 1951 because I remember sitting on an unmade bed in that apartment listening to the radio when Bobby Thompson hit his famous home run "heard 'round the world."

Avenue Z ran past our building. Two blocks away, straddling Avenue X, was an Italian neighborhood. The grammar school I went to, PS 216, was there. My mother, who was working at a laundry somewhere in Brooklyn, told me that Rosemarie, who was two, was my responsibility on weekends. That meant I had to push her in her stroller everywhere I went. Baseball games, where I'd ask other kids to protect her from foul balls when I was in the field since there were never any grown-ups around. Meeting my buddies at the drugstore, where we'd sit on the curb and spit thin streams of saliva through our front teeth, all the rage that summer, and exchange good-natured *ma fongools,* a phrase we picked up from our Italian friends. These two Avenue X girls thought I was cute and I was shy, so I would run from them, pushing Rosemarie's stroller, careening through the streets, Rosemarie screaming, the girls giggling, me panicked. Once, the girls in hot pursuit, the stroller smashed into the curb, sending Rosemarie flying out headfirst. Loud howls, a few scrapes, no lasting damage.

After our parents' reconciliation fizzled, my sisters and I started bouncing around again. For a few months, the three of us, or maybe just Pat and I, lived in Astoria with a couple whose life seemed to revolve around their sports car, although only their kids were allowed to ride in it. For a while Pat and I stayed with my father in a room with a kitchenette at the Greystone, a musty residential hotel at Broadway and Ninety-first Street where all my father's family seem to have lived at one time or another. I remember cooking smells that made me gag and middle-aged Jewish women with too much rouge sitting in the lobby smoking cork-tipped Herbert Tareyton cigarettes, which the ads said discriminating people preferred.

Just before the Kew Gardens apartment where we three kids and my mother finally landed in the summer of 1956, Pat, Rosemarie, and I lived for nearly two years in Queens with a family from the South. The mother was a warm, matronly woman and wonderful cook. Her husband was a heavy drinker who snarled at

everyone. He'd come home from work around four-thirty in the afternoon, go up to his room, drink beer from brown quart bottles,
and spend the evening cursing and smoking Pall Mall cigarettes
that he held in bony, yellowed fingers. He'd stay in his room the entire weekend, occasionally crash through the house looking for
something (I never knew what), then stumble back upstairs.

I didn't much like it there, but I didn't hate it, either. Every Saturday I'd go to the Savoy Theater under the Jamaica Avenue El and
watch three cowboy movies for twenty-five cents. My favorites
were Alan "Rocky" Lane, Charles Starett as the Durango Kid,
Wild Bill Elliott, Joel McCrea, Randolph Scott, Tim Holt, and
Lash LaRue. Some had sidekicks, a rotating crew comprised of
Gabby Hayes, Smiley Burnette, and Fuzzy Knight. I didn't much
like the singing cowboys—Roy Rogers, Gene Autry, Rex Allen—
or Hopalong Cassidy, who seemed too old and whose horse had
a stupid name, Topper, or any cowboy who tied his bandanna so
that both ends dangled foppishly in front instead of on the side,
one end in front, one in back. Bad guys, of course, always wore
the bib in front, a dead giveaway, as easy to read as women who
smoked so you knew they were easy or not to be trusted. I favored
the cross-draw and went back and forth on the issue of one six-
shooter or two.

In the summer of 1956, between my sophomore and junior years in
high school, my mother, my sisters, and I moved to a two-bedroom
apartment in Kew Gardens, at the junction of Union Turnpike,
Grand Central Parkway, and the Van Wyck Expressway. The
building resembled every other postwar apartment building in
Queens. Redbrick, functional, devoid of any element of architec-
tural distinction unless you counted the fire escapes that slashed di-
agonally across the sides of the buildings like jagged raised scars.
My sisters and I had no complaints about the aesthetic shortcomings. We saw the apartment as an end to our gypsylike existence
over the previous six or so years. If our parents weren't together, the

three of us were, and our mother was with us. More than anything, we needed and wanted stability in our lives, and it seemed we had finally found it.

That illusion lasted a few days. My mother, a tower of strength in so many situations, was as weak in her way as my father was in his. There were good times and bad, and my sisters and I persisted in believing that the bad times were an aberration, their end a matter of days away, once my mother recovered from her latest bout of drinking.

My father called two and three times a day, explaining that he was afraid that my mother might have fallen asleep with a cigarette burning. He didn't know the half of it, and out of a sense of loyalty to my mother we didn't tell him. At a certain point, my sister Pat and my mother became antagonists, Pat less willing than Rosemarie, who was only about seven, or I to overlook or rationalize her transgressions. I had my own room, complete with desk and radio. Pat, Rosemarie, and my mother had the other bedroom. They slept on a king-sized bed of sorts that consisted of two twin beds pushed together with a common headboard and footboard. Rosemarie slept in the middle. When Pat and my mother started arguing at night, as they often did, Rosemarie would slip unnoticed through the crack between the beds and lie on the floor, terrified, listening to the muffled voices above her, pretending the angry words were coming from another apartment.

I finally realized that our years-long quest for normalcy was a pipe dream on Easter Sunday 1957, less than a year after we moved to Kew Gardens. Thanks to my father, we had Easter outfits, a suit for me, pretty dresses and bonnets for Pat and Rosemarie. To celebrate, my mother had gotten tickets for the Easter Show at Radio City Music Hall. The movie was *Funny Face*, a musical about the fashion trade starring Fred Astaire, Audrey Hepburn, and a brassy character actress named Kay Thompson.

We had seats in the balcony, good seats, we could see everything. The show on stage was typically religious and kind of boring, but fine for the day. Plus we got there late and didn't have to sit through all of it. My mother said she was feeling ill, so every few minutes she would get up to go to the ladies room. She seemed shakier each time she returned, climbing with increasing unsteadiness over people to reach her seat. By the time the movie came on, she was having trouble finding the right row, and she'd call out, "Bobby, Patti, Rosemarie." People would shout "Quiet!" and "Siddown!" On screen, there was this terrific production number featuring Kay Thompson as a fashion editor who decided that pink was going to be the breakthrough color of the year. "Think Pink! Think Pink!" she sang as Audrey Hepburn appeared in one stunning pink outfit after another.

"Bobby, Patti, Rosemarie."

"Think Pink! Think Pink!"

"Bobby . . ."

"Think . . ."

". . . Patti . . ."

". . . Pink!"

"We've got to get out of here," I whispered to my sisters.

"Let's go," said Pat.

". . . Rosemarie . . ."

"We can't leave Mom," said Rosemarie, crying.

"The hell we can't," I said.

We got up and made our way down the row to the opposite aisle from my mother, ignoring her, pretending we had no idea who she was. As we departed, she was lurching, Lear-like, up and down the other aisle, calling to us. I had some money in my pocket. We went a block away to the Roxy and saw *The Buster Keaton Story*. Afterward, we had Easter dinner at Tad's, the discount steak place.

6
—

The Hoople

I met Tommy Wall in the summer of 1958, about the time I joined the Lynvets. A Stuyvesant friend, Bob Muffoletto, and I were working out together at a park in Astoria. Bob had captained the Stuyvesant team the previous year, made All-City as an end, and was heading for Lehigh on a football scholarship. Tommy, who was a couple of years younger than Bob and me, was at the park by himself and offered to throw passes to us. He had a fine, accurate arm, was funny and engaging as well, the kind of off-brand guy you meet and immediately like.

At the time, Tommy was still a couple of years away from the Lynvets and quarterbacking the Woodside Chiefs in the Pop Warner Junior Division. He would play just two years with the Lynvets and, as quarterbacks go, he was not in the same league as Bob Lulley or Bob Ferriola. But no Lynvet had a quicker mind or cared more about the team. Few were more well liked. And many years later, he became the magnet that brought the far-flung Lynvet nation back together. By then, his life had settled into an enviable equilibrium, an achievement at which his friends from earlier days could only marvel. In those days, off the field, his life was all rough edges. But the Lynvets gave him something that he hung on to through the good times and the many bad ones that lay ahead, the belief that if you did things the right way—practiced hard, kept your uniform clean, didn't complain, acted with courage, never blamed others for your mistakes—the outcome, of a game or your life, would be one you could be proud of. It was, of course, a ridiculous notion. Life was unfair, everybody knew that, even the most die-hard Lynvets like Tommy Wall. But the enduring legacy of the Lynvets, one that would play itself out in Tommy's life, was that you didn't waste your time worrying about whether the cards were stacked against you. Maybe they were, maybe they weren't, but this is where I start, let's see how far I can go. That was the key to life, Lynvet-style. Play with passion and get up no matter how hard the hit, even if, as in Tommy's case, many of the blows were self-inflicted.

◉

Off the field, sad-eyed Tommy Wall was his own worst enemy, a rebel and a small-bore delinquent, though he could never quite conceal a wiseass, Holden Caulfield–like charm. His demons were easy to finger. He drank too much and he ran with a rough crowd. Within the nation's most sophisticated city he grew up in an insular world of narrowly circumscribed choices. His father, an Irish immigrant, was the doorman at 50 Sutton Place, a luxury apartment building in midtown Manhattan, a decent job that put food on the table, nothing to aspire to. In the heavily Irish community of Woodside, so it was said, a young man became a priest, a cop, or a crook. The parents were children of the Great Depression. To them, a job with the city or a company generally immune to hard economic times such as the gas or electric company was much prized. Tommy's father once pointed to a neighbor and said, "Good man. Thirty-five years with the Edison company." Tommy wanted to scream. The guy had nothing, lived in a dingy apartment, never went anywhere except the corner bar. Was that what he could expect, on the off chance that he straightened out his life? Growing old in a horseshit job that offered a measure of security and nothing else?

On the field, Tommy was a different person. In the huddle, he was the picture of poise and professionalism, his helmet shined to a gleam, his jersey showing the crease from its weekly visit to the dry cleaner. An unlikely perfectionist, he demanded so much of himself that minor mistakes tormented him. During one game, mopping up for Bob Ferriola in a Lynvet rout, he was twice penalized for taking too much time between plays. Nobody cared, but Tommy was inconsolable afterward, talking to no one, refusing a ride home, walking the entire ten miles by himself, his equipment bag slung over his shoulder.

Tommy dreamed of playing football from the first time he saw the Woodside Junior Rangers take the field at St. Michael's Park, a WPA project that sat between the Brooklyn Queens Expressway and Grand Central Parkway. The team had uniforms, silver jerseys and red pants, though the players saved money on tape by using strips of inner tube to hold up their thigh guards. They had fans, too, boisterous ones who lugged cases of beer to the game, sometimes set up tables with bottles of booze on them, and lined the field three and four deep from end zone to end zone. After the star quarterback, John Hourican, scored a touchdown, someone ran onto the field and handed him a can of beer. He took a sip, handed it back to the fan, got penalized. "How the hell else was I gonna get that guy off the field?" Hourican complained to the ref.

For Tommy there was more than love of the game. In the back of his mind, he saw football as a way out. Forget that he was small and did not have an overly strong throwing arm. A quarterback is a general, he would tell himself, he's not just an arm. His role model was little Eddie LeBaron, who quarterbacked the Washington Redskins in the 1950s. Like LeBaron, the shortest player in the NFL, Tommy was gritty, smart, and smooth. His ticket to the big time—first college, maybe even the pros—would be someone like Spook Stegman, a freelance street recruiter who haunted the city's playgrounds scouting out undiscovered athletic prospects, mostly basketball players, and funneling them to big-time college teams, often kids known, in the vernacular of the day, as Hooples—guys like Tommy, who had talent but also a knack for screwing up their lives.

That Tommy actually became a fine quarterback was a triumph of will over talent. His parents struggled to send him to Mount St. Michael, one of the top Catholic high schools in the city. Academically, the Mount was among the best, but Tommy chose it because it was a football factory with incomparable athletic facilities at its campus in the Bronx. As a freshman, he stood four foot eleven, weighed ninety-four pounds, and could not reach the strap on the subway, which he rode to school an hour and half each way. The freshman coach, fearing for Tommy's safety, told him he was too small to play high school football and begged him not to even try out. On the freshman team, many of his teammates were a foot taller and a hundred pounds heavier. In the team picture, he looks like the mascot. The waterboy towers over him. Coaches and players alike called him Midget.

He earned their respect. A scrub in the defensive backfield, he was a fearless tackler, never shying away (or "pussying out," in the patois of the gridiron) from the driving legs and pounding cleats of players twice his size. In a scrimmage with the varsity, he intercepted a pass and streaked down the sideline. "I'm gonna score," he told himself as the goal line loomed. That was his last conscious thought before Vince Promuto, who went on to become a college All-American and captain of the Washington Redskins under Vince Lombardi, burst out of a pack of pursuers and crushed him. He landed on the cinder track that surrounded the field. He woke up in the locker room an hour later, stretched out on the training table, with a concussion, bruised ribs, and a bawling Promuto standing beside him, saying over and over again, "I didn't know it was you, Midget." That made Tommy feel even worse. Howie Smith, the varsity coach with the Notre Dame pedigree, didn't help matters. Pacing back and forth in his Knute Rockne knickers, he kept shouting, "Who put the goddamn Midget in the scrimmage?" Tommy was back on the field the next day.

The following year, Tommy grew to five feet, 105 pounds, and made the junior varsity. He was still a second-string defensive back, but his tenacity won him a following. Or so he thought.

For the final game of the season, members of the Mount's jayvee team, other than the truly irredeemable, were traditionally accorded the honor of donning varsity uniforms and warming up on the field with the big boys. Tommy couldn't wait. The list of players chosen, though, included everyone but him. At the game, he climbed to the top of the stadium, sat by himself, and choked back sobs as he watched his erstwhile teammates doing calisthenics, running out for passes, and performing other drills with the varsity.

The following Monday, riding the subway home from school, the varsity tackle, Dutch Leonard, worked his way over to him.

"You got the best compliment of all down in the locker room," said Dutch.

"Fuck you, Leonard," said Tommy, in no mood to be teased.

"No, I'm serious," Dutch persisted.

After the game, Dutch told Tommy, Howie Smith asked Brother Dennis Richard, the jayvee coach, which of his players might be ready to move up to the varsity the following year. Three or four of the obvious prospects were mentioned.

Finally, Coach Smith asked, "Who's the toughest kid on the team?"

"The toughest kid on the team is the Midget," the jayvee coach answered.

"Well, where is he?" demanded Smith, looking around.

"We didn't have a varsity uniform that would fit him," said Brother Dennis Richard.

Making the varsity never became an issue. The following June, Tommy flunked three courses, one more than permissible. That, combined with an erratic conduct record, resulted in his expulsion. It was a stunning reversal of fortune. He had done so well on the Mount's entrance exam that he had been put in a scholarship class, a tribute to his intelligence that also meant his tuition would be waived if he maintained an 85 average, no small matter to his parents.

Shocked at being expelled, but looking to rebound, he decided to make up two of the three courses—geometry and biology—at the Delahanty Institute, a private high school in Jamaica. Without consulting the Mount, he spent eight weeks in summer school, passed the two courses and the Regents exams in both. In late August, armed with his transcripts, he returned to the Mount unannounced to plead his case. He waited for two hours in the dean's anteroom before he was ushered into the office.

"Brother," Tommy began, "I went to summer school and made up the two classes I failed. I was just wondering if there was any chance—"

"No," said the dean, cutting him off. "If I let you back in, I would have to let everybody back in."

"But everybody didn't go to summer school and make up the classes. I have my grades here from Delahanty."

"No."

That fall, Tommy entered Bryant, his local public high school. Bryant did not have a football team so he turned to the sandlots and signed on with his neighborhood team, the Woodside Chiefs, quickly establishing himself as a mainstay in the defensive backfield. The next year he decided to become a quarterback. By himself, like a mime, he practiced the movements a quarterback had to master—the handoff, the pitchout, the reverse spin, dropping back to pass, setting himself to throw. To strengthen his arm, he stuffed an old football with newspapers and fishing sinkers, making it heavier, then practiced throwing it over and over again. To improve his accuracy, he threw passes to anyone he could persuade to play with him. When nobody was around, he threw at a tree for hours at a time, retrieving the ball himself after each pass. His work paid off. In 1959 he led the Chiefs to the Pop Warner Junior League championship game and was named All-League quarterback. On occasion, he indulged in some tension-relieving goofiness, making the palms-down crowd-quieting gesture he had picked up from watching college and pro quarterbacks even when there was only a smattering of fans on the sidelines.

He had leadership qualities and organizational ability. At seventeen, he started a Chiefs team for kids fourteen to sixteen, entered them in the Pop Warner Intermediate Division, and coached them to the league finals two years in a row. He handled everything from attending league meetings and raising money for uniforms to lining the field before games. He was just a year older than most of his players, but everyone knew who ran the show.

Away from football, his life was a wreck. He blamed no one but himself, just as he never failed to own up to his juvenile misdeeds, perhaps the saving grace in his relationship with adults, whether his parents, coaches, or school officials. The drinking age in New York at the time was eighteen. Tommy had been drinking since he was thirteen and he sensed now, at seventeen, that it was getting out of hand. Virtually every corner in Woodside had at least one bar—he once counted seventy-nine in a one-mile-square between Queens Boulevard and Northern Boulevard—and drinking was woven into the fabric of the community. The men he admired were not the middle-aged working stiffs like his father, who came home to their families each night from their lackluster jobs, but the construction workers, men slightly older than Tommy, who trooped into the bars like young knights late on Friday afternoons, muscles bristling, paychecks in their pockets, rolling home to slumbering wives at three or four in the morning.

In those days, in Woodside, real men smoked Luckies and drank Fleischmann's. Whiskey ads regularly ran on the sports pages, often amid stories on high school and sandlot games. One ad showed a dapper, mustachioed man decked out in trenchcoat, bowler, and walking stick cradling an oversized bottle of Fleischmann's in his arm. "In Fine Whiskey . . . FLEISCHMANN's is the BIG Buy! 90 PROOF is why!" (Progress can be hard to measure. These days, it seems, the whiskey ads are being squeezed off the sports pages by ads for massage parlors and X-rated video joints.) A popular drink was a ball and a bat, a shot of Fleischmann's with a beer chaser. A variation was the depth charge. You dropped your shot glass filled with Fleischmann's or another of the favored rye whiskeys—Four Roses, Seagram's, Carstairs, Pleasant Moments, Three Feathers—into the beer glass and chugged. Guinness wasn't on tap back then, so sometimes you'd order a bottle of the rich Irish stout and float two or three inches of it on your draft. That's as complicated as the mixology got at McCoy's, a favorite hangout of Tommy's. One time some swells and their dates blundered in and called for a round of martinis and manhattans. Old Man McCoy threw them out. "Don't be coming into the House of McCoy ordering your fancy mixed drinks," he shouted at them as they scurried for the door. McCoy's had a slogan, one it shared with kindred establishments in the neighborhood. "Never Trust a Man Who Doesn't Drink." Bars routinely had a dog or two stretched out on the floor, as men would tell their wives they were going to walk the family pet, then slip into the nearest tavern for a few beers.

Vaguely, Tommy understood that he was better than he was showing—that, in fact, he was smarter than most kids he knew. He loved history, kept up with current events, and read lots of books, in those days mostly popular fiction—*The Blackboard Jungle* by Evan Hunter, before it became a movie, *The Hoods* by Harry Grey, Uris's *Battle Cry*. He did well on those infrequent occasions when he applied himself academically. He also scored high on standardized tests. He flunked out of the Mount because he would get home each day and hang out with his friends on street corners or at Margie's candy store. At Bryant, he cut classes most afternoons and headed for Margie's, where his fellow truants, boys and girls alike, gathered to smoke cigarettes, drink Cokes, and play the jukebox. He gave the school the number of the pay phone at Margie's as his home number, so when school officials called to report he had cut a class, one of the girls there would answer, "Yes, this is Mrs. Wall. I know, he came home sick. Thank you for calling."

By the time he was seventeen, he was a nighttime regular at the local bars, first Austin's, later Brennan's, then McCoy's and the Shamrock, drinking, smoking, occasionally hot-wiring a car. His father, who landed in Boston when he came to America and briefly washed dishes at the Harvard faculty club, believed in education, begged his son to work hard in school, told him Harvard and MIT were possibilities. Tommy didn't believe him, thought of his dad as an innocent.

If Tommy put little stock in his father's words, he had in John Hourican, the beer-sipping star of the Woodside Junior Rangers, a role model closer to home than Eddie LeBaron.

"John Hourican was everything I wanted to be," said Tommy. "He was a regular guy, he was smart, and he took shit from no one. And he was a great athlete."

Like Tommy, Hourican was a quarterback, but teams rarely owned his rights for more than a year, the sandlot equivalent of a free agent before anyone had ever heard the term.

About four years older than Tommy, Hourican drank and hung out on street corners and at Windmuller Park, Woodside's main gathering spot other than bars. Unlike Tommy, he was soft-spoken and excelled in school, possessing a kind of survivor's instinct never issued to Tommy.

Hourican was protective of Tommy, as if he had appointed himself his big brother. One day Tommy came up with a deck of French playing cards, each card bearing the picture of a nude woman in a provocative pose. He was proudly showing them off at the park when Hourican wandered over.

"Whaddya got there?" he asked Tommy, glaring at him.

"I got this French deck," Tommy replied.

"Let me take a look at it," said Hourican.

Tommy passed the deck to him. Hourican glanced at the cards, then threw them down a storm drain. Tommy was angry. He was also surprised, then embarrassed, that Hourican disapproved so strongly.

"How much did you pay for them?" asked Hourican.

"I paid a buck, John," snapped Tommy.

Hourican reached into his pocket, pulled out a dollar, and handed it to Tommy.

"Don't mess with that shit anymore," said Hourican, walking away.

Tommy had a great eye for detail, but for a long time he missed the obvious. He admired John Hourican's athletic skills, but he also liked the fact that John was a street kid just as he was. So some nights he'd see Hourican in a bar, but not register the fact that it was just some nights, maybe twice a week, while he was there every night. And he noticed—though he thought of it as a mild curiosity of no special import—that John often had books piled next to him at the bar. Hourican was taking a full course load at St. John's University's Brooklyn campus, in addition to putting in an eight-hour day on a job near the school.

7

Switched at Birth

I knew after Easter Sunday at Radio City that nothing was likely to get better at home anytime soon and that the important thing was for my sisters and me to survive our childhood. It was easier for me. My mother had instilled in me a sense of my own worth. She may have transferred her dreams for my father to me, but I always knew I was special to her. My sisters, with good reason, didn't feel that way. Pat, in particular, never seemed able to impress our mother, who invariably dismissed her achievements with the infuriating phrase "small potatoes." Even so, Pat, barely into her teens, was the anchor for all of us. She imposed a kind of order on our apartment, vacuuming, cleaning the bathroom, making beds, doing dishes that my mother left sitting in greasy water in the sink, a sight that made me gag. Or I made myself gag, I'm not sure, I just made it clear I wasn't going to touch them.

As much as I hated to admit it, I played an important role, too. My sisters trusted me to protect them, to calm them in difficult times, to deal with my mother at her worst. To be normal.

I did little things, like helping my sisters sort out life. When Pat

had a problem, she'd suggest we walk up to the Kew Rest, a delicatessen on Queens Boulevard. Our order never changed. A rare
roast beef on rye for each of us, mine with a side order of potato
salad, a Coke for Pat and a Dr. Brown's black cherry soda for me.
Then I'd try to help her work out whatever was bothering her. Usually I could. Not always.

"Can we go to the delicatessen?" she asked one afternoon
shortly after she started high school.

"Sure," I said.

I usually had some idea what was bothering her. Not this time.
She held back until the gentlemanly white-haired waiter in the
black bow tie and white cloth jacket padded over and placed our
sandwiches and sodas on the table.

"I heard about something and I need to ask you about it," she
said.

"What?" I replied, suddenly feeling uncomfortable.

"It's about babies."

"Uh . . ."

"Do you know?"

"Uh . . ."

"Bobby!"

"Would you stop calling me Bobby!"

"Look, just tell me."

"What did you hear?"

"About stuff, you know . . ." She told me what she had heard,
bundling the crucial words in familial euphemisms, but getting it
pretty much right. I wanted to scream at her, "This isn't my job."
Instead, I said, "Jesus, Pat."

"I just have one question," she said.

I took a bite of my sandwich and chewed slowly but couldn't
swallow, so I took a swig of my Dr. Brown's, started coughing,
and tried to keep my composure as soda gurgled in my nostrils.

"What?" I asked. "What's your question?"

"All I want to know is . . ."

"Yeah . . . ? "

". . . do you believe it?"

I hesitated, searching for what today would be termed an age-appropriate response, finally said, "Uh, yeah."

"Oh, gross," she said.

I let that lie.

I also protected my sisters in various ways. Pat, a vivacious kid with long blond hair and blue eyes, attracted lots of boys. Being a boy myself, I didn't trust any of them. I worried in particular about a guy named Eddie Keegan, who was maybe a year younger than me. Eddie was okay, an Irish kid with black hair and a spit curl, and a slick line of patter. But I didn't want him around Pat. One wintry day, the phone rang and someone told me that Pat had been hurt in a snowball fight and something about Eddie Keegan.

My chance. I ran outside. Pat had clearly been crying, but she wasn't anymore. The small splotch of blood on her forehead had dried. Eddie was with her.

"What happened?" I asked, eyeing Eddie.

"I'm fine," said Pat, trying to smile. "Eddie was—"

Cool Eddie couldn't keep his mouth shut. "Hey, Bob," he said. "A piece-a-ice musta got in the snowball. The—"

I punched him in the mouth.

Eddie was tough. Before long, we were pounding away at each other. Pat was screaming that Eddie had nothing to do with it, that he had gotten there after the snowball fight and had been trying to help her. Nothing registered. At a break in the action, Eddie said, "Bob, why the hell we fighting?" I thought about the question, Pat's words finally sinking in. "I don't know," I said, jamming my hands in my pockets and storming away.

There was nothing wrong with Eddie Keegan. The truth was, he was more than okay. I kind of liked him until he started hanging around Pat. I sensed that he was too fast for her, though, so I stepped in. That was my role in the family, whether I liked it or not. One of many, few easily explained and none having to do with washing dishes. And no matter how much I tried to persuade myself that Pat and Rosemarie would be fine if I wasn't there, I knew I was kidding myself.

The problem was, I was nearing the end of my high school

years and college lay ahead. Curiously, I never doubted I was going to college even though no one on either side of the family had done so. That certainty was my mother's doing. On good days, she was the best mother I could imagine, and she caused me to think of college as a natural progression in my life, not a choice to be pondered. I don't remember a lot of talk about it. I just always knew I was going to college.

But that was about it. There was no discussion about where I was going to go. All I knew was that I wanted to go away to school, partly for romantic reasons, mostly to get away from home. But how was I going to leave home? Pat would be fourteen, Rosemarie nine when I entered college, too young to be left in a situation in which who knew what the hell was going to happen next. In school, my Stuyvesant friends had been talking about colleges since we were sophomores. I walked away from such conversations because they seemed to have no bearing on my life. Everyone I knew took the College Boards, as we called the SATs, for practice as juniors. I didn't. Come senior year, I may have been the only Stuyvesant student not to take them for real. It didn't help that, aside from surviving, I didn't have any idea what I wanted to do with my life. I do remember at one point asking a couple of classmates what they were going to be. Doctor, said one; lawyer, said the other. "Why?" I asked, expecting answers on the order of "To heal the sick" or "To defend the innocent." What I got was, "That's where the money is." I knew even then that this was not a representative sample, but those responses bothered me, made me realize I wanted to do something more with my life than make money. No idea what, of course. Show business was not an option. None of my parents' musical talent had rubbed off on me, which depressed me not at all since I didn't want to be like either of them and, in fact, my two left feet and tin ear allowed me occasionally to toy with the idea that I might be a changeling, switched at birth.

There were, I knew, plenty of good colleges in New York City. NYU, Columbia, CCNY, Queens College, Brooklyn College, Fordham, they were all over the place. The new St. John's University campus in Hillcrest was a ten-minute bus ride down Union

Turnpike from our apartment building. What did Harvard or Princeton or UCLA or the University of Michigan have that I couldn't find less than an hour away? Nothing except what I craved most, a normal life, the prospective joys of which I had to weigh against the concern I felt for my sisters and my mother. As my friends applied to colleges, I held off, looking for a way out that I could justify to myself. Around then I saw a movie about West Point, *The Long Gray Line*, starring Tyrone Power. A military academy was different. There were lots of colleges, but there was only one West Point, and it wasn't in commuting distance. The more I thought about it, the more I liked the idea. Even setting aside my hopes of getting away from home, West Point fit my desire to do something that had meaning beyond making a living. I wrote to my congressman to see what I had to do to obtain a nomination, which you had to have before you could even take the entrance exam for any of the service academies. I had waited too long. He wrote back to say all his nominations for the year were spoken for. So now what?

Sometime in the spring I found out you could get into St. John's without taking the College Boards. I applied and was quickly accepted. That settled it, at least for the next year, time for Pat and Rosemarie to get a little older, time for something good to happen, perhaps my mother realizing she had a serious drinking problem and doing something about it.

She was two people. Sober, she was smarter and more sophisticated than seemed possible for someone with an eighth-grade education. She had charm, common sense, and an acute sense of right and wrong, which she imparted to my sisters and me. During her periods of sobriety, Pat, Rosemarie, and I would wonder if she had finally gotten the message. Those hopeful times invariably ended when the doorbell rang and she raced to the door shouting, "I'll get it," which we knew meant she had phoned the liquor store and ordered another bottle of Gilbey's gin.

When she was drinking, she stumbled and staggered on the street and slurred her words in conversation, bringing on embarrassed silences before people discreetly turned away from her. At home, she seemed to live for days on beer and gin and sandwiches that included anything, often sliced bananas, with Durkee's salad dressing slathered on them while we three kids opened can after can of Dinty Moore beef stew or College Inn chicken à la king or poured Campbell's cream of mushroom soup over canned tuna and called it tuna à la king.

At times my mother's actions were outlandish. Angry with my sisters for not doing the dishes, she pulled pots and pans from the cold, scummy dishwater and nailed them to the door of the bedroom she shared with them. When friends came over, she was often fine, terrific really, other times she humiliated us. Late at night, she would scream the vilest things about my father and his wife, her words, graphic and hate-filled, ricocheting along the walls of the courtyard that our second-floor apartment overlooked.

She'd do it in the living room, after Pat, Rosemarie, and I were in bed. I'd go out there, try to calm her down, reason with her, do anything to get her to stop screaming, knowing Pat and Rosemarie were cowering in the bedroom, that our neighbors were learning our family's darkest secrets. Sometimes she'd be lying on the floor with all the lights off. In the warmer months the windows would be open, so I'd run around shutting them, begging her to be quiet. Sometimes she wouldn't, so I'd put my hand over her mouth and whisper, "Mom, Mom, please stop." She'd pull at my arm and twist her head, so I'd press my hand down harder on her mouth. Then she'd go limp, as if she had passed out, or worse. I'd try to revive her, check her pulse, even though I suspected that she was faking. She took her time showing signs of life. And then she'd start screaming again.

So, in truth, nothing was settled when I got into St. John's. I thought of St. John's as a placeholder, not somewhere I planned to spend the next four years of my life. If nothing else, it would give me a place to go each day and keep me focused on college. West Point still interested me, but that seemed a long shot. In truth, I was spinning, unable to get control of my life and increasingly doubtful as I approached my eighteenth birthday that I ever would.

It was about this time that I stumbled on the Lynvets.

8

The Man from Mars

*I*n early September 1958, I left our second-floor apartment in Kew Gardens, walked a few steps to the corner of Union Turnpike and 135th Street, and climbed aboard the Q44 bus. Ten minutes later, I hopped off at Union Turnpike and 164th Street and slid joylessly into my first year of college. My status as a freshman at St. John's University made no sense to me except as a ratification of my belief that I was a prisoner of my own family. That first day was a blur, although I learned one curious fact: I was a physics major. I had no idea how that had happened, and I was determined to change majors, an easy thing to do that first day. The more I thought about it, though, the more I realized that, one, I didn't have any idea what I would switch to, and, two, it didn't matter. St. John's was a harbor of convenience until I could sort out other options. And, if I was serious about West Point or Annapolis, which had also begun to appeal to me, then science and math courses might help. They couldn't hurt, any more than a year at St. John's could hurt. But I was running in place at St. John's from the moment I stepped onto the campus.

About this time, in the part of my life that was starting to matter a lot, the Lynvet part, Peter Connor arrived in our midst. This was early in my time with the team, so I was still feeling my way with the coaches and my new teammates. It was a Saturday in September, two weeks before our first game, which would be against the Lynvet alumni in the inaugural of a preseason contest to honor the memory of Father Lynch. We were practicing at Cross Bay Oval.

"What the hell's that?" someone said. A few of the players looked up. "Holy shit!" someone else said. Now everyone was looking. A vehicle that resembled the upright nose cone of a rocket was bounding through the gate in the fence. As it rambled across the field toward us, we could make out two smiling faces through the futuristic wraparound windshield. The vehicle only had three wheels, two in front and one in back, which added to the otherwordly aspect of the scene. Someone joked about being invaded from outer space. Finally, after bumping across the field, the vehicle pulled up in front of Larry Kelly. No one said a word. If this was the vanguard of some extraterrestrial force, it was not a very menacing one. More like a couple of zany, misguided aliens seeking directions back to the mother ship.

We were still gawking at the vehicle when the top cranked open and a stocky young man seemed to float up through the roof, like a genie emerging from a lamp. To this day I still see an old leather Notre Dame helmet encasing his head, a broad grin creasing his rugged Irish features, and a cigar cocked jauntily in his upraised hand, as if in salute. I've since been told that my imagination has gotten away from me, that there was no helmet, no cigar, just this mystery guest and his goofy, endearing grin, which—as any and all Lynvets will readily attest—was more than enough. He climbed out of the vehicle, which opened from the front like a freezer, and along with his more athletic-looking companion, presented himself to Larry Kelly. Peter Connor and Jimmy Farrell reporting for duty, here to play football, an entrance that every Lynvet knows about and scores claim to have witnessed though there could have been no more than twenty-five of us there that day.

Farrell looked the part. Tall and solidly built, he carried himself like a ballplayer. We didn't know him, but we knew him. Aside from the oddball car, he was like us. From out on the Island, one of the first Lynvets from beyond the city limits. But not Mars.

Peter was from Mars. With his short stature, stubby arms, stumpy legs, and nonexistent neck, he seemed like a mature gorilla whose growth had been stunted, or perhaps a not-fully-evolved man. On his arrival he knew nobody on the team, but by the end of practice we all knew him. He moved from group to group, smiling, shaking hands, talking about the great season ahead, conceding that, yes, he had played a little ball, never mentioning he had made All–Long Island; played with Bob Reifsnyder, who was then winning All-American honors at Navy; and captained the Baldwin High School team. Who is this guy, we wondered? We figured Kelly had recruited him, but we were wrong, Kelly didn't know who he was either. From the start, though, we understood that he was something special, a small package but nothing less than a gift from the gods to the Lynvets. As we got to know him, Bob Bushman, an assistant coach, said, "It's as if he had a sign on that car that said, 'This team will never be the same.'"

Peter Connor, like an ironclad in the age of sail, had no vulnerabilities. He stood five foot seven and weighed 180 pounds. He had a large, square head that was out of proportion to the rest of his body, and it seemed to rest directly on his shoulders, as if his neck had collapsed under the weight of it. He had round, muscular shoulders, a barrel chest, and thick, powerful legs. "Like a little refrigerator," said Tommy Wall. "Nowhere to hit him to hurt him."

As we soon discovered, Peter brushed aside the strongest, most savvy blockers with a combination of football smarts and quickness. He was a textbook tackler, ramming his shoulder into the ball carrier as he wrapped his arms around the runner's legs, then driving him into the ground. He was, of course, an intimidator. One day a running back—a big kid, new to the league and much her-

alded by his teammates during the summer brag fests at Rockaway—dove off tackle on the first play of the game. Peter leveled
him, then slowly rose to his feet, straddling the opponent. Looking
down at the stunned runner, Peter intoned, "I . . . eat . . . you."

Said Tommy Wall, "The guy's eyes go out. I don't think he
gained ten yards the whole game."

On paper Peter played linebacker. In reality, he was all over the
field. He sacked quarterbacks, mugged running backs plunging
through the line or running wide, and, when the situation required
it, dropped back into pass coverage. He was vocal at a time before
trash talk. To opponents, he would shout, "You! You! I want you!
You're mine! You're mine!" Always in motion, he slapped teammates on the helmet, urged them on, and let them know he expected more from them and was determined to get it one way or
the other: "Let's hit! Let's hit!" He made himself the embodiment
of an already-stellar Lynvet defense and in doing so made everyone
better.

At a critical point in an important game, Peter ran over to me,
shook me by my shoulder pads, and shouted, "Bobby! Bobby! This
is it!" Momentarily forgetting he thought I was Jewish, he added,
"Do it for Father Lynch!" Do what? I thought I had been playing a
good game. But I knew Peter wanted more, and I wanted to give it
to him. Was I afraid of him? No. At least I don't think so. What I
wanted more than anything was to plug into his fearlessness, his
refusal to let anything—another player, the tension of the game,
life itself—back him down. He was at that moment, and so many
others, a life force, someone who played with such pure joy and was
so good at what he did that you just shook your head in wonder. He
was the spirit of the team, the soul of the Lynvets.

Peter was born in Long Beach, a spit between the ocean and the
bay on Long Island, in August 1938, the fourth of six children. At
Baldwin High School, he played basketball and football. Back then
he was five foot five, and his basketball shorts came down below his

knees. It wasn't a style statement, not in those days. The shorts were the smallest size available. In a game against Valley Stream, he paired up for the tip-off beside an opponent who stood six foot six. "Are you the mascot?" asked the Valley Stream player. Not in a snotty way, more like he was confused, as if wary of becoming the butt of some pre-game hijinks.

Football was different. Early on, Peter found the formula for success. He knew he didn't have the size or the speed he needed to excel, so he trained himself to react quickly. He also discovered that he had extraordinary instincts. He just seemed to know what the other team was going to do. Then he added the most important ingredient. Toughness. He told himself that if he was tough enough, emotional enough, if he never gave up, it would compensate for his deficiencies. And he was right. Once, in subfreezing temperatures, Peter played so hard and perspired so profusely that his uniform literally froze on him. It had to be cut off, as if he was in a full-body cast. Or a mummy.

Baldwin lost more than it won in 1955, Peter's senior year when he was cocaptain, a far cry from two years earlier when, with the gargantuan Bob Reifsnyder mashing defenders from his fullback slot, the team had gone undefeated. They lost the last game to their great rival, Freeport, by three touchdowns in a blizzard that obscured the goalposts. The following morning, Peter wandered down to the field by himself, clomping through the snow from one end zone to the other and back again. Reliving the games, cherishing the memories, replaying the sounds—not the roar of the crowd, but a discordant reprise of the many bruising collisions of which he had been a part. He loved football as much that day as he ever had in his life. He wondered vaguely if he might be able to play for a college team, maybe one of the small schools out on the Island, such as Hofstra or C. W. Post, but he knew he was kidding himself. "April is over, April is over," F. Scott Fitzgerald wrote in his story "The Sensible Thing" as his young protagonist realizes that the freshness of his youth has been lost along with his passion for a first love. In much the same way, Peter said farewell to football that morning, never suspecting that the Lynvets lay in his future.

He did not graduate from high school. His pattern throughout his time at Baldwin was to work hard enough during the football and basketball seasons to stay eligible, then screw off after that. He wound up a few credits short, decided to go his own way. In October of 1956, he joined the Army under a six-month reserve program, and returned the following spring. By then his family had moved to Gramercy Park, in lower Manhattan. He took a job as a mail clerk for the American Cyanamid Company, sorting and delivering mail at the firm's headquarters in the RCA Building. On weekends he took the Long Island Railroad back out to the Island and hung out with his friends from high school. Many of them were in college and they would bring Peter to fraternity parties where his antics were worth more than the price of the free beer he consumed. At one party, his friends were talking up his football prowess. Other guys, clustered around someone twice Peter's size, laughed at the stories and said he could never bring down their pal. The revelers started moving to the sides of the large party room, egging on Peter and the other guy.

"Hey, you can't stop him," someone shouted at Peter.

"I can stop him," retorted Peter. To the big guy, he hollered, "You ain't gonna make it to the other side of the room."

The big guy pushed off the far wall and came rumbling at Peter. They collided in the middle of the room. The big guy went down. They went through the drill two more times. Same result.

Peter was more than a great sandlot football player, more than a tough guy. His personality, on the field and off, was kinetic. He was a happy person, and his effervescent temperament was infectious. You liked being around him because everything was more fun when Peter was part of it. He was without guile and, in some ways, devoid of limits. At one of his first Lynvet postgame parties, he dropped his pants and paraded around in his undershorts on the shoulders of a teammate. It became a tradition. He did it at every party, and everyone loved it. Why? Because it was Peter, and somehow, actions that might seem boorish or embarrassing if others indulged in them seemed high humor in his case.

One summer, Peter and some Lynvet cronies rented a house in

the Hamptons. Back then, you could do it for next to nothing. For reasons long forgotten, Peter convinced his friends that it would be great fun to put a rowboat on the roof. Somehow they did it, then dropped the anchor down the chimney. They were sitting in the boat, rowing, when the police arrived.

"What the hell happened?" asked a cop, shading his eyes from the sun.

"You wouldn't believe the fucking wave, officer," Peter called down.

Another time, also in the Hamptons, Peter and Chipper Dombo were arrested. They had been drinking and had stolen a bench from a picnic table on a nearby lawn. At the station house, a cop checked the file he was holding, looked sternly at Peter, and said, "You're a two-time loser."

"Did you see what that first one was for, officer?" Peter asked.

"No," said the cop. "It just says destruction of property."

"I ate a menu at the diner," said Peter. The cop broke up, but Peter and Chipper were still fined fifty bucks apiece.

Peter's closest Lynvet buddy was lineman Hughie Mulligan. Their friendship began at the first Lynvet party of the 1958 season. Peter was living in Manhattan at the time, so late in the evening Hughie told Peter he could spend the night at his family's railroad flat in City Line.

About four in the morning, Hughie's father, the night bartender at Baldoch's, in East New York, walked in and saw a dim light in the kitchen. The refrigerator door was open. Closer examination revealed Peter, whom Mr. Mulligan had never met, perched on a chair, head and shoulders in the refrigerator, shoveling leftovers into his mouth. Peter didn't notice Mr. Mulligan, went right on eating. Mr. Mulligan went to bed. The next morning, Hughie awakened and wandered into the kitchen. His mother and father were sitting at their small breakfast table, drinking coffee, chatting quietly. Peter, in his underwear, his hairy chest lending him a resemblance to a black bear, was asleep on the table.

Bob Ferriola would later say, "Peter was Belushi before there was a Belushi."

9

The Gold Dust Twins

*T*he 1958 season began with a celebration of Lynvet tradition that quickly transformed itself into something akin to fratricide.

It was billed as the First Annual Father Lawrence E. Lynch Memorial Bowl, but long before the kickoff everyone was calling it the Alumni Game. Players going back to the first Lynvet team in 1950 were eligible to suit up against the Lynvet Seniors. Most who did were twenty-five or younger. They were not slower, only bigger in the way that men in their early twenties seem finally to grow into their bodies.

That put us at a disadvantage because Pop Warner had a 185-pound weight limit. We told ourselves we were in better shape and better prepared. None of us knew quite what to expect, but Larry Kelly warned us that the Alumni were taking the game seriously—working out hard, drilling a couple of nights a week. Names of vaunted former Lynvets were in the air at all our practices. Hey, I hear Jimmy Sims is gonna play. Yeah, Tom McCabe, too. So it went. Our opponents, it seemed, were to be the heart of the great

Lynvet senior teams that had won four championships in six years, including those three consecutive titles from 1953 to 1955. What about Lulley, old Passin' Bob? He was our backfield coach.

"Hey, Bob," we asked, "you're not playing against us, are you?"

"Actually," Lulley said with a smile, "I am."

No surprise, Kelly's first move on taking over the Seniors was to install Bob Ferriola at quarterback and move the tall, angular Herb Tortolani, who had played the position the previous two years, to offensive end, essentially flip-flopping them. I started at left halfback, opposite Tommy Vaughan, back from the Marines along with Hughie Mulligan and Chipper Dombo. I couldn't run inside, I couldn't run outside. Making it to the line of scrimmage seemed a monumental achievement. Vaughan, who was bigger and faster than I was, did better, but not a lot better.

Despite Kelly's warnings, I did not take the game seriously until it began—and by then it was too late. Guys I had seen hanging around practice, nice guys, always a smile for a new kid like me, were suddenly crashing through the line and battering me, at least until Ferriola realized that any chance we had to pick up yardage on the ground lay with himself, Vaughan, or John Faulkner, the fullback, not me.

And there were no smiles from the Alumni, no slaps on the ass, no one offering a hand as I pushed myself up off the ground and scraped the grass off my facemask. In truth, I felt small, physically small in a way that I never had on a football field, a skinny kid who had no business trying to play with the big boys. And I knew why. The Alumni wanted to win more than I did, perhaps more than our whole team did. Why? Because that's what they did, they won, they had always won. Maybe they were a little older and not quite in fighting trim, but they loved to win and they hated to lose. I could see it in their eyes as they settled in at the line of scrimmage before a play, I could feel it in the forearm that cracked across my helmet, nearly taking my head off, as I tried to pass-block for Ferriola.

They wanted to win and they did. They beat us 6–0. Lulley's passing set up the lone touchdown, and he was voted Most Valuable Player. As the game ended, helmets came off, smiles reappeared, hands were proffered. Everyone—Seniors and Alumni alike—talked about celebrating that night at the Imperial Cafe in Richmond Hill, which I gathered was the bar of choice for Lynvet postgame parties.

I didn't go. It was Sunday and I had homework to do for school the next day. I was taking physics, calculus, English, economics, religion, and Latin. The last was my sister Pat's idea. She was starting St. Agnes High School in College Point and was required to take Latin. I had choices, including French and Spanish, either of which made sense since I'd already taken them at various points as I bounced from school to school. But Pat said, "Why don't you take Latin, too? We can do our homework together." So I took Latin, giving the matter just slightly more thought than I had when I did whatever I did to become a physics major.

That night, as I sat at my desk trying to puzzle out a physics problem, I couldn't get the game out of my mind. By all rights, we should have beaten the Alumni. We had been practicing two nights a week and Saturdays since August. We were talented and well drilled. But we had run into something I had never encountered before, a will to win that we could not match. That didn't just level the playing field, it tilted it so drastically that, the closeness of the score aside, we were backpedaling all game. I saw soft Irish eyes crinkled in postgame cheer, the same eyes that minutes earlier had blazed fire. What was that? And how did I get it?

After the Alumni Game our practices took on an added edge. Pop Warner league play began two weeks later. Our first game was against the Astoria Willows, a team new to the league that we had heard little about. But Kelly knew something. How else to explain his decision to start his third-string halfbacks in place of Tommy Vaughan and me? Unless he was sending us a message that he was unhappy with our play in the Alumni Game. That didn't seem likely since Tommy and I continued to practice as the putative starters.

What Kelly knew, I realized later, was that the Willows were not in our league, thanks to a scouting report from his mysterious adviser, Paul Frey, who drifted silently around our practices like a ghost from seasons past, speaking to no one but the coaches. On our first possession, Larry O'Keefe, a third-string back playing behind our first-string line, scored on a twenty-two-yard run. A few possessions later, Kelly sent in the second-string backfield, which also scored. Tommy Vaughan and I didn't get into the game until the second quarter, at which point we were leading 14–0. Tommy immediately went thirty yards for a touchdown, at least a blur rumored to be Vaughan vaporized on the snap and materialized in the end zone a split second later. The Willows weren't pushovers, and they played hard. But they made mistakes, like a pitcher in baseball who throws a good game except for three pitches that are knocked out of the park.

We won 42–0. I scored two touchdowns and loved it. I guess it was garbage time, but I didn't know the term then and wouldn't have cared anyway. The first score came on a sweep of right end from my left halfback position. Bob Ferriola faked to Vaughan diving into the line, then pitched back to me. I cut inside the defensive end and watched Hughie Mulligan, our big left tackle, level a defensive back. Two other Astoria backs converged on me as I broke toward the sideline. I reversed field, sliced between the two defenders, and almost sprang loose before they dragged me down. I got up slowly, angry that I had come so close to scoring only to fall a few yards short. Actually, I hadn't. The field wasn't marked all that well. I was three yards over the goal line. My teammates ran over, shook my hand, shouted congratulations. I accepted the kudos humbly, but with a slight swagger, as if it were no big deal. In fact, it was the first touchdown I had ever scored in anything but practice or a pickup game.

And it was not over. Not long after, even deeper into garbage time, I took a picture-perfect pass from Ferriola, split the secondary, and scored again. In all, pass and run combined, the play covered forty-five yards. As I flipped the ball to the referee and trotted to the sidelines, I felt undiluted joy, an emotion enhanced by the cheers of my teammates, especially Joe Aragona, who with an unstinting stream of "Wows" seemed even happier than me, and a slight, damn-near-imperceptible nod of approval from Larry Kelly.

We faced the Baisley Park Bombers in our second game. Kelly rolled his eyes when he talked about Baisley. The reason was Woody Wickers, who had joined the Bombers along with a coterie of pals that had formed the nucleus of the Nativity Crusaders and, before that, the Nat Paterson Panthers and possibly one or two other now-defunct teams that rarely won but made you pay a price for beating them. Their players were tough guys, and their strategy was to cause you to abandon your game plan by drawing you into an open-air bar fight. To beat them, you had to resist the temptation to forget about football and simply kick the shit out of them. And that was problematic. The Lynvets were better football players, not necessarily better bar fighters.

Woody Wickers was a sandlot thoroughbred. His father, Woody Sr., had played for Ozone Park's Kutie Kimball Klub in the late 1930s, before heading off to war in 1943 and winning the Bronze Star, two Purple Hearts, and the Combat Infantryman's Badge. Returning home to his wife, Helen, and three young sons, he began trying to put together football teams. He was always scrambling for players. Woodie Jr. remembers pulling friends out of bed on weekend mornings, guys who had never played organized football, and telling them, "We don't have eleven men. You've gotta play. Otherwise my dad's gonna have to pay a forfeit fee." Helen Wickers recalled a boy named Pendy, who her husband allowed on the team because he was a good kid even though he was at least three years younger than the twelve-year-olds Woody Sr. was then coaching. Pendy always wore a floppy cap and an overcoat that brushed the top of his shoes. He never got into a game, but he didn't seem to mind, he just liked hanging around the team. One day, though, an injury left Woodie Sr. short a player. "Okay, Pendy, you're going in," the coach said. Said Pendy, "Mr. Wickers, would you hold my lollipop?"

Woody Wickers hated the Lynvets. His reasons, those he could articulate, seemed skimpy. He was Ozone Park, the Lynvets were City Line. Sharks and Jets, that simple. Also, each spring he would receive a letter from Larry Kelly inviting him to join the Lynvets. Woody was infuriated by the letters. He couldn't believe Kelly was so lacking in class as to ask him to desert the team his father coached. Hell, why not? Kelly had already picked off two of Woody's best friends and onetime teammates, both now anchoring the Lynvets' formidable line. More likely, Woody reasoned, the letters were just Kelly's oblique way of breaking his balls. The key to Woody's hostility, I think, is that after losing to the Lynvets at one level or another for the better part of a decade, he did not want to cozy up to them—he wanted to beat their brains out.

So did his mother, the redoubtable Mrs. Wickers, who hated the Lynvets even more than her son did and could not conceive of his ever playing for them.

"We didn't cross over to the enemy," she said.

Mrs. Wickers was renowned for storming onto the field in the midst of a game and cutting loose with lefts and rights at helmeted, well-padded opponents whom she perceived as taking cheap shots at Woody, no stranger to the cheap shot himself. I asked her years later if her husband worried about her forays onto the gridiron. No, she said, he knew she could take care of herself. She added, "If I got mad at him, I'd belt him, too."

That Sunday, true to form, Baisley knocked Tommy Vaughan out of the game in the first quarter. Then Baisley suffered a more serious injury. Their best running back, Mike D'Amato, broke his collarbone on the opening kick off and was lost for the season. The game wasn't exactly a bar brawl, but the Baisley defense, led by Wickers, was stingy and hit hard. Bob Ferriola completed some short passes, but neither Joe Aragona, who replaced Tommy Vaughan at right halfback, nor I were picking up much on the ground. Late in the second quarter, though, we started to move. Mostly it was Aragona, who in his first sustained action of the season on offense was displaying not just speed, but balance and power. I was picking up two and three yards on straight-ahead dives into the line. Joe was going for eight and ten yards at a clip on sweeps. And whenever the drive, which started on our own twenty, began to stall, Ferriola would hit ex-quarterback Herb Tortolani, who was proving to be an extremely able receiver, with short possession passes over the middle. With a couple of minutes left in the half, we were on Baisley's one-yard line. In the huddle, Ferriola looked from Joe to me, then back to Joe, hesitated for a moment, and called my number, a dive play into the line. I was surprised. If we were going to score, and I felt confident we were, Joe deserved the touchdown. But Joe was unproven and I sensed that Ferriola trusted me more to get that final crucial yard that would break the unnerving scoring drought. Hughie Mulligan winked at me as we broke the huddle. Woody Wickers glared at me from across the line of scrimmage. I burst from my stance, felt Ferriola slip the ball into my arms, then drove forward behind Hughie. I hit some resistance, twisted to the side, drove my legs, and fell into the end zone. Joe was the first to congratulate me on the touchdown, throwing his arms around me as I climbed to my feet. As we ran off the field, Kelly murmured something barely intelligible, and probably sarcastic. All I could make out were the words "Gold Dust Twins." We won 12–0.

The season's third game, against the Greenpoint Crusaders, the only other undefeated team in the league, stood to be our big test. Greenpoint, the defending champions, always fielded a solid team. Two weeks earlier, they had beaten Baisley 26–0, routing a team that we had had trouble scoring against the week before. Unlike 1957, though, Greenpoint did not have Tommy Wall's self-appointed big brother John Hourican, the rugged, scrambling quarterback who had led them to the title that year.

Even though it seemed like a throwaway line at the time, it became clear at practice that week that others had heard Kelly's reference to Joe and me as the Gold Dust Twins. The nickname stuck, especially as Joe and I became close friends, though it was generally used in a slightly mocking, if affectionate, way. "Here come the Gold Dust Twins," someone would say when we arrived at practice or a game together. If a Lynvet saw one or the other of us alone, the standard greeting was "Hey, where's the other Gold Dust Twin?" The nickname was not a reflection of our mutual football prowess, which, as it turned out, was quite disparate. Or because we were often in the backfield together, since we weren't. I started at halfback with Tommy Vaughan. Joe was a defensive back that year who occasionally got some time on offense. More than anything, it was a commentary on our growing friendship, our physical similarities—we were built much the same, though Joe was darker and slightly heavier—and our presumed innocence, which sometimes came across as naïveté. We both fell into the category of clean-cut kids. Neither of us smoked. I didn't drink at all, and Joe rarely did even though we were both eighteen. We didn't have girlfriends. Moreover, I was a college kid and Joe wanted to be one. Not typical Lynvets.

The Greenpoint game fully established the identity of the 1958 Lynvet Senior team. The defense, led by Peter Connor and Kenny Rudzewick, had already proved itself against the Astoria Willows and Baisley, not to mention holding the Alumni to six points. But the offense, after running all over the Willows, had sputtered against Baisley in much the same way that it had in the Alumni Game. Greenpoint was tough, as tough as Baisley on defense, and the game was tied 0–0 going into the fourth period, a quarter in which the team we were going to be for the rest of the season announced itself.

Bob Ferriola, Tommy Vaughan and the tall, silent Herb Tortolani—those three in that fourth quarter sent the signal that the Lynvets of the glory years were back. They took a team that was playing well and made it great. Vaughan, held in check most of the day, suddenly began picking up huge chunks of yardage. And whenever a drive was about to stall, Ferriola would hit Tortolani over the middle on a slant pass that the big receiver would carry for a first down, always dragging at least two defenders with him. Everyone knew it was coming. Didn't matter. Finally, Ferriola lofted a pass downfield that Vaughan pulled in and carried into the end zone for a forty-five-yard touchdown. The next time we got the ball, Ferriola, Vaughan, and Tortolani reprised their performance from the previous drive, Ferriola finally carrying the ball over for a second and final touchdown. The game ended 14–0.

Thinking about the game afterward, I realized that something fascinating had transpired in that final period. Both teams had played at a very high level, but late in the game, when it counted,

Ferriola, Vaughan, and Tortolani had found something more, an inner fire that scorched all of us, made us run faster, block harder. In the huddle, it was Ferriola, Vaughan, and Tortolani, the lead singers, the rest of us a doo-wop chorus. All three seemed electrified, highlighted, the ones whose performance would determine whether we won or lost. Ferriola, calling the plays, never raised his voice. But his close-set eyes, which swept across every man in the huddle as he spoke, communicated a ferocity that no one could have imagined he possessed on meeting him in other circumstances. Vaughan, always cheerful, rarely taking anything seriously, a guy who loved to dance, stood like a statue, awaiting the words from Ferriola that would turn him loose once more. Tortolani, cool, self-contained, older and more mature than the rest of us, somehow ignoring the purplish bruises on his arms, legs, and face that go with catching passes in traffic.

By beating Greenpoint, we moved into undisputed possession of first place in the league. We won our next game, against Our Lady of Peace, in a 36–0 shellacking. Vaughan scored two touchdowns, Tortolani scored one on a pass from Ferriola, I ran for one. We had beaten every team in the league. Not only were we undefeated, we had rolled up 102 points in four games and no one had scored on us.

We were unstoppable. The following week, we demolished the Astoria Willows 42–0, the same score we had beaten them by the first time. Then we beat Baisley 24–0, rolling up sixteen first downs to their two. Greenpoint played us even tougher the second time around, but we pulled out a 14–8 victory. The win clinched the championship, the first for the Lynvet Seniors since 1955, but the defense left the field grumbling. Greenpoint scored in the game's closing minutes, the only time any team had crossed our goal line all year.

The final game of the season, against Our Lady of Peace, was meaningless. Even if we lost, we would still be the champs. Tommy Vaughan, the free-spirited Marine, stayed out dancing till four in the morning on Friday night and missed Saturday practice. Kelly benched him. Even on the bench, Tommy was assured an all-star berth and probably would walk away with the league's coveted high-scoring trophy as well.

Our Lady of Peace had gained some experience and improved substantially since we had beaten them 36–0 a month earlier. And Vaughan was out, which meant not only that we were shorn of our best runner but also that the Gold Dust Twins were in the backfield together for the first time since the second game of the season, against Baisley. On that day, Joe and I lived up to our nickname if not our reputation, since, in truth, we had no reputation.

The field on that last day of November was frozen, so every contact with the ground hurt. But not that much, not when you were having the kind of game Joe and I were having. In a reversal of our first pairing, I was picking up more yardage than Joe. With Vaughan stuck on the sidelines, I felt a special responsibility. I was not just running well, for one of the few times in my football career I was running mean. Instead of trying to elude tacklers, I was looking for contact, throwing a hip to the side then barreling right into a would-be tackler, reveling in the surprise and, yes, the fear I saw in his eyes when he realized too late that I was coming right at him. I probably could have gained more yardage by staying with my normal running style, but at a certain point I didn't care. I was playing as if determined to make up for all the frustrations of my years at Stuyvesant. No, I didn't suddenly turn into Lenny Rochester, or even Tommy Vaughan, but for that one game I knew I was something special, a guy you could count on, like Ferriola, Vaughan, and Tortolani, like Peter Connor, no one to fuck with.

Late in the third quarter, I scored on a pass from Ferriola, my second touchdown of the game, which put us up 18–0.

"You just tied Vaughan for high scorer," said one of my teammates.

"You're kidding?" I replied. I didn't know I was anywhere near Tommy's total. For a moment, I felt troubled. We would not have won the championship without Vaughan. With Vaughan, Woody Wickers's mom could have played in my place and we still would have won. Now Tommy and I were tied for the high scorer trophy? How unjust, I thought. How unfair. How ridiculous.

How cool!

We struggled on our next two possessions, but midway through the fourth quarter we started a drive from deep in our own territory. You can't get further into garbage time than this. We had already clinched the title and we were up 18–0 with about eight minutes left on the clock in the final game of the season against a team that had no offense. But Our Lady of Peace was still playing hard on defense and our offensive linemen were drooling for one more touchdown. By now, everyone knew that I would take the undisputed scoring title if I scored again. We rambled down the field, mostly me running behind blocks from Hughie Mulligan and guard Bob Crowley, driven not so much by the prospect of a trophy but by the feeling that I had been asked to pick up the slack in Tommy Vaughan's absence and I had done so and I loved it.

Suddenly, we were inside the five-yard line. As we moved into the huddle someone whispered to me, "Ferriola won't give it to you. He's Tommy's best friend." The choices were Joe or me or the fullback. Or Ferriola could keep it himself. Hughie Mulligan said, "You deserve this one." He was right, I did deserve the touchdown. What I didn't deserve was to take the high-scorer trophy away from Tommy Vaughan. So I said something in the huddle for the only time I can remember: "Give me the goddamn ball, Ferriola."

Sorry, Tommy.

Ferriola looked at me as if I were crazy. He had thrown people out of the huddle for little more than rolling their eyes. This time, though, he laughed and called my number, a dive into the line behind Hughie. I hit the frozen ground two yards over the goal line, and never felt a thing.

10

Can't Do Math

I went to my first victory party at the Imperial the night we beat Our Lady of Peace. Got drunk for the first time, too.

My winning the high-scorer trophy was like a gag that everyone was in on, yet I sensed that I had gained new stature among my Lynvet teammates. Even Larry Kelly, drinking quietly at the bar, congratulated me, though his expression said I should have known better. True, but so what? Tommy Vaughan was okay with it. The first thing I did when I got to the Imperial was find Tommy and offer a half-assed apology. It would have been hard to fake the way he laughed me off, threw his arms around me, and told me I deserved the trophy. As had happened on other occasions with Joe Aragona, Vaughan made me feel that he was happier about some accomplishment of mine than I was.

The Imperial was on 101st Avenue in Richmond Hill, not far from where the Bergin Fish and Hunt Club, the preserve of the Gotti family, would come into being a dozen years later. When the Lynvets first started hanging out at the Imperial, it was a dingy bar. By 1958, Old Joe, the elderly Italian who owned the place, had

spruced it up. He added "Lounge" to the name, removed the spit-
toons, placed a large sign over the bar that read No Spitting, and
pronounced it a "classa joint."

Old Joe, who stood five foot two, had a love-hate relationship
with the Lynvets. Lynvet parties occasionally ended in fights,
though usually only when players from rival teams thought it
would be great fun to crash the festivities. But there were other an-
noyances. Charlie McLaughlin, an original Lynvet, would always
sit at the end of the bar near the kitchen and steal the roast beef out
of sandwiches as they came out so that the customers would complain they had been served a meatless meal—lettuce, tomato, and
mayonnaise on bloody bread. Then there was Peter Connor and
Chipper Dombo's recurring prank. They would feed Old Joe's bull-
dog, Duke, bologna from the refrigerator at the back of the bar and
give him a bowl of beer to wash it down with. "You son of a bitch,"
Old Joe would say the next time he saw of one of them. "You got
the dog drunk and he shit all over the place."

On Sunday afternoons, though, the Lynvets were Old Joe's
boys. He'd be on the sidelines cheering like crazy, along with Duke,
IMPERIAL LYNVETS stitched in white on his maroon doggycoat.

The parties were held in the large back room, which had wood
paneling and resembled the basements of many homes in Queens
and Brooklyn. I saw much of the paneling up close after the Lady
of Peace game as I celebrated my high-scoring title by sliding
across tabletops and into the walls, much to the delight of my
teammates, who were only too happy to welcome me into the
drinking fraternity with endless rounds of Seven-and-Sevens.

I had fun that night, just as I always seemed to have fun with
the Lynvets, but the next day I was back at St. John's. To my surprise, I kind of liked the school. Even more amazing, I liked my
courses, particularly physics and calculus. Not only was I good at
them, I was at the top of the class or close to it. In the back of my
mind, and not all that far back, lurked the thought that my academic success was fraudulent, that my old Stuyvesant pals—many
no doubt taking similar courses at Harvard, Amherst, and Cal-
tech—were laughing like crazy at my possibly thinking I could ever

be a physicist of any consequence. But I didn't think that. I looked at the courses as valuable assets in my secret master plan for getting away from home. I was probably nearing the limit of my intellect as far as science and math were concerned. Still, I was having a perverse kind of fun. I also stood first in English, which seemed irrelevant at the time, near the bottom of the class in religion, and, predictably, last in Latin.

I blamed my sister Pat for my problems with Latin. She never told me—though I don't think she knew when she suggested we take the same language—that in addition to conjugating verbs, you also had to decline nouns in Latin. Nothing in my experience with Spanish and French had prepared me for that, and I was resentful, as if someone had played a dirty trick on me. It reminded me of when my family first broke up and Pat and I were put in an outwardly serene but hellish boarding school north of the city run by two mean-spirited old hags who introduced us to porridge, Wheatena, and similar delicacies from a menu inspired by Dickens.

I hated the place and quickly came to trust no one except a few of the other kids. I particularly distrusted our teacher, whom I suspected of trying to destroy our minds. This is why: division of fractions. The school I left was working on multiplication of fractions, which seemed fine. Take two fractions, multiply numerator by numerator, denominator by denominator, get the answer. At the boarding school, though, the class was beyond that, into dividing fractions. This is what we were instructed to do: invert the second fraction, then do the same thing you do when multiplying. Invert? Turn one of the fractions upside down? You're kidding, right? Nothing I had ever encountered in math before, or have encountered since, made so little sense. For a while, I refused to do it. Then, seeing that was getting me nowhere, I did it but didn't buy into it. I treated it like a pill that I put in my mouth but refused to swallow, determined to spit it out as soon as the coast was clear. Declining nouns in Latin was like that at first, though I soon realized that it was not a monstrous trick, just something destined to torpedo my chances of doing well in the course.

By then, I had decided that I wanted to go to Annapolis, not

West Point. For one thing, it was farther from home, 250 miles versus 50, well out of the impact area. More than that, I liked the idea of traveling, steaming into a new port every week or so and being led astray by exotic women rather than kicking around dusty Army posts in the Midwest and dating lumpy farmgirls. It was about that naive, and just as mindless. Both academies also had TV series on about that time, both terrible even to someone who truly wanted to like them, and the Annapolis guys seemed marginally less dippy than the West Pointers.

This time, in seeking a nomination, I didn't bother with my congressman. I went straight to Jacob Javits, one of New York's two U.S. senators. Not sure why, maybe because I had actually heard of him. At the same time, I was not unaware that statistically I had severely decreased my chances. Both senators and congressmen could fill the same number of Academy slots, rarely more than one or two a year, but senators drew applicants from all over the state, not just a single congressional district. Perhaps going to Javits had something to do with my ambivalence about leaving home, where things had not improved and the prospect of leaving Pat and Rosemarie to God-knows-what terrified me. If Javits chose me from his large pool of applicants, my resolve to break away would be stiffened. At any rate, I wrote to Senator Javits, explained my interest in Annapolis, and received a form letter saying he based his nominations on an examination that would be given in a few weeks at a federal building in downtown Manhattan. I was heartened by the news. I was acing English, physics, and calculus at St. John's. I thought I had a shot.

There were a lot of kids taking the test, which was not surprising but not encouraging, either. The English portion of the test was fine. But the math jumped me. Not a single calculus problem, a lot of intermediate algebra, the one math course I had difficulty with at Stuyvesant. Mixture problems. Time-and-distance problems. Consecutive integer problems. Leaving the building, I didn't feel good about the test—or my chances for the nomination.

Yet a couple of weeks later, I received a letter from Senator Javits asking me to come to his Manhattan office for an interview. I was excited. I had made the first cut. Now, it seemed, all I had to do was show him I was Annapolis material and I'd be on my way.

Wrong. The senator was known for an impatience with small talk, and I quickly learned that the reputation was merited.

"You did well in English, very well," he said. "You didn't do nearly as well in math. That troubles me. I don't think you can do the math at Annapolis."

I was stunned. Why interview me if he didn't think I could make the grade? I hastily explained that I was handling calculus exceedingly well at St. John's, that I had pretty much forgotten intermediate algebra but could relearn it if necessary.

I could tell from his eyes that my moment had passed. My hopes and dreams, which I had allowed to wander far and wide since receiving the second letter from Javits, suddenly seemed as stupid to me as they probably always were. I thought of myself as an honest, hardworking, smart, highly motivated kid who had finally found some direction. But to Javits, it was as if I was wearing a sandwich board on which were scrawled the words Can't Do Math.

Shit!

I'd had my chance and blown it. What now? I surveyed the situation. I was on a wild ride at St. John's, doing great in physics, but sensing that I would soon top out. Then what? Maybe I was a late bloomer as a physicist. In truth, I really liked it, was fascinated by it. Math, too. Differential equations, the second-semester math course, was almost as much fun as calculus, and I was doing just as well. Still, I remained suspicious of my aptitude for both and felt that sooner or later, probably sooner, I would hit a wall. The damn thing was, I hadn't yet and the semester was almost over and my life seemed as directionless as it had the previous spring at Stuyvesant.

Spinning again, I suddenly realized that Annapolis was still a possibility. Yes, it was out for the coming year, but the service academies accepted guys up to the age of twenty-two. I wasn't even nineteen yet. Maybe I should give it another try. I realized I had an advantage. I knew what the test was like. I could get a book and study up on intermediate algebra. I'd write a better letter. This time, in fact, I'd get someone to type it for me. But I wouldn't go to

Senator Javits again. He was convinced I couldn't do math. Fine, I'd try the other senator, Kenneth Keating.

The semester was nearing its end. I figured another year at St. John's couldn't hurt me. I'd be even further ahead if I ever made it to Annapolis, which had a prescribed curriculum that required everyone to start as a freshman no matter how many college courses you had taken. But I had a concern. A year as a physics major was one thing. But two? What if I again failed to get into Annapolis? Would I be committed to a field I hadn't chosen in the first place, but too deeply into it to switch to something else? At a school I had essentially stumbled into? I decided I'd stay with physics but keep my course load light—one physics course, one math course, no more than that. I'd dip into the electives and see if anything tickled some previously undeclared intellectual passion.

My adviser, an intense professor in the physics department, had other ideas. By now it was May and all the freshman physics majors had to confer with their advisers and select courses for the fall semester. Rumor had it that my adviser was going to push all his charges to take three physics courses and two math courses. Not a chance, I told myself. The day of the conferences, several of my friends and I lined up outside our adviser's office, each determined to stop short of the load we expected him to urge on us, though no one was looking for as light a schedule as I was. One after the other, my friends went in. Each came out shaking his or her head. Three physics courses, two math courses. "He's brutal," said one. "He says we have to do it or we'll fall behind."

I walked in, determined to stand my ground. I told him what I wanted to do. He told me what he wanted me to do. I tried to explain. He cut me off, questioned my commitment to physics in a way that I read as demeaning my willingness to take on difficult challenges, the kind of pitch that, for better or worse, I have always been a sucker for. I gave in, agreed to do what he wanted, and walked out more confused than ever.

That summer of 1959 I worked for my Aunt Flo on the fringe of Manhattan's garment district as a stockroom boy. Aunt Flo, the daughter of one of my father's sisters, was actually my cousin, but she was much older than I was. A recent widow, she was running the small company—Herbert Goldberg Handbags—founded by her late husband. My father got me the job, though I don't know why. I could have gone back to the Rapid Messenger Service, where I had worked the two previous summers, for the same minimum-wage dollar-an-hour I was getting from Aunt Flo. I think I took the job solely because it seemed important to my father, who felt he was doing something great for me. Maybe he thought I had a future there. Maybe I did. I worked hard, everyone liked me, I was family, and Aunt Flo had no kids. Suddenly a mind-numbing array of depressing professional possibilities confronted me, everything from purse peddler to third-rate physicist.

I worked in the back with a plump, middle-aged guy named Pete who kept a ragged, rarely lit cigar clamped in his teeth. We were very compatible and did our jobs well. Mostly what we did was take flat, unfolded boxes and fold them, then place a handbag inside. Next we put the handbag-laden boxes into larger boxes, taped them shut, slapped an address label on them and shipped them off to mail-order houses like Spiegel's or department stores like Marshall Field's. Once or twice a day I was dispatched on errands, usually lugging handbag samples to a buyer for his or her inspection. I liked getting out, walking the streets of the city, looking at New York women, the best, all cool elegance, fire and ice. I beamed my best clean-cut-kid smile at them when they caught me looking, wondering if they could possibly know what I was thinking, figuring they couldn't or they'd have me arrested on the spot.

About three weeks into the summer, I quit St. John's. Actually, I took a leave of absence, which would allow me to return if I didn't make it to Annapolis the following year. I needed breathing room. Caving in to my adviser had been a mistake, I told myself. I felt like a water skier who wipes out but refuses to let go of the tow rope and gets pulled helter-skelter through the water. I needed to take charge of my life somehow. Just turned nineteen, I thought of myself as a young man of substantial, if unfocused, promise. I needed to figure out how to do something with my talents, whatever they were. If not, I realized, I'd wind up like so many older guys I knew, locked into a job they didn't care about, wearing the pathetic look of someone who against all odds keeps thinking that life has bigger things in store for him. Or like my father, but without the excuse of genius.

11

Twilight Time

*A*t about this time, half a world away, a young man named Mike Montore was languishing in the U.S. Army stockade in Mannheim, Germany, a prison the Army had taken over after World War II and trimmed in concertina wire as a home away from home for its hard-core criminals and lesser undesirables. Mike had reached a point in his life at which he felt totally alienated from the outside world. To his mind, he was working toward a place where he could be devoid of feelings, where nothing anyone said or did could affect him, where he was afraid of nothing because he had nothing he cared about losing. His ambition, to the extent he had any, was to turn himself into a stone.

Mike had a book. He felt the writer was talking directly to him. The message seemed to be that you can survive anything if you can hate it enough. The author said he learned young that "it was better to be anything than afraid." At another point, he wrote of a need to prove "that I couldn't be scared or broken or driven to my knees, that I didn't give a damn." Further on, he talked of another need, "to prove one can do without—without love, without faith, without belief, without warmth, without friends, without freedom."

The book was *Cell 2455, Death Row,* written by convicted kidnapper-rapist Caryl Chessman, then awaiting execution in the gas chamber at San Quentin. Mike was a few weeks shy of his nineteenth birthday.

When Mike Montore was twelve, he was walking home from school along Grand Avenue in the Long Island town of Baldwin as it started to pour. Drenched, his blond hair plastered to his forehead, he ducked into the nearest doorway. A sign said Baldwin Public Library. He had no idea if he was allowed to be there. It was quiet, but a soothing quiet, not the eerie kind. His eyes lit up when he spied shelf upon shelf crammed with books. He tiptoed around the stacks, hoping to make himself invisible to the adults behind the counter near the front. Some grown-ups and a few kids were lined up there, cradling books in their arms. Spotting a book about the All-American running back Red Grange, he pulled it from the shelf and sucked in his breath. Sooner or later, he knew, one of the adults was going to tell him to buy the book or put it back. But no one said anything, so he figured they hadn't noticed. He searched out an isolated corner, dropped to the floor, and started to read. Two hours later, he looked up to see a woman standing over him.

"We're closing now and you have to go," said the woman in a firm but friendly voice.

Mike, flustered, his soft brown eyes brimming with guilt, scrambled to his feet and hurried off to return the book to the shelf.

"Don't you want to take it home?" the woman called after him.

Swinging around, Mike replied, "I don't have any money."

The woman smiled. "You don't need any money."

"You're kidding me," said Mike.

"No," said the woman.

"What a deal!" said Mike.

Mike understood his family didn't have much money, but he

never thought of himself as a poor kid. Paul, his dad, had a good job, in fact two good jobs. He was the foreman of a five-man gang that repaired and maintained the electrified third rail on the New York City subway system. That was during the week. On Fridays, after his subway shift ended, and Saturdays he worked in a butcher shop in Morningside Heights. As the family grew he also put in a few hours each week as a furniture mover for McDermott's, a moving company. Molly, Mike's Irish mother, always seemed to make do. By 1952, the family had expanded to eight kids, Mike the third oldest. The two bedrooms of Apartment 4E at 136 Seaman Avenue in Inwood each contained two fully engaged bunk beds. Paul and Molly slept on the sofa in the living room, as they had for as long as any of the kids could remember.

Whatever the sleeping arrangements, Mike thought of Inwood as a child's paradise. It nestled on the northern tip of Manhattan, above Harlem and Washington Heights, encased by the Hudson and Harlem Rivers. There were parks and ballfields on which he and his friends played baseball, football, basketball, roller hockey, and a game similar to lacrosse using a Spaldeen and sticks fashioned from ends of fruit crates. Inwood Hill Park, much of it unspoiled wilderness with huge granite bluffs jutting up above the river, lay behind Mike's mottled beige five-story building. The park provided a natural playground and hideout for Mike and his young cronies, who would disappear into a forest of majestic trees and long-abandoned Indian caves. On summer nights, the kids caught fireflies in the park, pulled off their wings to expose the light, then pressed them onto their arms to spell out their names.

They skinny-dipped in the Harlem River, dived off Slant Rock under the shadow of the Henry Hudson Bridge and cliffs with names like Lucille and Geronimo. They always tried to launch themselves beyond the Shit Line, the foul, slow-moving water that drifted along the shore in which there accumulated garbage, debris, human waste, and what Mike and his friends called "white eels," more elegantly described by T. S. Eliot as "other testimony of summer nights." When you were coming back in, you jackknifed down just outside the Shit Line and swam underwater toward shore. As you were about to break the surface, you flailed your arms like a crazy man to clear a spot to emerge. When the Circle Line tour boat passed, the guide pointed to the naked youngsters on the rocks. The passengers waved and shouted "Jump! Jump!" as if they were watching some urban variation on the cliff divers of Acapulco.

Mike's building had no elevator, so two nights a week the superintendent would ring a bell and haul on a rope, sending the dumbwaiter up to each floor to collect the garbage. Mike and his friends employed the dumbwaiter for a youthful test of courage. A kid would squeeze into the bin, then pull himself up as far as he dared. After scratching his initials on the wall of the dumbwaiter shaft to signify how high he had gone, he would release the rope and hurtle downward in something very close to free fall. Mike was the champion, his mark somewhere between the third and fourth floors.

The commingling of Italian and Irish blood in Mike produced a youth mercurial and impulsive. At an early age, though smaller than most of his friends, Mike was independent and self-reliant, a natural leader. By the time he was nine, he was leading his gang downtown by subway to Times Square where they explored the cavernous station and played on the escalators. Other times he guided them along Riverside Park on the shore of the Hudson to the George Washington Bridge and across the bridge to the Palisades on the New Jersey side. Or he'd take them to the Cloisters, a museum that sat like a medieval fortress amid a panoply of towering oaks, elms, and maples high on a hill in Fort Tryon Park. They played cowboys and Indians on the stately terraces and, when they could slip past the guards, in the cool stone interior with its vaulted ceilings and priceless artifacts.

He was a happy kid, but also a scrappy one, often coming home bloody. That combative strain would deepen as he grew older. At a neighborhood gathering when he was seven, he noticed a man who seemed to be making his mother uncomfortable. The man was leaning against the wall, kind of trapping Molly. Mike's father was at work. Mike watched for a while, finally had enough.

"Leave my mother alone," snapped Mike, grabbing the man's shirt, pulling him away.

"Oh, no, Michael, it's okay, it's okay," said his mother.

Mike felt like a little jerk. He had embarrassed his mother, the man, and himself. A few minutes later, though, his mother walked over to him and said, "Thank you, Michael."

He was an above-average student at the grammar school run by an order of Catholic brothers a few blocks from his apartment. He was smart, but the strict discipline at the school was the key to his grades because he was an undisciplined kid and classes were large, which meant scant individual attention. His classes were never smaller than fifty-five, all boys from the fifth grade on, and at least once the class size broke seventy. But the brothers were determined to keep control and hammer some knowledge into the kids. Sometimes they used yardsticks as teaching tools. Either you bent over or you held out your hands. The brothers charged three cents an inch if they broke the yardstick on you. The worst offenders, of which Mike was one, would be taken to the back stairs and smacked across the face, usually four times, left, right, left, right, smack, smack, smack, smack. Once, to his surprise, Mike started crying as he was being slapped around. Said the brother, seemingly offended by Mike's reaction to the beating, "Get off it, Montore, you've taken a lot more than this before." Which was true. Mike didn't understand his tears, prayed no one would find out.

Eventually the family expanded to ten kids, four boys and six girls, but it wasn't until the ninth child was born in 1953 that the Montores moved from their two-bedroom apartment on Seaman Avenue to a small house out on the Island in Baldwin. Mike's father quickly built two rooms in the attic and after at least a decade the parents were able to move from the living room to a bedroom of their own. That lasted a month, until Mike's grandfather moved in. Then it was back to the living-room sofa for Molly and Paul.

Mike did not make a soft landing in Baldwin, although because he was fun loving and engaging he made friends easily. His new school was less demanding academically than the one in Inwood, which meant he should have done well, but there were fewer restraints on his behavior, so his performance diminished. And he was becoming a wild, unruly kid. He started drinking at fourteen, by fifteen he was going regularly to bars.

By then he was pretty much on his own. He lived at home, but that was about it. He bought his own clothes, even paid his own dentist bill. He never resented it, thought of it as the way the world worked.

He had been imbued with the work ethic by the example of his father, who was still working two jobs in the city, commuting on the Long Island Rail Road. His dad worked hard, so he'd work hard. That's what men did, and all too quickly Mike was becoming a man. He caddied and had a paper route. In the mornings before school, he worked behind the counter at Liggett's, a drugstore near the train station that was always jammed two and three deep with harried commuters in suits and hats picking up coffee and buns for their trip into the city. He reported to work a few minutes after six, finished up at ten to eight. School, a half mile from the drugstore, started at eight. He had to run the whole way to avoid being late. Weekends he worked at Nunley's Carousel for ninety cents an hour.

He went out for the freshman football team at Baldwin High School, Peter Connor's old stomping ground, but because he was short and slight he had to wait for others to quit or be cut before he was issued any of the limited equipment available. He inherited some within a couple of weeks. Not long after, he got sick, spiked a 104-degree fever, and missed practice. When he returned the next day, his equipment had been given to someone else. So ended his freshman football career.

Soon he was cutting classes and hanging out in bars with greater frequency. He was getting into trouble, and the punishment was harsh and laced with ridicule. "You'll never amount to anything," his father would say. "You can't do anything right." To Mike, that sounded pretty much on target. Something was happening to him, and it wasn't healthy. Behind the easy smile, he was developing a cold spot deep within himself, a place to which he retreated when parts of his life ganged up on him. It was lonely there, but loneliness was preferable to being connected to a world that seemed to disapprove of him on those rare occasions when it bothered to notice him at all.

In his junior year, the desire to play football returned. His parents still housed and fed him, but otherwise he was supporting himself. So going out for the team posed a problem. At that point, he had a revelation.

"I've got my whole life to work two jobs and three jobs and four jobs," he told a friend. "I really should be a high school kid for these two years because I'm not going to get to do it again."

He made the junior varsity as a halfback and later moved to quarterback. At some point during the season he found that the excitement and violence of football provided a temporary salve for his growing sense of rootlessness and the frightening recognition that his life was heading nowhere worth the trouble to get to.

The following season, his senior year, he made the varsity as a defensive back. Though he had grown some, he was still small at five foot seven, 145 pounds, but he made a lot of tackles and proved a rugged, savvy pass defender. Midway through the season, the Asian flu hit the Baldwin team, which was undefeated, and Mike was pressed into service on offense as a halfback against Hempstead. Baldwin's blocking scheme in pass protection often paired him against Hempstead's big end, a fellow named John Mackey. Mackey played both ways and would go on to Syracuse University, then the Baltimore Colts, where he starred at tight end, one of the best ever to play that position. Against Baldwin, he beat Mike's brains out. But Mackey never got to the quarterback that Mike was protecting. Even so, Baldwin tumbled from the ranks of the unbeaten.

The following week, against Lawrence, as Mike and his teammates awaited the kickoff, he surveyed the players lined up at the opposite end of the field. He couldn't believe how big they were. One guy went 285 pounds. Several others seemed close to that. Mike, already suffering from bruised ribs aggravated by his run-in the week before with John Mackey, experienced what for him was an odd sensation. He was scared. You know, he thought, you can really get hurt playing this game.

Then he had another thought:

Yes, you can get hurt, but you almost never die. And you recover from everything else.

Mike had a great game. Late in a scoreless first half, he intercepted a pass on his own ten-yard line and ran it back ninety yards for a touchdown. He made several key tackles in the second half and pulled in another interception as Baldwin got back on the winning track.

Football paid an unexpected dividend. During the season he met a girl, a cheerleader two years behind him in school. Just when he thought he had shut down his emotions, she came into his shrinking world and brought it magically to life. He met her after each class, carried her books to the next one, then raced to his own class. More often than not he got there late. He didn't care.

At fifteen, she was cute, edging toward true beauty. Dark hair, dark eyes, a fabulous figure, a great sense of humor. She was tall for a girl, possibly a shade taller than Mike. They joked about it, but resisted measuring because they didn't really want to find out.

He graduated in June 1958, just barely. Not that it mattered. It never occurred to him that he could go to college. It was never discussed in his family.

"I didn't even know that different colleges had different prices," he said.

In fact, there was no talk within the family about the future. On graduation day, though, his father finally came through with some career guidance. Get a job as a plumber's helper, he said, learn the trade, you could be a plumber. Years later, Mike would think of his father's advice as the blue-collar equivalent of the guy whispering "Plastics" to Dustin Hoffman in *The Graduate*.

It didn't matter. Mike had the girl, a first love that he knew would be his only one. They saw each other throughout the summer. The fall was a different story. She was in school, Mike wasn't. He was working construction during the week and caddying on weekends. Her father, an Italian who followed strict Old World ways, didn't like Mike, saw him as a loser. The one time they met, the father didn't speak to him directly and used an Italian phrase to his daughter to describe Mike. Mike insisted that she translate.

She hesitated but finally said that it meant something like "a golf ball washer," a big nothing.

Her father forbid her from going out on school nights. But she and Mike found a way. Most evenings, right after supper, she was able to slip out of the house for a few minutes, a very few, rarely more than five. With the sun starting to set, Mike would walk the two miles from his house to hers and wait for her at the grammar school at the end of her street.

Each evening, he'd lean against the bricks of the school, watching for her, seeing her silhouette materialize in the fading shadows of the trees that lined her street, recognizing the bouncing step that seemed to him an expression of youth and optimism and the promise of a lifetime of happiness. When she reached him, they gently pressed themselves together, locked eyes, cheeks touching, lips brushing. Not much talk. And then she was gone.

She would apologize to him, tell him she felt terrible that he had to walk so far for so little. He smiled and said there was nothing he wouldn't do for her, that the walk was a small price for the chance to see her.

"I love you, Michael," she'd say each evening before she ran off, turning once to wave just before she disappeared into the shadows.

For him the walk became an extension of their brief time together. On the way over, there was the anticipation; on the way back, he held on to her warmth, the feel of her as she leaned against him. And both ways, he sang a song, usually to himself, sometimes loudly because he couldn't contain his joy, a song that was popular that year, "Twilight Time," by the Platters, which seemed to capture their few moments together:

Deep in the dark your kiss will thrill me like days of old
Lighting the spark of love that fills me with dreams untold
Each day I pray for evening just to be with you
Together at last at Twilight Time.

His love for her became the touchstone of his existence, the torch that melted the cold spot inside him, that made him deliriously happy and happily open. Wherever life would take him, he knew it would be with her. And that was enough for him.

It wasn't enough for her. As the fall gave way to the first chill of winter, something changed. Though he wouldn't accept it, he suspected that she had found someone else, another football player, a guy in her class whom she saw every day in school the way she used to see Mike. Mike saw them together over Christmas but refused to make the connection until she did it for him, on the phone, a few days into the new year.

He couldn't believe it was over. Didn't she understand the depth of his love for her, that she would never be loved this much again? He waited for her to come to her senses, fought down the temptation to call her or confront her on the street, beg her to take him back. Gripped by sorrow, he longed for the cold spot that he had worked so hard to develop only to have her turn it into a place of warmth and joy.

He knew he was on the verge of making a fool of himself. He also knew he had the ability to make her life miserable. He understood what had happened. He had allowed his love for her to define him to the exclusion of everything else. Which wasn't much. He had no plans for the future and no belief in himself, just a love that cast a rosy glow over a life of little promise. "Golf ball washer" didn't seem far off the mark.

He never told her about "Twilight Time." He might have, if they had stayed together, and she would have understood. Now it was all his, not a lot to take from their time together, but something, more than nothing.

He joined the Army. An act of both love and self-preservation. He was a tough kid. He knew he would do something stupid if he didn't get away, something that would hurt both of them, maybe others.

Soon, with a mixture of sadness and relief, he felt the cold spot reforming.

12

Morose Delectations

*T*he Lynvets were a rough-and-tumble crew, hard-drinking, easily baited into fights, but because most were Catholics they attended church on Sunday. Those living close to one another, like the City Line crowd, often went to Mass together at St. Sylvester's before a game. It was a religious event, but also a social one. My sister Pat, when she became a cheerleader for the Lynvet Juniors, would go to Mass at our parish in Kew Gardens with Lynvet friends Larry Sifert, who lived in the neighborhood, and Mike Faulkner, from nearby Flushing and the younger brother of two stars of the Senior team, then take the bus with them to the game.

Religion mixed with football. When *Father Cyclone,* Daisy Armoury's book on Father Lynch, was published in 1958, Larry Kelly told everyone but me to read it. A lot of the Lynvets did; others picked up the high points and passed them on. And Kelly often spoke of Father Lynch as an example of fortitude in circumstances far more dire than those we were facing on the football field. In time the tale of Father Lynch was embroidered. Jackie Meyer, one of the toughest of all Lynvet linemen, reduced to tears the lone

Jewish player on the peewee team he was coaching with a dramatic recounting of how Father Lynch had died giving last rites to a Jewish soldier. Father Lynch did give last rites to Jewish troops and he did die on the battlefield, but I'd never heard that the soldier he was ministering to at the time of his death was Jewish. But who knows?

Because of my last name, most of the Lynvets assumed I was Jewish, which probably explains why Kelly did not put *Father Cyclone* on my reading list. I wasn't. When I was fifteen, I became a Catholic. Up to then, though I believed in God and knew a few Catholic prayers, I was officially nothing. My mother told me to put "nonsectarian" on school forms. Whatever their other problems, religion never seemed a point of contention between my parents. Neither practiced their religion, though my mother seemed closer to hers than my father to his, and sometimes she would take me to church with her on those occasions when she went. No doubt because of my mother's influence and my father's indifference to his Jewish heritage, I gravitated toward Catholicism.

I liked going to Mass on Sunday, especially when I had been to confession and could receive communion. When I couldn't, it was uncomfortable, as if I had been fingered in a lineup, people climbing over me to get to the aisle, watching other teenagers, their hands clasped before them, walking beatifically to the altar rail like the soldiers of God they were, kneeling, awaiting the priest. Suffering through that portion of the service in our pews, the rest of the teenage contingent tried to look nonchalant, as if we had done nothing more to deny ourselves the sanctified wafer than blurt out a "goddamn" in the course of a tightly contested ballgame. Or maybe French-kissed, a badge of honor that seemed unlikely to draw God's full fury.

It was almost impossible to be a casual Catholic because sin kept us on our toes. Tommy Wall prayed that he'd be hit by a truck as he left church after confessing his sins. He figured that was the only way he could be sure to die in a state of grace, the prerequisite for entry into heaven, the temptations for a teenager in the 1950s being such that he knew his run of restored purity might last only minutes, possibly hours, rarely more than a day or two. I was different. I was convinced in those moments of blessed relief after confession as I was kneeling and saying my penance—the standard was ten Our Fathers, ten Hail Marys, and what the priest always called a "good" Act of Contrition—that I would never sin again. I was so happy to be absolved of my infamy that it seemed inconceivable that I would ever again get myself in a similar predicament. But Tommy had it right.

The Catholic Church recognized two kinds of sins, venial sins and mortal sins. Venial sins were no big deal, things like calling your sister a dope, telling a small lie, or, with a single exception, cursing. Venial sins, though regrettable, did not have to be confessed, though they could be, lending them value because the penitent could employ them to lard more serious infractions in the hope that the priest would miss the big one in all the clutter. I pulled my sister's hair twice, I teased her four times, I made her cry once, I was impure with myself three times, I told a lie in school once, I answered my mother back twice. Like that.

Mortal sins were serious stuff. Unconfessed, they meant the flames of Hell for eternity, no possibility of parole. Murder, logically, was a mortal sin. So were stealing and blasphemy, and sex outside marriage (a lot of sex inside marriage, too). The oddball sin was taking the Lord's name in vain, which as I understood it meant saying "God damn." You had to figure God would wink at that one, or at most give you a hot foot. It was useful as a distraction in confession, maybe confusing the priest into thinking that taking the Lord's name in vain was the mortal sin you were hiding amid all the hair-pulling and answering back so that he didn't tip to the Hell-for-sure heavyweight you dropped in further down the line.

Sex was the problem. There was nothing you could do in that area that was not a mortal sin unless you were married. There was impure touching. There was self-abuse, which seemed anything but. There was prolonged kissing, which was loosely interpreted as beyond five seconds, and its derivatives, French-kissing and soul kissing. The trickiest to handle were impure thoughts, which meant thinking about doing it and related matters. The Catholic Church was unusually reasonable on this transgression. You were not deemed to have committed a mortal sin simply because an impure thought flashed through your brain. That was considered natural, even unavoidable. The thought registered as a sin only when you entertained it, that is, set up a screen in your mind, flipped on the projector, and allowed the movie to run uninterrupted for any length of time. At that point, it became a morose delectation, and that meant Hell. You knew the difference between the random impure thought and a morose delectation. If you had time to enjoy it, you had let the show go on too long.

My church, Queen of Peace (not to be confused with Our Lady of Peace, which sponsored the football team), held confessions on Saturdays from four to six and seven-thirty to nine, though you have to wonder why the confessionals didn't run twenty-four hours a day and have a hotline to boot considering the consequences of dying with a mortal sin on your soul. Usually two priests, sometimes three, manned the confessionals. You maneuvered to get the best priest, meaning the one who got you in and out as quickly as possible, thus precluding any detailed discussion of your sins. I always tried to get Father Scanlan, a young priest who had baptized me, taught me catechism, and prepared me for my first Holy Communion and Confirmation. Because Father Scanlan didn't ask questions—just listened, then assigned penance—he was very popular with the teenage crowd, which led to jammed pews outside his confessional. If you were on a tight schedule, you'd have to take your chances with one of the other priests, which could be dicey.

There were always a lot of teenagers at confession. I assumed the girls were there as a social thing, because what could they have to confess? The guys, I figured, probably had taken the Lord's name in vain, maybe lapsed into a morose delectation or two. I knew I was the worst, unless there was a murderer in our midst. Sometimes someone would go into the confessional and be in there as long as ten minutes. As he or she emerged, my friends and I would exchange nervous glances, decide we needed to stretch our legs, casually drift back to Father Scanlan's line.

Temptation could jump you anywhere. At one of the junior high schools I went to, there was this girl named Hildegarde. She was blond, clean-cut, and beautiful, then overnight she went trashy, wearing tight sweaters and hanging out with the guys in pegged pants, big belt buckles worn on the side and black motorcycle jackets that oozed zippers. One day she was in the back of the bus with her hoody friends and the driver ordered her off, I think for smoking. She sauntered the length of the bus, her head thrown back, her middle finger making insinuating little circles that ascended ever higher. When she reached the front of the bus, she thrust her finger defiantly into the air and stepped off. I thought I was going to pass out.

Paperback books were a real temptation, especially the covers. People called them dime novels, though by the early fifties they ran a quarter, some thirty-five cents. Fortunately for budding sex fiends like me, the book racks at the drugstore always had a wide enough selection that I could pretend I was looking at serious stuff as I ogled the covers of such classics as *This Woman* ("His life was ashes—she made it flame anew"), which showed a vamp sitting on a bed dragging on a cigarette, her robe open to show the swell of her breasts and sufficiently disheveled to reveal the inside of her thigh, *B-Girl* ("No life for a virgin"), *Sintown U.S.A.* ("Wide-open vice . . . Sucker traps . . . Mob Murder"), *No Time For Sleep* ("A Blonde, a Brunette, and A Man Spell Trouble"). The women on the best covers had several things in common. Upturned breasts, with at least a hint of nipple. A skirt or dress, often ripped, that afforded a glimpse of thigh. A look of availability or sexual hunger. Even paperbacks by fine writers like Norman Mailer, George Orwell, Irwin Shaw, and Nelson Algren were dressed up with lurid covers designed to dupe the unwary.

I don't know how many of those books ever delivered on their promise, because I was afraid to buy them. Except for one: *Ask for Linda* ("She Made Men Pay For What They Wanted"). The cover: A cool young blonde in a flimsy black negligee, a wisp of smoke curling from the tip of her cigarette. The negligee falling from her right shoulder to reveal most of one breast. Her legs positioned to create the dizzying illusion that, were her negligee hiked up another inch . . . I was twelve or thirteen and I don't know how I ever mustered the courage to pluck the book from the rack, take it to the druggist, and hand him my quarter. I got the book back to wherever I was living at the time and that night snuck it into the bathroom. As I thumbed through it, I could tell something was going on, I didn't know what. Then I found out. As my breathing returned to normal, I understood that I was going to die. For the next half hour I stayed in the bathroom and said Our Fathers and Hail Marys, which I had learned from my mother even though I wasn't officially a Catholic yet. Then I climbed into bed, put my arms at my sides as if already in the coffin, and continued to pray, knowing I'd soon fall asleep for the last time.

I don't know if Catholic girls had the same problems the boys had. It was hard to tell, especially with the girls who went to Catholic schools. The two I dated both kissed with their mouths closed and backed away when they sensed trouble. I think they received good training in purity at school. My sister had a teacher in the eighth grade named Sister Mary Leticia who seemed a hundred years old when Pat took biology from her. Naturally everything was sanitized. The class studied the body, noting from the illustrations that men and women were built differently, though there was never a hint from Sister Mary Leticia that the differences related to anything of consequence. And two or three times in the course of each lesson Sister Mary Leticia would gaze toward the window and blurt out, "Don't do it, girls," as if she were in the throes of an exotic form of Tourette's syndrome. Pat and her classmates would look at each other, but so far as Pat could tell none of them had any more idea than she did what the elderly nun was talking about.

Pat got caught up in the novelty of being a Catholic when she and Rosemarie began attending Catholic school soon after we moved to Kew Gardens. For a time she would come home and dress up like a nun, tying our mother's black slip around her head to fashion a veil and placing a strip of toilet paper across her forehead to serve as the white headband. Then she'd collect Rosemarie and five or six of her little friends, line them up, and march them along the sidewalks and through the grassy areas near our apartment building as if they were a first grade Catholic school class. She used the benches in the playground as her classroom, where she would drill the kids in spelling and arithmetic, probably teaching them something in the process. They addressed her as "Sister Mary Patricia." This went on for several weeks, until one of the parents complained to our mother.

As Pat became a more seasoned Catholic, she became less starstruck by the nuns and by the church in general. In high school a nun, mistakenly thinking Pat had looked at another girl's paper, slapped her across the face. Grabbing the nun's habit, Pat pulled the nun toward her and said, "If you ever lay a hand on me again I'm going to knock you through the wall." And once at confession she told the priest that she had prolonged kissed three times. "At some point this could get more difficult," said the priest, "because when you get older there are going to be body kisses." Pat was startled. Body kisses? She had never heard of body kisses. Then she asked herself, Why is he telling me this?

Many parents saw corporal punishment as part of the Catholic school package, even when it went beyond a rap on the knuckles. By the time Tommy Wall reached the eighth grade, he had been thrown out of two or three schools. His father took him to a Catholic school in Brooklyn known for its strict discipline. The headmaster sent Tommy to another room to fill out an application form while he conferred with Tommy's father. For his address, because there was little space on the form, Tommy wrote "Wdsd." The headmaster came in, looked at the card.

"What does W-D-S-D-period mean?" the brother asked.

"That's Woodside, Brother, that's the abbreviation for Woodside," Tommy replied.

"We don't like abbreviations here," said the brother.

With that, he balled his fist and swung, smashing Tommy in the face, causing blood to spurt from his nose and spray his clothes. When his father saw him, he said, "That's what he needs, Brother."

Whatever its problems (and back then few could conceive of the misdeeds that would come to light with the dawn of the new century), the Catholic Church worked for me because the rest of my life seemed so tumultuous. I needed an institution that didn't change, that I could depend on to be the same from one week to the next, wherever I might be living. Did I believe all the teachings of the Church? Yes and no. I remember non-Catholic friends scoffing at the concept of the Virgin Birth. That didn't bother me. If God was all-powerful, that didn't seem like heavy lifting. I never quite came to grips with Original Sin or the belief that babies who died before they were baptized were denied a place in heaven. My major problem was reconciling the idea of an all-merciful God with all the pain and suffering in the world. The most obvious question: How could He sit quietly by as Hitler sent 6 million Jews to the gas chambers? I asked, got implausible answers, decided to set the issue aside for a time as many Catholics older and wiser than I seemed to have sorted it out.

And there was more to my becoming a Catholic than my mother's influence. Perhaps because I had seen too many war movies with Irish kids and guys called Ski as heroes, or because both my mother's brothers had served in World War II and no one in my father's family had, I associated Catholics with strength and courage. I had grown up in a time of duck-and-cover classroom drills in which we were instructed to climb under our desks and cradle our heads with our arms when we saw the blinding flash that, we were told, would precede an atomic attack by thirty seconds. I never took that stuff seriously. I did sense, though, that I would someday be called to the battlefield, and it mattered to me that I not only survive but perform bravely.

13

Hurricane Season

*A*s the summer of 1959 faded, I quit Herbert Goldberg Handbags and took a job at Hangar 14, the Pan American headquarters building at Idlewild Airport. Aunt Flo asked me to stay on, but the hourlong commute didn't make sense. I made what we now call a lateral move, from stockboy to mailboy, but cut the commute in half.

The Lynvets had started practicing for the fall season. There were a few changes. Larry Kelly was gone. After saying for years that he was going to get a college degree so that he could coach at the high school level and maybe higher, he headed south to the University of Tampa. Jim Bertsch, who coached the line the previous year, took over.

Jim had been a fiery lineman for John Adams, and later the Lynvets, and now was teaching high school math. The older guys knew him as someone who carried so little cash with him that he often paid for ten-cent beers with personal checks—by the beer. Jim worked hard, knew what he was doing, but lacked Kelly's football knowledge, attention to detail, and intensity, which, though understated, had infused all of us. Still, we reasoned that a team that had dominated the Pop Warner Senior Division the previous year should be able to get by with a competent manager, if not a stirring leader, as coach. Especially since we had only lost two key players. As it turned out, we had a lot to learn.

Herb Tortolani, our big, dependable receiver, had turned twenty-two and was no longer eligible to play under league rules. Yes, his absence would be felt, especially in third-and-long situations where his ability to snare Ferriola's short slant passes and battle for first downs had kept many of our drives alive the year before. But we had picked up an All-City end, Bob Hoenig, a solid blocker with good hands.

The other player we lost was Chipper Dombo, whom Larry took with him to Tampa. A scrappy, undersized guard, Chipper had captained the Seniors the year before, anchored our offensive line, and provided more than his share of laughs, though he never seemed to get the joke himself.

Women and cars, in combination with beer, were Chipper's undoing. Any girl who went out on a second date with him was sure to get a proposal of marriage. He was known to chase women up stairs, along beaches, through parking lots. One night that summer, Chipper, Hughie Mulligan, Peter Connor, and a couple of other Lynvets got into a bar fight in Long Beach. Peter needed stitches, so they went to a nearby hospital. As they waited in the emergency room, a shapely teenage girl caught their attention. She was in a wheelchair, having suffered a sprained foot, her mother attending her.

At some point, Hughie noticed that Chipper was missing. Just then the door to a treatment room swung open. Chipper, clad in a doctor's smock three sizes too big, stumbled out, a stethoscope dangling from his neck, a crew-cut Groucho absent the mustache. Pointing to the girl, he yelled, "Next!" The mother started to wheel the girl in, but Chipper edged the mother aside and stammered, "I'll, uh, do that. Only patients are, uh, allowed inside." Hughie watched the mother silently fuming, figured that Chipper's beery aura and inability to take two steps without tripping on the smock had triggered her suspicions. Within seconds she rushed into the treatment room, ending the examination before it got started.

Another time, Chipper's battered Volkswagen was discovered resting upside down on a six-foot snowbank outside the Imperial. To this day, no one has been able to explain it.

Losing Chipper mattered. His madcap escapades, which he invariably denied, had become part of the texture of the Lynvets, as had his occasionally vacant stare, as if he had somehow lost the thread of a conversation in which a moment before he had been deeply engaged. Self-effacing and endearing off the field, he was a tiger on it, small but able to perfectly leverage his moves so that he could put an opponent thirty pounds heavier on his back with what seemed little more than a shrug. Once, sensing an absence of fire in me, he grabbed my shoulder pads, bared his teeth, and stared into my eyes. He never said a word, but the stare, accompanied by a nearly imperceptible bobbing of his head, told me more about myself than I wanted to know.

Still, even without Tortolani and Chipper, we were loaded. Bob Ferriola was back. So were Tommy Vaughan, Peter Connor, Kenny Rudzewick, Hughie, John and Paul Faulkner, Joe Aragona. Lots of other guys, including me. Maybe the high-scorer award was tainted, but I wasn't a bad guy to have playing alongside Vaughan. The way we figured it, we would cruise to a second-straight championship.

Our confidence was reinforced in late September when we beat the Alumni 6–0, the identical score as the previous year when we were on the losing end. With more than a thousand fans in the stands at Woodrow Wilson Vocational High School, Tommy Vaughan took a pitchout from Ferriola in the second half and scampered thirty-five yards for the game's lone touchdown.

A week later, we played our final preseason game against a black team from St. Albans that competed in an unlimited league, which meant they were older and bigger than us. Meaner, too. Bob Ferriola didn't suit up. He had been hurt late in the Alumni Game when a lineman crashed over center and twisted his right ankle. It didn't seem like much at the time, but it turned out that the lateral ligaments of his ankle were torn, putting him out of action for at least a month. We won the game in the mud 6–0, once again on a stunning run by Vaughan, sixty yards in the blink of an eye. My father came to the game with my Uncle Frank, both rabid baseball fans who knew nothing about football. The game was not my best, in fact I did little of note except give Vaughan a chance to catch his breath every few plays, but it was the only time my father saw me on the gridiron. Because of the mud, you couldn't see our numbers, not for long. Still, my father was thrilled after the game.

"Bobby, Bobby, all I could hear was Timberg did this, Timberg did that, the guy never stopped talking about you," he said, meaning the field announcer, a bonus at the Alumni Game.

What he had heard, I realized, was, Timberg thrown for a three-yard loss, Timberg loses a yard, Timberg can't get outside, dropped behind the line. Stuff like that. My Uncle Frank, drawing on his long cigar, smiled benignly, said little. I was grateful he was hard of hearing, though I suspected he had heard enough to know the reality of my performance.

For the second game in a row, we lost a key player without initially realizing the severity of the injury. In the fourth quarter Tommy Vaughan took a punishing hit from a St. Albans linebacker. The collision left both players writhing on the field as teammates gathered around their fallen comrades. Vaughan struggled to his feet, but we soon learned that he had bruised his kidney. He didn't play another game, not that season, not ever.

We opened the 1959 Pop Warner season the following Sunday against Greenpoint, the team that had played us toughest the previous year. We did so without our two biggest offensive threats, Ferriola and Vaughan. Bobby Schmitt, who had played quarterback out on the Island, stepped in for Ferriola. In Vaughan's spot, right halfback, was the largely untested Joe Aragona. The Gold Dust Twins together again, not exactly cause for celebration.

Greenpoint was no match for us. We romped, 27–6. I scored one touchdown, Joe scored two. Joe was unstoppable. Vaughan may have had a step on Joe, but Joe simply didn't go down, not without at least two and usually three players hitting him. His balance was striking. Time after time he'd spin away from tackles, leaving opponents grabbing for air, at times actually cartwheeling over them and landing on his feet. Other times, and this was the most incredible thing, he'd be hit so hard that he seemed to be hurtling toward the ground only to somehow stop his fall, regain his footing and resume his run. Really, he'd put a hand out in front of him as if to break his fall, touch the ground with a finger—a single finger—and bounce up again and continue on his way. Suddenly the loss of Vaughan didn't seem such a disaster.

As the gun went off, Joe bounded over. "Bob, wow, you had some game," he said, hugging me.

"Joe, thanks, but you're the one that had the great game," I said as teammates moved past, slapping Joe on the back, more than a few shouting "Gold Dust Twins!"

"You think so?" Joe asked.

"Jesus, Joe, yes! Everybody thinks so."

"I don't know, Bob. I missed a few blocks. And I should have scored on that last run."

"You mean where you damn near carried the whole Greenpoint team into the end zone with you? That run? Joe, relax. You were great."

"You really think so? Wow."

"Besides," I said, "you never block."

About that time, Joe started calling me Brother.

To hear Joe Aragona tell it, he was born Fortune's child. If so, he had a short run in that role. His father was a master electrician who installed the lights at Marine Park, where the Lynvets played some of their games, and the traffic lights along Atlantic Avenue, a main thoroughfare that traversed Brooklyn and Queens. His mother handled the books for her brother-in-law's clothing company. The Aragona family, which also included Joe's older sister, Theresa, had a car and enough disposable income that his parents were looking for a house in the upscale Queens neighborhood of Jamaica Estates when Joe arrived. Before they found one, the good fortune ran out. His father, after an extended illness, died from a heart condition that may have had its roots in a childhood battle with rheumatic fever. Joe was three.

In the years that followed, Joe moved around. Not as much as I did, but enough, and in tougher neighborhoods. Always the new kid, he found himself getting in fights, which was fine one-on-one. But everyone who came at him seemed to have an intimidating support system—either a gang or a crowd or brawny older brothers. Though outgoing and gregarious, he became something of a loner—for Joe, an unnatural state. When he was in grade school, because his mother worked and his sister was too young to take care of him, he lived with his grandparents. When I met him, Joe, his mother, and Theresa shared a two-bedroom apartment in Rego Park.

He went to a rough high school, Franklin K. Lane in East New York, a huge institution beset by gangs and racial problems. For a time, because he felt threatened, he thought about joining a gang, or at least taking on the protective coloring of the tough kids at the school, the hoods, as they were known. But his mother, tiny and soft-spoken, had a will of iron. He told her he wanted a DA, a haircut popular with teenage thugs that swept back like the rear end of a duck. You're getting a crew cut, she said, and made it stick. They went to a clothing store. Joe said he wanted a motorcycle jacket, black, with lots of zippers. She walked out of the store. They went for shoes. He asked for motorcycle boots. She walked out of the store.

He was playing pick-up football at a local park in the fall of 1956 and one of the kids told him about the Lynvet Juniors. The team had one game left, and Joe went to watch. He was impressed. He had played some baseball at Lane, but the school had no football team and he had never played the sport in an organized way. The following year he went out for the Lynvets. Late in the season, before a game against Resurrection Ascension, Jack Clark, the head coach, announced that some scouts from Yale would be in the stands. Joe was probably the only guy on the team that believed

Clark and he had the game of his short football career. He was so good that some RA players came to the locker room after the game looking for Number 5 so they could shake his hand. Joe was flattered, but he had bigger things on his mind.

"Excuse me, Jack, where are the scouts from Yale?" he asked the coach in that deadly serious tone that reveals the terminally gullible.

Clark gave Joe a sheepish grin: "I'm sorry, Joe. I just said that so you guys would play good."

Joe was crestfallen. He had convinced himself that the Lynvets could be his ticket to college and a new life and in that moment reality jumped him with the ferocity of all the big brothers who had ever ganged up on him.

But Joe was as resilient a person as he was a football player. You could hit him, but he never seemed to go down. When I met him in 1958, he was going to Queens College at night, trying to muster the B average that he needed so that he could attend tuition-free as a fully matriculated day student. He kept falling just short, his average each semester over the next two years a B-minus. Was he discouraged? Yes. Would he give up? Not a chance.

Joe had his own way of preparing for a game, one that drove us all crazy. By the season of 1959, the jukebox in the basement of McLaughlin's bar where we dressed for games had been repaired. To psych himself up, Joe would cram nickels into the machine and play the Della Reese hit "Don't You Know," over and over again. God, I hated that song, almost as much as "Doggie in the Window," "Que Sera, Sera," and anything by Percy Faith.

My pregame preparations probably were just as odd, though less intrusive. Once in uniform, I'd sit there reading a volume of verse by the English poet A. E. Housman that reflected my increasingly melancholy temperament and ridiculously heroic aspirations.

> *Here dead lie we because we did not choose*
> *   To live and shame the land from which we sprung.*
> *Life, to be sure, is nothing much to lose;*
> *   But young men think it is, and we were young.*

The Senior Division in 1959 consisted of just four teams, which meant we'd play each team three times. The Astoria Willows and Our Lady of Peace, the teams that I had scored all but one of my touchdowns against the previous year, had dropped out of the league. That left two teams from 1958—Greenpoint, whom we had just crushed, and the Woody Wickers–led Baisley Park Bombers, whom we knew we would always beat even if we had to pay a price.

The fourth team, the Rockaway Knights, was new to the league. They were said to have some fine players, including Tommy Chapman, one of the few black players in Pop Warner, an all-purpose back known for his speed, elusiveness, and pass-catching ability. We played Rockaway next, and at practice the week before I kept hearing another name—someone called Hurricane, Rockaway's quarterback, whom several of the Lynvets seemed to know and think a lot of. But, really, the minor buildup to the Rockaway game was mostly to keep us interested. The week before, in its first game, Rockaway had been beaten by Baisley 12–2, which meant that the newcomers fell well short of the offensive juggernaut they seemed to be on paper.

Rockaway beat us 24–0. Mopped the field with us. Hurricane turned out to be John Hourican, Tommy Wall's friend. Hourican starred as a hard-hitting third baseman at Bishop Loughlin High School, and, because Loughlin had no football team, tore up the sandlot leagues as a quarterback. Like Bob Ferriola, he was a franchise player, the kind of guy who brought credibility and often a championship to any team he played with. He was not the classic quarterback, standing just five foot ten and having only a moderately strong arm. But he was muscular and powerful, could run over defenders, and specialized in a vanishing art, the jump pass, which he threw on the run with stunning accuracy. More than anything else, he brought a mind-set to the game on which the Lynvets liked to think they held the copyright.

"Bob Ferriola was stylish," said Tommy Wall. "John Hourican's attitude was 'I'll beat the shit out of you one way or the other. I'll beat you running or I'll beat you passing. But I'll beat you.' "

And he did. He ran, passed, blocked, killed us. According to The *Wave,* the weekly Rockaway paper that referred to him in print all season as John Hurricane, he completed ten—ten!—of his passes to just one receiver, Don Moran, a strong, tall end whom we simply could not cover. That didn't include the seventy-five-yard touchdown pass he threw to someone else.

Joe and I did little to obscure the absence of Bob Ferriola and Tommy Vaughan or to live up to our nickname, which had begun to seem less fanciful after our big game against Greenpoint. For me, the loss to Rockaway included my lowest moment as a Lynvet. In the second quarter, Bobby Schmitt, filling in again for Ferriola, called my number, a dive into the line behind Hughie Mulligan. Hughie opened the hole, but two yards downfield Rockaway's big tackle, Roger O'Gara, hit me, wrapped me up, and flung me down. I fumbled as I crashed into the ground. These days, the rules say the ground can't cause a fumble. Back then, the ground almost always did. I lay there like a splattered egg. Everything hurt as I struggled to my feet. But the physical pain was nothing compared to the anguish I felt as I saw the look on Hughie Mulligan's face. Total disbelief. A fumble. The Lynvets never fumbled. At that moment I fully understood the warning John Heisman issued to his Georgia Tech teams at the beginning of each new season: Better to have died as a small boy than ever to fumble the football.

In mid-October, I wrote to Senator Keating telling him of my interest in Annapolis. He replied a week or so later, saying he had only a single slot for the coming year and promising to let me know the date of the test on which he would base his nomination. This again brought home to me the very narrow window I had given myself. I bought a book on intermediate algebra and started studying regularly. I had time. My job at Pan American did not exactly make intellectual demands on me.

This is what the job consisted of: Mail pouches came in constantly. We dumped them out on a big table, sorted the envelopes and packages, placed the bundles in tublike carts, and pushed off on our rounds four times a day. John Henry, the head mailboy and my closest friend at work, had the executive offices, where the secretaries were the prettiest and best dressed. The junior man, I had the maintenance area, where I delivered to heavyset men in overalls.

Actually, I liked the job, viewed it as the perfect holding pattern, though I had a few dark thoughts, not for the first time, about my affinity for mindless tasks and where that might be leading. The mailroom supervisor, Bob Perez, was a warm, considerate boss in his early twenties. He always wore a suit to work and kept his jacket on all day no matter how hot it got, like Ronald Reagan years later in the Oval Office. The mailboys wore white shirts and ties. The mail came not just from the post office but from all of Pan Am's far-flung overseas outposts as well. The pouches carried three-letter station designations—LHR, ORL, BER, TYO, CPH, ROM, SPL. As I decoded the letters, I pictured the fabulous cities they represented, wondered whether I would make it to Annapolis and eventually have the chance to see them myself.

The week after Rockaway, we played the Baisley Park Bombers. Bob Ferriola suited up for the game, but his ankle was still giving him problems and he didn't start. Our offense was ragged, out of synch—eleven guys straining to get it right but unable to put together two good plays in succession. By late in the second quarter Baisley led by a touchdown, thanks to the running of Woody Wickers and Mike D'Amato, a big back who had been hurt the previous year.

Coach Bertsch, on the sideline, said to Ferriola: "Can you play?"

"I'll try," Ferriola replied.

As he ran onto the field, Hughie Mulligan broke into a big smile and began clapping. Soon we all were clapping. On the other side of the line, I saw Woody Wickers measuring Ferriola. "Okay," Bob said as the huddle formed around him, "let's get something going." And that was it, we were back to normal. Pass, run, run, pass, touchdown. The offense was purring again, a missing part restored. Wickers went after Ferriola on every play, but it didn't matter. We won by two touchdowns, the scoring drives fueled by Ferriola's passing and the running of Joe Aragona.

The following week we murdered Greenpoint, 32–0. John Faulkner, our taciturn fullback, scored twice on short runs set up by Joe's lengthy scampers and Ferriola's strong and accurate arm. Eddie Steffens, a slim, rock-hard defensive back, intercepted a pass in the end zone and ran it back 102 yards. I scored a long touchdown, about forty yards, behind a block from Hughie Mulligan and a drawn-up Greenpoint secondary that allowed me to run untouched from the backfield to the end zone. In the second quarter, I was knocked senseless when someone's knee caught me flush on the helmet as I was throwing a block for Joe. I returned to the world early in the fourth quarter, aimlessly wandering the sideline. Coach Bertsch and someone else ran over to me, asked how many fingers they were holding up, sent me back into the game when I came within two of the right answer.

That same day Baisley, having beaten Rockaway in the first game of the season, tied them, catapulting us into first place with just a single loss and no ties.

We played Rockaway for a second time on Sunday, November 1. The first game, we decided, had been a fluke. Ferriola had been out. Worse, we had underestimated the Knights. No way that was going to happen again. And it didn't. Ferriola, though hobbling, played the entire game. And we played as hard as we could, which was really depressing since we still lost.

The game was much closer, but Hourican did it to us a second time. The headline in *The Wave* read:

Knights Conquer
Lynvets Again, 8–0

Moran Goes Over in 2d

Period on 20-Yard

Pass from Hurricane

Back in second place. Time to take stock. We were not, it seemed, as good as we had been the year before. What was missing? Chipper, for one, though John Schmauser had done a fine job in his stead. Herb Tortolani? Yes. Bob Hoenig was terrific, but not quite Tortolani. Tommy Vaughan? Yes, yes, and yes. Even so, Joe Aragona had moved into Tommy's spot and begun building a reputation as daunting as Vaughan's.

What about me? In truth, I was playing just fair. I could explode out of the backfield if I got a good block, which I could usually count on from Hughie Mulligan and Bob Crowley, the left guard. And I could cut as sharply as anyone in the league. But I didn't seem to be able to get outside on pitchouts as often as I had the year before. I also lacked the ability to take a hit and keep going or to right myself if a defender's hand caught my ankle, deficiencies that Joe's incredible balance threw into bold relief. At least, that's how I saw it; no one else seemed to notice.

Another problem was our pass defense. If not porous, it clearly had some weak links since Hourican had picked it apart twice, even with Peter Connor on the loose and putting together an even more impressive All-League season than the year before.

There was something else. Though I hated to admit it, I didn't care as much about football as I had before. I wondered if my unsettled future, combined with the ongoing madness at home, had drained off some of my desire. The decision to quit St. John's had seemed a wise one in August. By November, with nothing going for me except a long-shot hope of getting into Annapolis, my post–high school career pattern—college student to stockboy to mailboy—had me second-guessing myself. But looking around the team, the intensity of 1958 seemed to be lacking in nearly everyone except perhaps Peter. I mean, Christ, a team damn near identical to the one that had gone undefeated a year ago, that had scored over two hundred points and given up one lousy touchdown, had two losses and was sitting in second place, a spot in the standings previously known to us only by hearsay.

Something else was missing, and almost as soon as we began to focus on it, the situation was rectified. We had team meetings at the

Imperial on Wednesday evenings to review the previous game and
prepare for our opponent the coming Sunday. On the Wednesday
after the Rockaway game, we were greeted as we entered the bar by
a familiar figure.

"I'm back," said Larry Kelly as we took seats in the backroom.
"Forget the losses. It's a new season."

College, it seemed, had not worked out. Kelly offered no explanation. What was clear was that Larry had reclaimed the head
coaching job, displacing Jim Bertsch through a meeting of the
minds or, more likely, some sort of coup—hopefully bloodless, but
probably not. Truly, I didn't care and I don't think anybody else on
the team did, either. The blond crew cut, the apple cheeks, the
piercing blue eyes, the precise, needling diction set off now and
then by an easy laugh, yes, even the stupid white bucks—God, it
was good to have him back. Within half an hour, he had transformed us from a team reeling from a very big loss to what we had
been the previous year whether we knew it or not, agents of his will.

He quickly displayed a quality that had always worked for him,
the ability to infuriate. Turning off the lights, he switched on a
jerky eight-millimeter film of the Rockaway game. In one sequence, Joe took a pitchout and ran wide around end as I threw a
block on the outside linebacker and missed him completely. "Nice
block, Bob," murmured Kelly, to muffled laughter. As the film continued, though, it clearly showed me scrambling to my feet, racing
toward the sideline, and taking out a Rockaway player with a vi-
cious cross-body block just as he was about to tackle Aragona.

"What about that, Larry, did you see that block?" I said.

"What block was that, Bob?" asked Kelly in a tone of puzzle-
ment, setting off a fresh round of laughter, no longer muffled.

I knew I had made a fool of myself. I was angry and humiliated.
I would show Kelly. I only started feeling better when I realized I
hadn't felt that much emotion about football all season.

After the meeting, we all went out to the bar. Joe and I went
over to Larry.

He greeted us with the words "Gold Dust Twins," employing
the mocking tone that no one used anymore.

"Hey, Larry, we're doing pretty good," said Joe.

"Are you?" asked Kelly. "We'll see Sunday."

"Ah, Larry," said Joe, walking away, shaking his head, disappointed that Kelly seemed unaware of his enhanced stature on the team. Which, as the next few minutes proved, was not true.

"I need to talk to you," Larry said to me, gesturing for me to follow him to a quiet corner of the bar.

"Our pass defense is having problems," he said. "I'm going to move you to defensive halfback. Steffens and John Faulkner are fine. But I want you at right defensive halfback. I need your speed there."

My heart leaped. Good, great, I'd just as soon play both ways. But there was more.

"I'm taking you off offense," Larry said. "At least I'm not going to start you on offense."

I was flabbergasted. Joe and I were a team. The Gold Dust Twins were not a joke anymore. And all I ever wanted to be was a running back.

"Why, Larry?" I asked, seemingly mystified, wondering if he knew what I knew and, if so, how the hell he had come upon that knowledge.

"You're going down too easy," he said.

"What are you talking about?"

"You're not breaking tackles. Arm tackles are bringing you down. You're still a good back, but you're more valuable to the team right now in the defensive backfield. We'll score points with Ferriola and Aragona. You'll still play some offense, but what we have to do is stop Hourican, and that means we need to keep Chapman and Moran from getting free in the secondary."

Larry knew. My guess was that he had been tipped by Paul Frey, the mysterious adviser to Lynvet coaches whom I now thought of as an enemy spy. I felt dizzy as I rode home on the bus. Oddly enough, I felt less troubled about losing my first-string offensive halfback position than I did about living up to Larry's expectations for me on defense. Still, there was no way to sugarcoat the fact that I had been demoted, which I tried with only middling success not to view as symbolic of the way my life was going.

Thanks to the Baisley Park Bombers, who had beaten and tied Rockaway, we still had a mathematical chance at retaining our title even though the Knights had beaten us twice. First, though, we had to beat Baisley for a second time and Greenpoint a third time. If we did, our game with Rockaway on the Sunday before Thanksgiving would be for the championship.

The game with Baisley ended in a riot. We were well ahead as the fourth quarter began. A couple of dustups, featuring Woody Wickers and Peter Connor, excited the increasingly lubricated fans of both teams. With the clock winding down, the ranks on opposite sides of the field surged toward each other with every pileup. Mrs. Wickers was patrolling her sideline, firing up the Baisley partisans. I was in the defensive backfield next to Eddie Steffens when the volatile mix of whiskey, beer, and football ignited. The Baisley quarterback had just moved over center when one of our players— probably Peter, but it was hard to tell—went flying over the line, grabbed the signal caller's face mask, and pulled him down.

Our fans were cheering, Baisley's fans were screaming, the wide-eyed officials were turning from one sideline to the other. Suddenly Mrs. Wickers stormed onto the field, hauling her oversized handbag, a Herbert Goldberg no doubt, and cut loose with a string of obscenities at Eddie.

The imperturbable Steffens, a man of few words, listened with a blank stare, then said, "Get off the field, old woman."

At that, Mrs. Wickers swung, catching Eddie on the side of the head with her purse. That did it. The fans swarmed onto the field, some running, others staggering forward like Roman legions summoned to battle in the midst of a bacchanal. "Game over," the refs shouted, scooping up the ball and disappearing through an opening in the fence.

I hollered over to Steffens, "What do we do now, Eddie?"

Eddie replied, "Keep your helmet on."

Very good advice.

Afterward, Kelly said to assistant coach Bob Bushman, "Steffens is the perfect player. He's tough, he's smart, and the only one he talks to is Mrs. Wickers."

The following week Rockaway edged its nemesis, Baisley, 14–6, a victory highlighted by a sixty-yard run by Donny Knott, the younger brother of the coach, Richie Knott. We beat Greenpoint handily as Ferriola seemed to finally shake the ankle injury that had dogged him all season. After the game, Kelly said we would be practicing Monday through Friday under the lights at Victory Field. On Sunday, the Lynvets and Rockaway would meet for the title. Kelly had one week to figure out how to tame a Hurricane.

14

The Coach

*L*arry Kelly rarely revealed himself to anyone. He had drinking buddies, but the bar talk hardly ever moved beyond football. If it wasn't Lynvet football, then it was Notre Dame football or New York Giants football. When I joined the Lynvets in 1958, I surmised—because of the precision of his speech, the self-assurance with which he carried himself, the crispness of the players in responding to his directions—that he was a high school principal or some sort of junior executive. No one I asked, though, seemed to know for sure where he worked, let alone where he lived. Someone thought he sold women's shoes, someone else said he worked for Schaefer Beer, others reported, none too confidently, that he drove a Singer sewing machine truck. There was also talk of a post office job or that he sold life insurance.

In fact, he did all those things, none for very long. One day in 1958, Eddie Keane, an end on the Lynvet Junior team that Larry had coached to a championship the year before, cut his afternoon classes at Holy Cross High School in Bayside and ducked into the

Loew's Willard on Jamaica Avenue to kill time before he could safely go home. He ran into Larry, then selling insurance.

"What are you doing here?" asked Kelly.

"Same thing you're doing," Eddie replied. "I'm someplace I'm not supposed to be."

There was only one place Larry Kelly was supposed to be. That was on a football field, instructing young men how to play the game and preparing them to take on the rest of their lives. Off the field, his life—ragged, undisciplined, seemingly without direction—was the polar opposite of the character he imposed on his teams. In his role as coach, he seemed electrified, always in sharp focus, a vivid and quietly commanding figure to those of us who played for him. In other circumstances, the lighting changed, revealing an all-too-human character struggling without great success to fit into those parts of the world not defined by sidelines and end zones. But if Larry struggled, those of us he coached gained from him qualities that we clung to as we stumbled into adulthood and that few of us ever gave up without a fight.

The young men filed dutifully into the funeral parlor, Larry Kelly's friends, there to pay last respects to Larry's mother. One by one they approached the casket, gazed at the woman lying there, a rosary threaded through her fingers, then moved on. All but Tommy Marshall, a close friend and Lynvet teammate who knew the real story, reacted curiously, as if perplexed by what they had seen. As quickly as they could politely do so, the young men left the establishment and gathered outside. Shaking his head, one of them, reflecting the confusion they all felt, said, "Who's the strange lady in the box?"

Tommy Marshall explained. The woman in the casket was Larry's mother. The woman whom they all knew as his mother, the one he lived with and called Mom, was his foster mother.

The young men marveled at the news. Most had grown up with Larry, gone to school with him, played baseball and football with him, been drinking in most of the local bars with him. And yet he had never gotten around to telling them the truth about the woman they thought of as his mother. Or that all along the woman who had given birth to him was living somewhere nearby in Brooklyn.

At the time of his mother's death in 1953, Larry had been living as a foster child in the City Line home of Kitty Messbauer, a widow with four kids of her own, for nearly two decades. She had taken him from the Angel Guardian Home in Bensonhurst as a six-week-old infant in 1934. Not long after, Kitty took in his sister, Mary, who was three years older, couldn't walk properly because of rickets, and had just been returned to Angel Guardian by a couple who couldn't contend with her physical problems.

Nora Grace Mullins Kelly, the lady in the box, was either widowed, as she claimed, or unmarried, of which there was some evidence. The children's birth certificates identified their father as Patrick John Kelly. Nora's differing explanations for Patrick Kelly's death raised suspicions, though. Sometimes she said a train had hit him, other times that he fell off a ship and was impaled by the anchor.

Whatever the reality of the children's parentage, Kitty Messbauer, a McKeon by birth, provided a warm, loving home for Larry and Mary. She tried to adopt them more than once, but Nora refused to sign the papers. Kitty's home was filled with music from the upright player piano that you pumped with your foot and the phonograph that you wound by hand. There were hundreds of records. And Larry loved to perform. He knew all the Al Jolson songs and would belt out "California, Here I Come," "Mammy," and "Swanee" at family gatherings. He could run through George M. Cohan's repertoire—"Yankee Doodle Dandy," "You're a Grand Old Flag," "Over There," "Give My Regards to Broadway." At an American Legion party he sang "God Bless America," pecking out the tune with one finger on the piano. His favorite song was "When Irish Eyes Are Smiling," recorded in 1916 by the much-beloved Irish tenor John McCormack, viewed as next to God in Irish-American homes.

As he grew older, Larry became a nomad, appearing unexpectedly at the homes of friends and frequently asking to spend the night. For a time, he all but moved in with Tommy Marshall's family. One night he climbed into the bed of Tommy's older brother, Pete. Pete came home and turned on the light, awakening Larry. "Who the hell are you?" Larry groggily demanded of Pete.

Nora remained in her children's lives, riding the subway and the El from her apartment in Manhattan to the station at City Line, where on Kitty's orders Larry and Mary would meet her and bring her to the Messbauer home to visit. Later, Nora moved to Brooklyn, not far from the kids. She liked to dance and drink and play the two-dollar window at the track. She did piecework in a factory, before that scrubbed floors for a quarter an hour. She'd give Larry two dimes to get her a pack of Chesterfields from the vending machine in a nearby bar. "You can keep the two pennies," she said, meaning the change that came inside the cellophane wrapper.

She seemed to have little fondness for Mary, but she doted on Larry. She bought a TV so he could watch football games. And over and over again, she fed a dream she could never make come true, telling him, "I'm going to send you to Notre Dame, Larry."

For young Larry, as for all the Irish in New York, Notre Dame was the only team that mattered. The first movie he ever saw was *Knute Rockne, All-American,* about the legendary coach of the Fighting Irish. His heroes were players like Angelo Bertelli, an All-American quarterback who quit the team six games into the 1943 season to join the Marines, and Johnny Lujack, who took over from Bertelli, went to war himself, then returned to win the Heisman Trophy, college football's highest individual honor.

For a few years, Larry believed Nora when she promised to send him to Notre Dame. As he moved into his teens, though, he realized that his mother had no way to deliver on her promise. Nor could Kitty. To make ends meet, she had to go out to work, first at a Lucky Strike factory, later handing out towels at the YMCA.

If the dream died hard, Larry did not show it. He was happy-go-lucky, friendly, and well liked, though none of his pals looked

on him as a leader. At a certain point, he developed a wise-guy attitude that some found engaging, others annoying. At team meetings in the early Lynvet days, he peppered Charlie Fitzgerald with
questions that often seemed to have little purpose other than to
torment the coach.

"Okay, Kelly, take a walk," Charlie said one night, throwing
him out of a meeting for neither the first nor the last time.

Larry left. A few minutes later he returned.

"Kelly, didn't I tell you to take a walk?" said Charlie.

"I took a walk," said Kelly. "Now I'm back."

Hoping to catch up with his best friend and Lynvet teammate,
John Weber, Larry joined the Marines in 1953, near the end of the
Korean War. He enlisted July 13; John stepped on a land mine and
died July 14.

Larry missed the war, did most of his duty aboard ship as a
seagoing Marine. Tommy Marshall was still in the Corps when
Larry was discharged. "I'm out, how you doin'?" Larry asked
Tommy on a postcard he scribbled at McSorley's Ale House in
Lower Manhattan. Not long after, Tommy learned that Larry was
dating his girlfriend.

People forgave Kelly's indiscretions. "That's Larry," they'd say,
as if the rootless quality that led him to spend so much time with
the Marshalls was a reflection of his confused parentage. Others
sensed he was searching for an anchor. Friend and Lynvet teammate Kevin Glynn detected something darker: "There was something troubling him that we never understood."

Larry did not play high school football. Neither Kitty nor Nora
could afford the tuition to a Catholic school with a team, and
Larry's mixed grades denied him a scholarship. That meant the
local public school, Franklin K. Lane, which didn't have a team.
Hoping to play at least one season, he finagled an out-of-district
transfer, to John Adams in Jamaica before his senior year, a shift
that caught the attention of the sports pages because of his exploits
as the Lynvets' vaunted pass-catching end. But something went
wrong, and the authorities ruled that as a transfer student he was
ineligible to suit up. Making the best of it, he became the team

manager, lining the field before games, keeping the water bucket full, and handling other odd jobs. But he was often seen huddling with the coach and they seemed to be talking strategy, not water discipline or the condition of the locker room.

By 1956, the last year he was eligible to play for the Lynvet Seniors, Larry began to gravitate toward coaching. Kenny Rudzewick, new to the team that year but with a gilt-edged sandlot résumé, was shocked to see Kelly routinely arguing with the coaches. Equally shocking, he would force the quarterback, Herb Tortolani, to change plays in the huddle. "I'm not running that pattern," Larry would say, stubbornly standing his ground until Tortolani switched to a play more to Kelly's liking.

One day Larry trotted over to Kenny and said, "You're tipping your shoulder, you're telegraphing your block."

Kenny fumed: "What are you, a coach?"

Said Larry, pausing, his eyes twinkling, "Actually, I'm sort of a coach."

Kenny decided to listen, was glad he did, concluded that Kelly knew what he was talking about.

By then, Larry was in his first season as an assistant coach for the Lynvet Junior team, which was led by a young quarterback named Bob Ferriola. Two years later, taking over as head coach of the Lynvet Seniors, Larry made it clear from the start that he was in charge. He also moved quickly to head off the kinds of coach–player tiffs that he himself had frequently instigated in the past, telling the team when it assembled for spring practice in 1958, a few months before I showed up, that there would be no more postgame gripe sessions that had been a fixture during the Fitzgerald years and the years that followed.

"I don't really care what you think," he said. "Don't think. Just do what I tell you to do."

He started with an ace, several aces, up his sleeve. The cream of the previous year's championship Junior team had moved up to the Senior ranks with him. Soon, though, his eye for talent—more precisely, his ability to see a player in one position and realize that he could be more valuable to the team in a different one—became his trademark. Installing Ferriola at quarterback and turning the lanky Tortolani into a receiver was just his first move. Bobby Schmitt, a quarterback at Valley Stream High School, became a ferocious defensive end and a capable receiver. Al Schneeberg, a standout player on the Junior team but so small at five foot six and 135 pounds that he seemed destined to be a career benchwarmer as a Senior, became an All-League center, anchoring the offensive line for four years. Not everyone welcomed Kelly's version of musical chairs, but most of the players flourished in their new roles.

Bob Bushman, whom Kelly recruited as an assistant coach to help put the Seniors back together, was another major asset, especially in reinvigorating the offense. Bushman had been an All-City quarterback at Brooklyn Prep in 1952, as well as a running back and defensive back with the Lulley-led Lynvets, so he knew the territory.

There was another ingredient in Kelly's success, some say a vital one: Paul Frey. Paul, who worked for the post office and lived with his sister, went back to the beginning with the Lynvets. He was usually an adviser to coaches rather than a coach himself and, so it was said, football's version of a mad scientist, the man who devised the offensive and defensive schemes employed by Lynvet coaches from Charlie Fitzgerald on. Paul also scouted Lynvet opponents, which gave Kelly and his predecessors another edge. Paul was, as well, a perfectionist. "Larrreee, back to the drawing board," he moaned after the Lynvets had crushed a team 53–0.

By the time I joined the Lynvets, Paul was in his forties, and well established as a man of mystery. He was gaunt, almost cadaverous, with pointed features. He wore his jet black hair slicked back, dressed in dark blue or black and invariably had a five o'clock shadow. There were the inevitable comparisons to Dracula. "He climbs out of his coffin to help out," Bob Ferriola deadpanned when I asked about Paul. Hughie Mulligan claimed to be surprised when Paul showed up in daylight. When Paul spoke, he did so almost exclusively to the coaches and did not attend postgame parties. He was said to maintain a lively correspondence with a number of college coaches around the country. He often wrote to Kelly in the off-season, his missives carrying over to the backs of the envelopes, which were covered with the X's and O's of football formations.

"Paul has the ability to appear and disappear," Bob Bushman once joked to a friend. "He can become invisible or cloud men's minds like The Shadow. When he's scouting, he can stand in the middle of the opposition huddle and never be seen. You see him standing there in the dark at practice. Not much later there's nothing there. Then he appears somewhere else." Kelly once turned to Bushman at a night practice and said, "I know Paul is around. I can hear his pencil taking notes."

Bob and Paul and others helped, but the Lynvets were Larry Kelly's team. He imposed discipline, paid attention to detail, believed in repetition, and was a fine teacher. It was as if he transferred intact from the Parris Island drill field to the Cross Bay Oval practice facility the Marine Corps's time-honored technique of military instruction: Tell 'em what you're gonna tell 'em. Tell 'em. Then tell 'em what you told 'em.

Discipline started with our uniforms. "If your uniform isn't clean before the game, you won't play," he told us. "If it's clean after the game, you won't play next week."

But practice was the key. Under Kelly, there was no excuse for missing a practice other than a job or school. And you were expected to be on time, an expectation that proved infectious. When Tommy Wall quarterbacked the Seniors, he'd fire the football at the head of a teammate who showed up late. Our offense, though innovative, was not complicated, which meant we had little more than a dozen plays. We'd run through them over and over and over again as Kelly and his assistants looked for flaws in our stances, the way we came off the ball, personal quirks that might alert an opponent to the direction of the upcoming play. It should have been boring, but it almost never was, because Larry moved between offense and defense, linemen and backs, nodding here, correcting there, easing the drudgery with a wisecrack or well-aimed barb.

His put-downs were frequent, often memorable. Frustrated with Bobby Gibbs, a quarterback, he said, "Didn't you learn anything at Brooklyn Prep other than how to iron your socks?" To Rich Sardiello, a fine running back, he snapped, "Are we calling two plays in the huddle, one for you and another for the rest of the team?" He was especially impatient with players who tried to explain why they had ignored his instructions. "Don't think," he told one lineman. "When you think you put the team at a disadvantage." To another lineman: "If you want to think, you'll have to borrow somebody else's head." Of Joe Aragona, whose penchant for improvising on pass plays drove Kelly and Bushman crazy, he said, "Aragona never even runs the wrong pattern the same way twice in a row." And if the two coaches went along with the Gold Dust Twins sobriquet that had attached itself to Joe and me, they occasionally blurted out their private nicknames for us—Disease and Disaster.

A nod from Larry mattered. For reasons that may have said more about us than it did about him, we cared what Larry thought of us, even those players who knew him outside the context of football, where he cast a less imposing shadow. Perhaps it had to do with the chariness with which he dispensed compliments; more likely, it was tied into where we were in our lives, on the uneasy threshold of adulthood, and in the absence of recognition from any authority figures whose opinions meant something to us. With Larry on the sidelines, we knew we were the best at what we did, which may have been, to borrow my mother's maddening phrase, small potatoes, but not to us, not then, when most of us needed to feel good about ourselves because other than football there was little in our lives to make us feel anything but ordinary. We were Lynvets, and Larry Kelly was our coach. That made us special.

There was more to Kelly than football. Handsome, seemingly unflappable in his khaki slacks and white bucks, he was more collegiate than the college kids on the team. He favored such Manhattan nightspots as P. J. Clarke's and Toots Shor's, where he rubbed elbows with actors, professional athletes, and sportswriters. When someone else was buying, he drank scotch—Dewar's or Grant's— unlike most of the Lynvets, for whom the beverage of choice remained beer, rye, or a Seven-and-Seven. He vacationed in what seemed like exotic locales to those of us whose travels were largely circumscribed by the New York City subway system and the Long Island Railroad. "Cape Cod? Where the fuck's that, Larry, next to Mars?" asked Tommy Wall, who never missed a chance to flash the dead-end kid demeanor that he knew drove Kelly crazy.

Larry was irrepressible, too. One night, with Peter Connor in tow, he double-parked his Singer sewing machine truck outside an East Side nightspot known to be a celebrity hangout. As they were drinking at the bar, Rocky Graziano, the onetime world middleweight champion once suspended for failing to report a bribe attempt, pulled up the stool next to them. They chatted with the champ, a good guy who seemed to enjoy their company, at least until Larry said, "So, Rocky, how many fights did you dump?"

That side of Kelly was consistent with his persona on the sidelines. The rest of his life wasn't. During those years he was fired from a series of dreary jobs. Driving the Singer truck was one of the better ones, though the truck was curiously thin on sewing machines, packed instead with tackling dummies, blocking pads, helmets, and other football paraphernalia. For a time, he also did what he called "missionary work" for Schaefer, which billed itself as "the one beer to have when you're having more than one." Stopping at a saloon, Larry would tell the bartender to give everyone a round of drinks on "the Schaefer guy," then try to persuade the proprietor to drop Piel's or Rheingold or Pabst or Ballantine or whatever else he had on tap. For Kelly, who loved the conviviality of bars, it seemed a dream job, but it lasted only a year or so, until he wrecked the company car a second time.

Not long after, he went to work for the insurance company. One day, Peter Connor and some other Lynvets called him at work, said they wanted to drop by and say hello. They were impressed to find him behind a large desk in a spacious office. Then a coworker poked his head in the door and said, "Kelly, you better get out of here. The boss is on the way back."

Larry dated occasionally but, unlike Bob Bushman, who was known to escort Broadway actresses, he was not a ladies' man. For a time he dated Kenny Rudzewick's sister, Nancy. Kenny, who knew Kelly better than most, told friends, affectionately but pointedly, "The greatest thing that ever happened in my Lynvet experience is that Larry didn't marry my sister."

One time Larry brought Peter, Kenny, and Chipper Dombo to a football clinic put on by college and professional football coaches at the Taft Hotel in the city. Afterward, Larry and his entourage talked their way into the hospitality suite, where Kelly told an alternately bemused and flabbergasted Allie Sherman, the coach of the New York Giants, what he was doing wrong with his team, all the while enjoying the food and drink set out for Sherman and the rest of the clinic's bigwigs.

To Larry, there was nothing ludicrous about his lecturing an NFL coach. He had been to lots of clinics and discussed the game with other established coaches. He never felt a sense of inferiority. If anything, he saw himself as at least their peer in terms of football knowledge. In his mind, he could walk on the field in South Bend tomorrow and lead the Fighting Irish to a national championship. All he lacked, he believed, was the opportunity. That opportunity, his friends told him, would not come without a college education. "Hell," they said, "you can't even coach a high school team without a degree." Did he believe it? To an extent. He occasionally made head fakes in the direction of college, but he was unable to follow through, much like my father, who seemed invariably to shy away from chances to affirm his talent on a larger stage. Somehow, it seemed, Larry half expected to be discovered and elevated overnight to star status, the sandlot equivalent of Lana Turner catching the eye of a talent scout at Schwab's drugstore.

Was he tortured by what seemed to others dim prospects for achieving his dream? Not obviously, certainly not to those of us outside his inner circle who knew him almost entirely as a football coach. To us, at times, he had an imperious quality, as if he had done more, seen more, traveled more, read more.

"He was arrogant, he was sarcastic, he could be derisive, he was irritating, he could get you furious at him," said Bob Bushman. "But Larry was Larry and he did what he did better than anyone else could do it and he knew it and he told you he knew it and he knew you knew it and he'd shove it down your throat if you didn't like it. He was the best."

For most of us, that was Larry Kelly. One of the few to see another side was Bob Ferriola. After the fabulous 1958 season, a newspaper friend of Larry's arranged for Ferriola, the league's reigning MVP, to try out for the team at the University of Tampa. Larry said he'd ride down with Bobby, cheer him on, maybe see a bit of Florida. They rode down with Bob's brother-in-law, who was moving to the Tampa area. Shortly before they got there, Kelly startled Bob by revealing that he was trying out for the team, too. When they arrived at the school, no one seemed quite sure who they were, but they were given ratty old uniforms and equipment and instructed to report to the practice field the next morning.

They were put up in what looked like an attic to Bob, but may well have been one of the minarets that adorned the school's architecturally eclectic main building, originally a resort hotel. It felt creepy to Ferriola. That evening Larry seemed uncharacteristically subdued. Unsettled as well. "Wear this," said Larry, handing Bob a scapula, a Catholic medallion worn around the neck. "For spiritual guidance." Bob slipped it over his head even though, as Larry well knew, Ferriola was a Protestant, the only one on the Lynvets. Bob was worried about the next day. He wanted to play well, but he sensed that something was fishy. He finally fell asleep, only to awaken in the middle of the night. He heard mumbling coming from the other bed. Bob listened more closely, realized that Larry was praying. "I was kind of scared and I was kind of nervous and I was thinking, 'What am I doing here?' " Bob later told a friend.

The next day they reported to the practice field. They were treated as walk-ons, not as players the coach was looking to recruit.

Larry had not played football in nearly four years, and it showed. Bob, convinced that no one cared how he performed, played passably. Afterward, a team functionary said, "We'll be in touch." They hitchhiked back to New York, barely exchanging a word the whole way home. Ferriola knew he had been afforded a rare glimpse of Larry—off his game, rattled, an uncertain man.

15

"Let Me Have Steffens"

*T*here should have been a desperation about our practices in that week before the 1959 title game with Rockaway—the Knights had not only beaten us twice, they had shut us out both times. Instead, a sense of inevitability gradually took hold, building from practice to practice, as if Kelly's return had begun to reweave the cloak of invincibility that had clung to us the previous year.

"Everybody wants to win," Kelly said at the week's first practice. "If you really want to win, you've got to work at it. You cannot just win."

We worked at it. For two hours each night Monday through Friday, we practiced in pads and sneakers on the barely illuminated aphalt playground at Victory Field in Woodhaven. Those of us on defense spent most of the time on pass coverage, everything aimed at stopping the elusive John Hourican from getting the ball to Tommy Chapman, Don Moran, or Donny Knott.

A single play during one of our practices that chill late-November week has stayed with me through the years. Ferriola was the quarterback, I was at right halfback, Kelly figuring, I guess, that he might need me as a backup on offense. On the snap, I slipped between right tackle and right end and broke downfield in a pattern that curled gently back toward the center of the field, like a banana. I ran hard the first ten yards, but held back a bit. At ten yards, I broke into a full sprint, blowing past the defensive back as Ferriola cut loose a long, towering pass in my direction. Three light towers provided the illumination, but it was uneven. Glancing over my left shoulder, I saw Ferriola throw the ball. Or appear to throw it—I did not see the ball leave his hand. Running full tilt, I saw the ball for the first time as it intersected the glare from the initial bank of lights. Then it was gone. At this point, even though I was running as fast as I could, I felt the world downshift into slow motion. Looking up, I saw the ball sail majestically across the second bank of lights, moving in a tight spiral at nosebleed altitude, shimmering for a split second before it again went into eclipse. I continued sprinting, aware that I was closing on the tall chain-link fence that surrounded the playground. Searching the sky, I saw the ball a final time as it crossed the last bank of lights. It was coming down. Then it was gone again. About ten yards from the fence, never breaking stride, I stretched my arms out and the ball settled perfectly, if invisibly, into my hands. As I knew it would. I tucked the ball in, veered to the left to avoid the fence and jogged back upfield. Those few seconds, while the ball was in flight and I sprinted heedlessly toward the fence fueled by nothing but faith, remain the closest I have ever come to an out-of-body experience.

As practice ended Friday night, we felt razor-sharp, ready for Rockaway. Spontaneously, or so it seemed, we all piled into the few cars available and headed for a bar. Or bars. First one place, then another. Eventually we wound up at the Flora Dora on Roosevelt Avenue in Jackson Heights, not a usual hangout.

The crowd seemed older, but we didn't care. A trio composed of three heavily made-up older women, the Flora Dora Girls, was playing German songs and show tunes. Within minutes, Peter took over. Soon he was on the bar, telling us how good we were, how we were going to murder Rockaway. And then he shouted to the women to play the World War I standard, "Over There." We were all singing, Lynvets and non-Lynvets, as Peter trooped up and down the bar like a drum major. And he made a small adjustment to the lyrics:

Over there! Over there!
Send the word, send the word over there,
That the 'Vets are coming, the 'Vets are coming
There's drum, drum, drumming everywhere.

It wasn't terribly original, but we sang the song off and on for hours, along with just about everything else George M. Cohan had written, until we got thrown out. By then, we had christened an anthem.

The fix was in. Kelly and Bushman, in league with Peter, had cooked up the night at the Flora Dora. The team was missing one thing, Bushman later explained. Earlier Lynvet squads had been like a brotherhood, the players knowing each other from the streets, the schools, the churches, mostly the bars in and around City Line. Our team was geographically diverse, with players coming from all over Brooklyn and Queens, even Long Island. The brain trust decided we needed to spend more time together, to deepen the bond beyond the gridiron.

It worked. We left the Flora Dora with more than a team song. Said Bushman: "The outsiders were now insiders. Peter had pulled the sword from the stone. They would follow him to Hell. Or to jail, whichever came first."

On Sunday we were back at Victory Field. Not on the concrete playground, but on the torn-up grass field that adjoined it that had neither lights nor electrical outlets for our generator and thus was foreclosed to us for night practices. At least a thousand fans crowded the sidelines, evenly divided between the two teams. We felt confident as we ran onto the field for our pregame warm-up drills. Kelly and Bushman, with a big assist from Peter, had managed to persuade us that the team that Hourican and the Rockaway Knights had put down for the count twice were imposters, ersatz Lynvets, a bunch of guys masquerading as us, but not us at all. Kelly's return had immersed us in the past, our past, and transformed us into the team we had been the year before. And Kelly's arrogance, however improbable, had rekindled our swagger. As we lined up for the kickoff, we did not feel like underdogs battling for our lives. We felt like champions, defending our crown. Against a worthy foe, yes, but a foe that had never beaten a Larry Kelly–coached team or faced Bob Ferriola at full strength. Or played the real Lynvets.

We scored first, a disciplined drive highlighted by the running of Ferriola, Aragona, and fullback John Faulkner. We also had some luck. Ferriola, running right on a quarterback keeper, cut between the tackle and end and unaccountably fumbled the ball on Rockaway's nine-yard line. Just dropped it, with one defender between him and the goal line. Then his foot hit it. The ball rolled forward and tumbled out of bounds on the two just as the lone defender dove for it. Rockaway claimed its player had touched the ball before it crossed the sideline. The referee disagreed. Lynvet ball, first and goal to go at the two. John Faulkner pounded it in behind a wedge of blockers. We failed to convert, but we had drawn first blood and were up 6–0.

The Knights, convinced they should have had the ball after Ferriola's fumble, were furious. It was early in the game, so there was plenty of time for them to come back. But I know what I was thinking, and my guess is Rockaway was thinking the same thing. Going into the game, they held an important psychological edge. In the two earlier meetings, we had never scored on them. Now, in the game that counted, we had broken through and scored the first time we touched the ball.

Rockaway battled back. No one intimidated John Hourican, certainly not the Lynvets, to whom he had lost only once in his long sandlot career. Most recently, he had beaten them for the Warner title as Greenpoint's quarterback two years earlier and dominated them this year. And Hourican had weapons—receivers

like Don Moran, running backs like Donny Knott, and the sleek
and powerful Tommy Chapman. And they came at us. Bruising
runs, quick, sharp passes, in some ways a mirror image of us.

Emotionally, I had become a defensive back. My job was to defend my territory against anyone who ventured into it and that was
all I thought about. I no longer pictured myself catching long,
arching passes or breaking loose on dazzling forty-yard touchdown
runs. I envied my mates in the secondary. John Faulkner and Eddie
Steffens were punishing tacklers. I was quick and smart and I could
tackle, but no one ever limped off the field after colliding with me.
Can't even remember anyone getting up slowly. Still, if Kelly had
been leveling with me about needing to plug a hole in the defensive
backfield, I had plugged it.

On Rockaway's first two possessions, no one had come my
way. I was ready for trouble, but I wasn't looking for it. I wondered
if possibly the word had gotten around that going at Timberg
meant courting disaster. Just in time, reality hit me, thanks to Peter
Connor.

"Bobby," he shouted from his center linebacker spot.

As I looked his way, he pointed to the ground, his turf, and said,
"Nothing here! Nothing here!"

Glaring at me now, his finger tracing an arc across my area of
responsibility, he said, "Nothing there, either, right, Bobby?"

Peter knew. And now I did, too. Hourican was setting me up.

"Got it, Peter," I said. "Nothing here!"

Two plays later, Tommy Chapman took a swing pass, swept
around end, and headed toward me. The only player between
Chappie and the goal line, I hit him, and tried to wrap him up as
one of his knees crashed into my shoulder, another into my helmet.
I felt him starting to break loose, but I held on and rolled with my
arms around one of his legs. He went down after only a modest
gain. He bounced to his feet. I felt woozy as I stood up. Peter was
already there, slapping me on the helmet, hollering, "Way to go,
Bobby! Way to go!" I accepted the praise humbly, as we all did in
those days.

"Thanks, Peter," I said. I knew I had played over my head in taking down Chapman one-on-one in the open field. And I knew why. Peter had briefly convinced me that I was him, and it had been one helluva ride. I would have been happy if the game had ended right then.

The game, in fact, had just begun. Midway through the second quarter, Rockaway scored, Hourican passing for a touchdown to a kid named Mercer, whom I had never even heard of. Jesus, I thought, these guys are loaded. Rockaway missed the extra points, as we had after our touchdown, but on the next series the Knights caught Ferriola in our end zone and dropped him for a two-point safety.

Nothing much happened the rest of the half, although there was a mildly odd incident. Ferriola went through some fakes with his back to the line, then spun and threw the ball a mile downfield. But nobody was there. No receiver, no defender. Watching from the sideline, I could see that Bob was unusually animated in the huddle. I suspected that someone had run the wrong pass pattern.

At halftime, Rockaway led 8–6.

Both teams moved the ball well in the third quarter, but neither could penetrate deeper than the opposition's thirty-yard line. The fans were getting raucous, especially Rockaway's, who sensed that even Ferriola was not going to be able bring us back. We were playing well, but our offense kept bogging down.

Late in the third quarter, we were on Rockaway's forty-five-yard line, which is where we seemed to be most of the period, when Ferriola called a time-out and trotted over to the sideline.

"Let me have Steffens," he said to Kelly.

Kelly looked at Ferriola. Bob Bushman, an old quarterback, seemed to understand immediately and nodded emphatically. Standing nearby, I was puzzled. Eddie Steffens was a fixture in the defensive backfield, but he rarely played offense. True, he was a more than adequate runner and a fine receiver, but he hardly seemed to merit a time-out and this council of elders.

"Eddie, go in for Aragona," said Kelly.

Joe trotted off the field, shaking his head. "Holy smokes, Larry, what'd you do that for?"

The first play after the time-out was a plunge by the fullback that gained a yard, if that. Steffens flanked out to the left on second down. On the snap, Ferriola turned, faked to the fullback, then to the halfback. Spinning toward the line, he started backpedaling. Then he planted his rear foot and cut the ball loose downfield. It was the same play that had caused the consternation in the first half, with one difference. This time, there was a receiver there, Eddie Steffens, who caught the ball in stride on the fifteen-yard line and carried it in untouched for the score.

As Eddie crossed the goal line, a Lynvet fan ran up to him, hugged him, and shouted, "I just won two grand!"

Afterward, Bushman explained the switch from Aragona to Steffens. Along with Ferriola, Aragona was our greatest threat. A runner of uncanny intuitiveness, he was the Lynvets' ultimate play-maker. But Ferriola sometimes got frustrated with Joe because he had a tendency to freelance, and not just when he had the ball under his arm. He also did it on pass plays, often choosing his own route rather than the one that had been laid out for him. Which meant that Ferriola on occasion could not find him in the sea of maroon-and-white jerseys. Steffens, Ferriola knew, would run the pass pattern as drawn. Steady Eddie, strong German stock, silent but deadly. Plus, Eddie was fast, perhaps the fastest man on the team. There was one other factor. Aragona drew defenders like a magnet; Steffens would not. The switch looked like Kelly was just giving Joe a breather.

With a quarter to go, we led 12–8. Suddenly Rockaway was on fire. Hourican was hitting Chapman and Moran with short- and medium-range passes. Chapman, with an occasional assist from Donny Knott, was grinding out yards. Peter Connor was all over us, shouting, slapping us, but we were still giving up too much yardage. With less than ten minutes to go, Rockaway was on our one-yard line. Rockaway called a time-out. Peter lost it.

"I eat dirt! I eat dirt!" he shouted as he jammed chunks of the field into his mouth. He ran from one Lynvet lineman to another, shoving grass and dirt in their faces.

Kenny Rudzewick, less mercurial than Peter but just as tough, grabbed him and said, "Do that again, Peter, and I'll kill you!" Kenny may even have thrown a punch at Peter.

But Peter was in his own world. As Rockaway broke from its huddle, Peter was still screaming "I eat dirt! I eat dirt!" as brown spittle dripped from his chin and sprayed across the line of scrimmage at the gaping opposition linemen.

Peter, Kenny, and two other linemen stopped Hourican on the next play, driving him back to the nine. But the refs allowed him forward progress and again marked the ball at the one. On the next play, Rockaway fumbled and we recovered. Out of the woods.

Not quite. Our offense couldn't kill the clock, and we had to punt. Rockaway began what both sides knew would be its final drive. Ferriola, now playing defensive end, crashed through the line on one play and put Hourican down for a loss. But John Hourican in his own way was as much a force of nature as Peter Connor. There was a relentlessness about that last drive and, for me at least, an inexorability. I had been feeding off Peter and Kenny and Faulkner and Steffens and the blood from a gash that Chapman had put in my lip, but now I was getting anxious. Is Hourican setting me up again? If so, he was taking his time about it. They were back on our ten, with maybe a minute and a half to play. A pass over the middle hit Peter in the stomach, but he couldn't hold on to it. He raged. Had he made the interception, the game would have been over.

Rockaway had one last play. Fourth down and goal to go from the eight. Chapman was flanked to my side. As Rockaway was in the huddle, I told myself I wanted them to come at me. Now, though, seeing Chappie out there, I knew that was precisely what was about to happen, and a chill went through me. A name flashed in my mind: Lenny Rochester. Now another black guy, Tommy Chapman, was about to make me feel like a piece of shit. Just stay with him, I told myself, just stay with the son of a bitch.

Suddenly everything was in motion, Hourican dropping back to pass, Chapman sprinting toward me, then cutting sharply across the field. I was with him. And then I wasn't. He had kept something in reserve and left me behind. Not far behind, but far enough and he was over the goal line and the ball was coming toward him at warp speed. I was out of the play and Chapman was reaching out to gather in the pass that would give the championship to Rockaway—when John Faulkner came from nowhere and took the ball off Chappie's outstretched fingers.

John returned the ball only about ten yards, but that didn't matter. It was the Lynvets' ball, with thirty seconds left. Ferriola took a knee, the referee's gun went off, and the game was over. The Lynvets were champions once again. Car horns blared as our fans celebrated. I tried to find Chapman and Hourican to shake their hands, but the Rockaway team had departed quickly. In the locker room, we sang endless choruses of "Over There."

Chipper Dombo, who had stayed in school in Tampa when Kelly left, was sitting in a Florida bar when the phone rang.

"Chipper, a call for you," said the bartender.

Dombo walked over to the phone. It was Peter Connor, as he knew it would be.

"Chip, we did it," said Peter. "We beat those Rockaway fucks. We're champs again."

Chipper hung up the phone and reclaimed his seat at the bar. He looked at the beer in front of him for a few moments, then lifted it. Not loudly, but loud enough for those around him to hear, he said, "Three cheers for the Lynvets."

The date was November 22, 1959, a day of triumph for the Lynvets. Four years later to the day, another gun would echo the one that ended that greatest of Lynvet victories and the world we knew would begin its rapid fade to black.

16

The C-I-R Brick

*A*s 1960 began, the glow of the Lynvet victory over Rockaway was wearing off and I was again brooding about my future. I was nineteen and still working in the mailroom at Pan Am. Other than trying to get a nomination to Annapolis, I had done little to impose a direction on my life, neither deciding to give St. John's another try nor applying elsewhere. Things had not improved at home. In fact, they had gotten worse, if only because it had become clear that either my mother had no idea of the devastation her drinking was inflicting on Pat, Rosemarie, and me or she knew but was powerless to do anything about it.

The situation was very confusing to us. We thought we could help her. We thought she could help herself. We told ourselves that it was only a matter of time. Then she would do something outrageous and we knew were kidding ourselves. On her good days, which by a slim margin outnumbered the bad ones, she was there for all of us, if more for me than for Pat and Rosemarie. She was smart, she had common sense, and when she was sober, she was kind and generous. For a time, she provided a home for the two sons of a younger sister, who had perished in a mysterious fire in her room at a state mental hospital. Of all my mother's five surviving siblings, she was least equipped to take in the boys, who were roughly Pat's and Rosemarie's ages and, unlike the three of us, very high-maintenance kids. But she did it, and she did everything she could to make it work, but in the end it didn't.

Was I really needed at home? I thought so, by my sisters, yes, but also by my mother. My concern for all of them immobilized me. I had given myself only one way out, Annapolis. I had taken Senator Keating's qualifying test for a nomination even though my chances of getting one seemed remote. That worked for me. If I somehow got in, I figured it would be the hand of God, which one does not lightly ignore, and I told myself that I would beat down the feeling that I was abandoning my sisters and my mother and just go.

The Western Union telegram arrived in early February:

Congratulations Am delighted to advise you have been nominated as one of my 6 candidates to the naval academy. You are highly deserving of this outstanding honor. The academic board at the academy will appoint the young man they believe most qualified. Please advise return wire if you will accept nomination.

Kenneth B. Keating

US Senator

The door had been opened a crack. This was my chance and, unlike my father, I was not going to let it slip away. The Academy used the College Boards as its entrance exam and I figured I'd be faced with the same kinds of questions as the ones on the tests for the nomination—vocabulary, reading comprehension, and math through intermediate algebra. I got a book and once again applied myself to mixture problems, time-and-motion problems, and all the other types of problems that had convinced Senator Javits that I couldn't handle the math at the Academy.

About this time, I ran into Tommy Wall at the Lynvets annual

Valentine's Day party. He was there at Larry Kelly's invitation, part of Larry's effort to recruit him to eventually replace Bob Ferriola at quarterback. Though we hadn't seen each other since we'd met in Astoria a year and a half earlier, we greeted each other as old friends, much the way onetime college roommates fall into an easy familiarity, as if no time had passed, despite the toll of the years and differing stations in life.

Because Annapolis was beginning to look like a solid possibility, my future with the team was uncertain that night, and I was feeling both anxious and melancholy. If things broke right, this would be my last Lynvet party as a member of the team. As a result, I drank too much, unusual for me. My teammates, who persisted in thinking of me as as a clean-cut college kid even though I had started smoking and was still pushing a mail cart around the Pan Am hangar, delighted in egging me on. Well past midnight, Tommy, sensing that I was in trouble, calmed me down, eased me out of the bar, and rode the buses with me back to Kew Gardens. We sat on the cold concrete in the passageway outside the laundry room in the basement of my apartment building and talked for hours. He could discuss just about anything. From time to time I would run outside to vomit on the grass. He stayed with me until I was sober enough to go up to my apartment. By then it was past dawn. The whole episode was an act of great kindness toward someone he had met only once before and might never see again.

I had to take a physical for the Academy a week or so later. A battery of military doctors examined me. The one who took my blood pressure said mine was high. That had never happened before.

"How high?" I asked.

"High enough to keep you out of Annapolis if we can't get it down," he replied. "It's probably just nerves."

That was about ten in the morning. The doctor put me in a room with a cot in it and told me to rest. I worked at not being nervous. *Not much riding on this,* I thought, *just my whole goddamn future.* Every hour someone would come in and take my blood pressure. Then they'd say, "Rest some more."

At five, the first doctor came in, wrapped the blood pressure cup around my arm, and listened through his stethoscope. I was really nervous now.

"You're fine," he said. "Go home."

I looked at him. He met my gaze, held it a split second longer than necessary. A winkless wink. My heart pounding, I thanked him and left quickly, before he could have second thoughts.

Not long after, I took the College Boards. I felt I had done well, but I knew I faced stiff competition. I was at practice with the Queen of Peace baseball team on a warm Saturday in late March when my mother and sisters suddenly appeared behind the fence and hollered to me. Pat and Rosemarie were jumping up and down.

"You've got a letter from the Academy," said my mother, passing an envelope to me through the fence.

The next day the Lynvets were holding their first spring practice. I took the bus to Cross Bay Oval and got there on time, but I didn't bring my uniform or equipment.

"Didn't we once talk about being suited up when practice begins?" Kelly asked me.

"I guess I'm not going to practice today, Larry," I said.

A frown crossed Kelly's face. Bob Bushman, who was standing beside him, understood. "You got in, right," he said. "You made it?"

"Right," I said.

Suddenly the Lynvets, among them the new kid, Tommy Wall, engulfed me, shaking my hand, slapping me on the back. Everyone, it seemed, was happy for me.

"Way to go, Brother," said Joe Aragona, whose B average continued to elude him. "Wow, Annapolis, that's some school."

We agreed to get together at the Imperial that night to celebrate, but I never made it. I decided to stay around and watch the team practice. During the scrimmage, I was standing about fifteen yards behind the line talking to the coaches when the defense converged on the quarterback, who started scrambling back toward us. The defensive line caught up to him as he reached us, and we all went down in a pile. I heard something pop in my left knee. The pain was terrible. Someone took me to the hospital. My knee was wrapped and I was sent home. I could barely walk. I lay on the couch in our living room, under the mirror that covered the whole wall, and tried not to think about what my injury might mean. I stared at the lamps on our end tables, focusing on the yellowed cellophane that covered the shades and wondered if there might be a time when you could safely remove it.

What am I going to do? I asked myself. I could see my knee swelling. I didn't know much about life at Annapolis, but I did know it was not sedentary. There was marching, sports, drills, who knew what else? You had to be able to run, the faster the better, and walking was damn near impossible for me. The next day, I went to our family doctor, who sent me to an orthopedist. He examined my knee, told me there was no cartilage or ligament damage. I had torn the meniscus, he said, not great, but not the worst thing, either. He drained what seemed a quart of blood from my knee, using the largest needle I had ever seen.

"Can I still play football?" I asked.

"Maybe," the doctor replied. "We'll have to see how it heals."

"What about Annapolis? Can I still go?"

"I don't know. You should get in touch with them and find out how this affects you."

"This is going to heal, right? And I'll be able to walk, and run."

"It should."

Later that day, I thought about how I would inform the Naval Academy of my injury. Should I write a letter? To whom? Or should I call? Who would I call? Maybe I should let Senator Keating know so that he could arrange for one of the other guys to take my place if the Academy disqualified me.

That evening I finally decided whom I was going to tell.

No one.

I was ordered to report on July 3. One weekend in May my father and I took a trip to Annapolis. My knee was still tender, but I could walk without a limp. We just wanted to look over the place, so we didn't tell anybody we were coming. We took the train to Baltimore, then a bus to Annapolis, about an hour away. Halfway there, the commercial portion of the road we were on, Ritchie

Highway, gave way to rustic scenery, tall trees lining the road, here and there a gas station, a different world for a New York City kid. A sign: Annapolis—Naval Academy. As the bus slid onto the exit ramp, I peered out the window, searching for the Academy, anticipating my first glimpse. Within minutes we crested a rise and there it was, over the drawbridge ahead of us and off to the left, massive buildings with green roofs, solid and imposing, as if an assemblage of monuments had migrated to the shores of what I knew to be the Severn River and settled on a promontory of softly manicured grass, tennis courts, and athletic fields.

We arrived on the grounds in time for Saturday noon meal formation. The midshipmen, in their dress-white uniforms, were arrayed on a yellow-brick courtyard in front of a gargantuan edifice that I knew to be the famous dormitory, Bancroft Hall, the largest in the world, capable of housing all thirty-eight hundred midshipmen, the broad expanse of steps leading up to its doors guarded as if it were a fortress by cannon mounted on concrete stanchions.

We watched as midshipmen officers walked along the ranks, turning crisply to look over each man.

"Bobby, what the hell are they doing?" my father asked.

"Inspecting the troops," I said, having seen enough war movies and *Men of Annapolis* episodes on TV to know that much.

The inspection over, the crowd of onlookers gathered in front of the fierce statue of the Indian chief Tecumseh beheld a silent sea of white. Then, from one of the midshipman officers:

"Re-port!"

And the replies:

"First Regiment formed, sir!"

"Second Regiment formed, sir!"

I had chills. This was, I had no doubt, the place for me, the clean, well-lighted place where people lived normal, if demanding, lives as they prepared themselves for something that mattered.

After the Brigade of Midshipmen marched off to the strains of "Anchors Aweigh," my father and I crossed the broad brick courtyard known as Tecumseh Court and climbed the steps to Bancroft Hall, with its vaulted ceilings, marble floors, and arching windows.

We went up an interior marble staircase into Memorial Hall, where Captain James Lawrence's dying words, "Don't give up the ship," were stitched into a faded battle flag.

On our way into Bancroft, as I would soon learn, we passed near a special brick among the thousands that made up Tecumseh Court. They called it the C-I-R brick, those letters having been carved into it ages before by some long-forgotten midshipman. If I had known about it that day it surely would have tempered my enthusiasm.

C-I-R. Christ I Resign.

It was fun being with my dad that weekend, as it almost always was. I loved my father, but I sensed a weakness at his core that I was wary of, as if it were catching. Once remarried, though he continued to write popular music, he couldn't get it published or recorded. Not that he didn't try. Bankrolled by his wife and royalties he collected from previous work, mostly cartoon ditties, he took important people in the music-publishing business to expensive dinners, fawned over them, but seemed incapable of turning these social occasions into professional opportunities, which was his game plan for getting his songs to artists like Sinatra and Tony Bennett. I thought of my father's scheme as benighted and unworthy of him. My sister Pat has since challenged that interpretation, angrily shouting at me, "These days they call it networking and everybody does it!"

Pat may be right, but my mother was my role model on such matters. Whatever her faults, she refused to kowtow to anyone. She told me that she once complained to my father that his sister Hattie, who twice married well, neither time to Benny Leonard, had insulted her. His response? "Rosemarie, I can't say anything to Hattie because someday we may have to borrow money from her."

That fit, true or not. My father was always telling me to be nice to some big-deal guy or his kids because the guy could help him and maybe down the line the guy could help me, too. He often explained why it was important to bullshit people. "Bobby, Bobby, you've got to flatter people, tell them what they want to hear, it doesn't cost you anything." And he was always extolling the virtues of his wife's family back in Scranton, kids from her first marriage, all much older than me. Those may have been his true feelings, but I sensed that he was afraid of them, feared that at any moment they might kick down the door of the suite that he and his wife occupied at the Mayflower Hotel and reclaim their mother and her dwindling but still reasonably robust checkbook.

My mother was always comparing me to my father, in the process delivering a poisonous message. "He's afraid of everything," she would say. "He's afraid to fail. He's afraid of his own shadow. You're everything he's not."

I wasn't so sure about any of it. To begin with, I wasn't convinced that my mother had my father pegged accurately, though there was ample evidence, if viewed in a certain light, that she wasn't too far off the mark. He once explained to me why he had passed up some opportunity by saying "You know, Bob, I'm a fearful person."

I didn't want to hear that. The truth was, I was hardly fearless. Other than Peter Connor, the only truly fearless person I knew was my mother. And she had other problems. When I thought about it, Annapolis was perfect for me, met my highest standards, not just because I liked the idea of being a midshipman and a naval officer, but because of what it seemed to foreclose. In those days, what I didn't want to be was as important, maybe more important, than anything else.

17

"Don't Shoot Me, I'm Only Sixteen"

John Hourican, when he wasn't embarrassing the Lynvets, was as good a friend and mentor as Tommy Wall could hope for. But Hourican wasn't always there to save Tommy from himself. Tommy was hanging out at the recreation center in Woodside one evening a couple of years before he joined the Lynvets when the attendant, a moonlighting gym teacher, aroused his anger, never a hard emotion to evoke. Tommy had borrowed a pencil from the teacher, then refused to give it back, punctuating his refusal with an expletive. The teacher pushed Tommy and Tommy punched him. The teacher said he was calling the cops. Tommy couldn't understand it; he hadn't really hurt the guy. But he took off. The authorities didn't know who he was since he had registered under a false name. Everyone did. It only made sense. If you broke a Ping-Pong paddle, the center sent a letter to your parents.

Tommy was back at the rec center a week later. He figured the whole thing had blown over. Out of the corner of his eye, he saw three men in porkpie hats climbing the stairs. Cops. Coolly, he headed for the stairs and slid quickly through the trio.

At the top of the stairs, one of the cops asked, "Where is he?"

"He just ran down past you," the teacher said.

Tommy was gone. But he still didn't realize that others were taking the incident seriously even if he wasn't. A week or so later he returned to the rec center. So did the cops. This time they grabbed him and threw him up against the wall.

"When we get you down to the precinct, we're going to kick your ass, you little punk," said one cop.

Tommy bolted, hitting the double doors, scrambling down the stairs. The cop, just a few steps behind him, yelled, "Stop, you son of bitch."

Outside, Tommy crashed into a parked car, rolled off it, and started tearing up Skillman Avenue. The cop hit the car, too, harder than Tommy. The cop was even angrier than before. Tommy saw him pull his gun. Tommy was petrified, felt his legs turn to rubber. He scooted past PS 11, thought of cutting down the concrete path near the school, decided against it when he remembered it was a dead end. Straining to reach a trail into the woods at Windmuller Park, he was so scared he felt as if his heart would blow out of his chest. He glanced over his shoulder as the light of a streetlamp caught the barrel of the policeman's weapon.

"Stop or I'll shoot," shouted the cop.

Tommy, his heart pounding, his legs buckling under him, hollered back, "Don't shoot me, I'm only sixteen."

A moment later, Tommy found the trail, regained his composure and his legs as he heard the cop stumbling around, cracking his knee against a log, losing his enthusiasm for the chase.

Well, fuck this, Tommy thought, catching his breath and feeling his cockiness return, I'm not going back there again. And they can't get me because I registered with a phony name. So I'm safe.

He was right, or so it seemed, until the *Long Island Star-Journal* ran a team picture of the Woodside Chiefs, complete with names. A few nights later, he heard footsteps on the staircase, peered through the peephole in the door and saw porkpie hats. He scrambled out through the fire escape. The cops told his sister, the only one home, to tell her father to make sure Tommy was there the following night. We just want to talk to the kid, the cops said.

"You'd better wait for them," Tommy's father told him. "The guy said he just wants to talk." Tommy stayed home. The cops arrived. "Let's go," they said. "Go where?" asked Tommy.

At the station house the cops booked him for felonious assault. Then they hauled him to the Tombs in downtown Manhattan, where he was fingerprinted, photographed, and arraigned. The cops told the night court judge that registering under a fake name at the rec center was evidence of "a premeditated criminal mind." The teacher said Tommy had tried to stab his eye out with the pencil. The judge set bail at $2,500. His father didn't have the money and knew nothing about how the bail system operated. They transported Tommy to the Brooklyn House of Detention in the middle of the night. His fellow inmates, an experienced crew, told him that as a first-time offender he'd get off easy. "One to three," they said, meaning years. Tommy didn't think he could handle one to three days.

He spent a week at the House of Detention in a one-man cell on the twelfth floor, Cell Lower C 12. The first morning, a scrub brush for wiping out toilets was passed from cell to cell. Tommy didn't understand its purpose. Neither did the guy next to him. "What's this for, man?" Tommy's neighbor asked the prisoner on the other side of him. "That's your mammy's toothbrush," came the reply. Everyone laughed, Tommy's introduction to jailhouse humor.

In the cafeteria, stewed prunes were served at breakfast. "I jerked off in them," said the guy with the ladle. At lunch, the same guy said, "You want stew? I shit in the stew." Later, Tommy walked into the rec room, and saw a gang of prisoners watching *American Bandstand* on TV. Every few minutes someone would find fault with Bob or Darlene or one of the other regulars and spit on the screen. "Look at that guy," an aggrieved member of the audience would say. And cut loose. An inmate with a rag stood beside the TV, as if on sentry duty, to wipe the saliva from the screen. Tommy could relate. Dick Clark's crew of clean-cut teenagers were the envy of most of their contemporaries. Tommy and his friends sometimes talked of driving to Philadelphia, where the show originated, and beating the shit out of them.

After lights out, Tommy lay on his paper-thin mattress listening in terror to the other inmates hurling insults seemingly at random, an obscenity-laced game akin to bingo.

"Hey, Upper B 12, I've got your momma in here sucking on my dick."

"Lower A 2, I got a big prick for your sister."

He was sentenced to indefinite probation not to exceed five years. After a year, he got a new probation officer, a Mr. Gault, a tall, athletic-looking man who did not treat Tommy as a criminal. In December 1958, Mr. Gault said he had read about Tommy and the Chiefs in the paper, that they were going up against the College Point Klowns in the Pop Warner League play-offs. Tommy invited him to the game. College Point was favored, but Tommy led the Chiefs to an upset victory. After the game, Mr. Gault found Tommy.

"I really enjoyed the game," he said. "You were terrific."

"Thanks," said Tommy.

"I'm taking you off probation," said Mr. Gault.

A year later, Larry Kelly recruited him in the stands. In the spring of 1960 Tommy started practicing with the Lynvets. The match was a good one. He liked the Lynvets, and they liked him. He was playing so well that he even entertained the notion of beating out Ferriola.

Football aside, nothing got better for Tommy. That summer, his uncle got him a job at the Pepsi-Cola bottling plant in Long Island City, across the East River from Manhattan. The job paid ninety-four dollars a week, good money. His job was to throw cases of empty Pepsi bottles onto a conveyor belt.

By late summer the job had become unbearable. One Friday on his lunch hour he took his paycheck and headed for a local bar. Soon he was knocking back Skindivers—a volatile concoction composed of vodka, green crème de menthe, dry vermouth, and club soda. He had four or five before returning to work.

An hour or so later, the foreman called for a volunteer to spread tarpaulins over cases of Pepsi sitting outside in the motor pool. The cases were stacked easily two stories high. The tarps were to shield the bottles from the sun over the weekend so they didn't explode before the distributors picked them up Monday morning. Tommy said he'd do it. Minutes later he was hoisted to the top of the mountain of Pepsi cases. Reeling from the booze and the steamy heat on the floor of the plant, he struggled with the tarps as his feet slid between the bottles. Down below, the foreman called to him: "You, Wall, hurry it up."

Tommy continued to struggle and kept slipping. From below, "Hey, Wall, move it." Seeing red, Tommy grabbed a bottle of Pepsi and hurled it at his tormentor.

"Fuck you!" Tommy shouted as the bottle shattered on the concrete.

He grabbed another bottle, then another. Each time he fired off a Pepsi, he hollered, "Fuck you!" Soon the plant's managers, in their ties and white shirts, were out in the yard, along with Tommy's uncle, dodging shards of bottle glass and soft drink spray, trying to talk him down. Finally, he stopped throwing bottles and just stood there, fighting for balance, screaming imprecations for reasons he only vaguely understood, a solitary figure silhouetted against the changing New York skyline—the Empire State Building and the Chrysler Building, the new United Nations Building in front of them, the even newer Seagram Building, all green glass and relentlessly modern.

About that time, the Lynvets started summer practice. Tommy looked at himself and made a grim appraisal.

"Away from the Lynvets, I'm an eighteen-year-old bum."

18

Jersey On My Mind

*A*s Tommy was getting initiated into Lynvet football, I was making my way by rail to Baltimore, where I was to board the bus to Annapolis. I should have been excited. A new world was opening up to me. Plus I was free of my family. Instead, as my southbound train rolled under the Hudson River on that early July day in 1960, I found myself in the grip of an aching melancholy. I recalled how my mother always described those parts of the world that were not New York.

Jersey, she would say. All the rest is Jersey.

I was leaving New York for a new life among the Jerseyites, be they Texans or Californians or Iowans. A better life, I hoped, but certainly a different one. And as the train rattled through settings I knew almost totally from movies and TV, I felt that I was losing something, a city about which I had long been ambivalent, but now sensed I would miss greatly. My thoughts were jumbled as fragments of my life and its connection to the city bounced about willy-nilly in my brain.

From the time I was eleven, I could look at the subway map on the station wall, figure out where to change trains, and get wherever I wanted to go. I had no idea how Brooklyn and Queens connected to one another, only that both were across the East River from what we called the City. I didn't know east from west, north from south, except in midtown Manhattan, which was laid out so that you couldn't help knowing. But who needed a sense of direction? I wasn't riding out to the North Forty or searching for the West Fork; I just needed to know how to get from Union Turnpike station to Broadway and 86th Street or First Avenue and 14th. I'd read about how kids in other places considered it a big deal when they were finally given the keys to the family car, but I never understood that. To me, cars meant only clogged traffic, screeching brakes, and blaring horns. A fifteen-cent subway token was my passport to the world, at least the world I cared about.

I always had jobs, all over the city. One summer when I was living with a family in Brighton Beach, I shined shoes on the boardwalk at Coney Island, New York's mildly seedy middle-class playground. I made a shoeshine box out of an old drawer, which was bulky and lacked panache but worked. All my friends charged fifteen cents a shine. I undercut them, charged a dime, worked three hours longer a day than they did, and made the same money. My dad hated the idea that I was shining shoes.

"You don't have to do that," he said. "I'll give you money."

"Thanks," I said, "but I like doing it."

You'd think that not many people on the boardwalk would be wearing the kind of shoes that needed a shine, but you'd be wrong. Lots of guys, mostly older men, sat on the benches looking out at the ocean across the thousands of people crammed onto the beach glistening from Coppertone suntan oil. They didn't care about the Parachute Jump or the Cyclone or Steeplechase Park or the Wonder Wheel or the Star Penny Arcade arrayed behind them like a world gone happily berserk; they just wanted to look at the ocean and dream old-guy dreams.

"Hey, kid," they'd say, "don't get any polish on my socks or I ain't gonna pay you." Or they'd say, "Ten cents? You're a thief, kid. A go-niff. You know what a goniff is?" I'd answer, "A thief?" They'd say, "Right, kid. You're okay. Gimme a shine. Watch the socks."

I turned sixteen in June 1956 and immediately got my working papers. My first real job, one where I worked for someone else rather than shining shoes or selling icy soft drinks to softball players in schoolyards on weekends, was with the Rapid Messenger Service, which operated out of a dingy office on 42nd Street, amid a string of terrific gross-out movie theaters, adult bookstores, and doorways filled with luckless souls who in those unenlightened times we called bums. The job paid a dollar an hour and gave me the run of the city, at least that part of the city I cared about, Central Park South down through the theater district to Macy's and Gimbels at 34th Street. I was a West Side guy, never set foot in B. Altman's or Saks or Lord and Taylor. Mostly I delivered in the garment district, usually packages, sometimes pushing a cart hung with dresses or coats. I had to use the delivery entrance, where the elevators took forever and my colleagues in the messenger trade—mostly bulky older men with unshaved faces—grumbled and killed time by unleashing at the whitewashed walls great gobs of saliva that would splatter, cling, lose traction, and begin a meandering journey to the pitted concrete floor.

New York in the late 1950s was a great place for a young man to get lost. The city was cold and impersonal and I could disappear into it. The crowds and the lights and the noise and the cars and the buildings conspired to render us all anonymous. That was for me. I didn't want people to know who I was—that my parents were divorced, that my mother was an alcoholic, that my father seemed to be living off his wife, that I didn't know from one month to the next where I would call home or, later on, that my life was going nowhere. Walking the streets of New York, I felt like the star of a movie of my own devising, with the city as the set. Young man with promise, awaiting fortune's touch.

One of my father's best friends was Johnny Shubert, who owned many of the theaters on Broadway, so he could gets us house seats for the hottest shows in town—almost always free. Pat, Rosemarie, and I saw all the great musicals from seats rarely worse than fourth-row center. I saw *West Side Story* five times. Pat saw it thirteen times, falling in love with a succession of actors who played the Anglo gang leader Riff.

Around this same time, I had a brush with show business, a minor one, but more than enough to keep alive the vague suspicion that I had been switched at birth.

I was a junior at Stuyvesant when I finally decided it was time to learn to dance. I wasn't looking to do much—a slow dance and a fast dance, meaning the fox trot and the Lindy. My sister Pat was a great dancer and could have taught me, but she would have teased me about having a girlfriend, which I didn't, or wanting a girlfriend, which I did.

"How about Arthur Murray's?" I asked my mother.

"God," she said, arching her eyebrows, as if I had suggested we move to Paramus.

She explained to me that, yes, I could probably learn the fox trot and the Lindy at Arthur Murray's, but I would develop no sense of rhythm, or movement, or lots of other things that she convinced me were important. That's how I would up at Oliver McCool's.

Oliver McCool, tall and bony and bearing a faint resemblance to Fred Astaire, ran a tap-dancing studio on the second floor of a building on 53rd and Broadway. He was the younger brother of my mother's late tap teacher, the legendary—or so we had been told—Tommy Nip. Soon, twice a week, I was going to Oliver's after school. As far as I could tell, I was the only student in the class who was not an aspiring performer or a professional already. Even so, I quickly realized I loved tap dancing and desperately wanted to be good at it. Alas, my alleged genes notwithstanding, I was bereft of talent. After six months, I had managed to learn three tap steps, which every newcomer to the class had mastered within the first half hour of his or her first one-hour lesson. My father came by one day to watch me. Afterward, totally befuddled, as if I had committed a crime against nature, he kept saying, "Bobby, Bobby, how come you don't hear the beat?" My apprenticeship to Oliver Mc-

Cool, who put us through our paces from atop a short wooden stool, a cigarette drooping from his lips, his left foot pounding the floor in what I gathered had something to do with the elusive beat, eventually ended. I liked him and he kept assuring me I was getting there, but even I could see this was a fool's errand. Needless to say, when we said goodbye I still could do neither the fox trot nor the Lindy.

New York at night was the best. After a show, alone, walking along Broadway, bouncing off people, the Camel guy puffing away above the street, blowing beautiful smoke rings that drifted lazily through the charged air, tipsy sailors in their jaunty white hats and bell bottoms, all the stores still open, so much neon that everyone seemed electrified, the newsstands with the early papers and garish displays of girlie magazines, the air filled with perfume and ciga-rette smoke and limitless possibility if you were young and strong and smart and had an eye for it.

In 1958, around the time I started playing for the Lynvets, thanks to my dad I discovered the Hickory House, a steakhouse and jazz club on 52nd Street. In the 1930s and 1940s, 52nd Street was known as Swing Street, more often as just The Street. Jazz clubs lined both sides of 52nd between Fifth and Sixth Avenues— the Three Deuces, Jimmy Ryan's, the Famous Door, Kelly's Stable, the Onyx Club. By the late Fifties, most had closed and several had become strip joints. In their day, though, virtually all the jazz greats performed on The Street—Charlie Parker, Miles Davis, Billie Holiday, Dizzy Gillespie, Thelonious Monk, everyone. The Hick-ory House, a block west, was a survivor, with its horseshoe bar sur-rounding a raised stage, muted lighting, and dark wood booths where you could cut a deal, engage in a seduction, or, if you were like me, delude yourself that you were up to something along that line. Marian McPartland was usually there, sometimes Billy Tay-lor. I used to go to the Hickory House after seeing a Broadway show, arriving about eleven-thirty, usually with my father, a friend or, less frequently, a date. My dad taught me not to eat before a show and save my appetite for after, when I wouldn't feel rushed and could enjoy my meal. So I'd sit there, listen to the music, have a scotch on the rocks, order a steak, maybe a piece of cheesecake (not as good as the Turf's, but close), have another scotch, then head to the subway for the trip back to Queens. That was the downside of not having a car. The Hickory House did its part in getting young women to consider indulging in the unthinkable. In the glare of a subway car, they quickly reverted to the virgin persuasion. On that score, sadly, I was their co-religionist.

I came out of my reverie as we were speeding through the Maryland countryside and I wondered how a New York City boy would fit in with the Jerseyites. What did a guy from Idaho also making his way to Annapolis that day think of a place where more kids probably mobbed the balcony of the Brooklyn Paramount for one of Alan Freed's rock-and-roll shows than lived in his entire state? Did the Idaho kid judge it by movies like *Blackboard Jungle*, which portrayed juvenile delinquents in a dumpy New York City high school terrorizing their teachers? The kid must have seen it— everybody had seen it, and everybody had danced to the song that gave the film its electicity, Bill Haley and the Comets' "Rock Around the Clock," with a beat so insistent that even I could pick it up. Or *On the Waterfront*, with guys who challenged Johnny Friendly and his labor goons hung from meathooks or beaten within an inch of their lives. Magazines, newspapers, television, even Broadway musicals focused on gang violence in the city. Some of that must have made its way across the Continental Divide to a state best known for its potatoes. Teen gangs were at the heart of *West Side Story*, along with *My Fair Lady* the toughest ticket on Broadway and already in production as a movie. Books like Harry Grey's *The Hoods* glorified New York mobsters even if the bad guys ultimately paid a price. What about Jack Kerouac, Allen Ginsberg and the rest of the Beats, many bred at Columbia and now clustered in the East Village? What did the Idaho kid think of their contemptuous, antiestablishment style, their outrageous novels and verse, and their hipster's familiarity with drugs? Ginsberg's "Howl"—"I saw the best minds of my generation destroyed by madness, starving hysterical naked, dragging themselves through the negro streets at dawn looking for an angry fix"—hardly the

speech patterns I associated with Boise and Pocatello and Soda
Springs.

"Baltimore next," shouted the conductor as the train pulled out
of Wilmington. I thought of Johnny Unitas and the great Colts
teams, recalled that the dreadful St. Louis Browns had moved to
Baltimore a few years back and become the slightly less dreadful
Orioles. That brought to mind the most embarrassing episode of
my boyhood, one that affirmed my addiction to baseball in the days
before football claimed me.

All my early sports heroes were baseball players, most of them
Yankees. This was the era of the Clipper, "Scooter" Rizzuto, Yogi,
the young Whitey Ford, Steady Eddie Lopat, Vic Raschi, and the
Chief, Allie Reynolds. But my favorite, my first hero, was Number
15, Tommy Henrich, "Old Reliable," as the great Yankee right
fielder of the late 1930s and 1940s was known.

I was eight, so this was 1948, possibly 1949. My father had
taken me to Yankee Stadium to see the Bronx Bombers play the
Detroit Tigers. At least I think it was the Tigers. Late in the game,
the Yankees were down by two runs. As usual, I was eating hot dogs
and downing Cokes and growing ever more anxious as the game
progressed. I was afraid to leave my seat even to go to the bathroom
lest the Yankees sense a diminution, however brief, in the collective
will of their fans to fight to the very end. With the game on the
line, the Yanks, I truly believed, needed me in my seat, cheering as
loudly as I could, at one with the other fans, who needed no prodding from electronic scoreboard gadgetry. As the Tigers came to
bat in the top of the ninth, still leading by two runs, reality as-
saulted me. I needed to urinate so badly that even my loyalty to the
Yankees would have to give, if only for a couple of minutes. I turned
to my father.

"Dad, I have to go to the bathroom."

My father, who was as big a Yankee fan as me, replied, in a disbelieving tone, "Now? Hendrich could get up in the ninth." My
dad always said Hendrich, not Henrich, just as he invariably referred to people named Henry as Hendry, don't ask me why.

"Dad. Yes. Now. I really, really have to go."

We edged our way toward the aisle past other spectators—most of them men, nearly all in suits and ties, many wearing fedoras, porkpies, or Panamas—then down the steps of the grandstand and made our way to the men's room. There was a line. The Tigers were still up, though they didn't seem to be doing anything to add to their lead. Old Reliable was scheduled to bat fifth in the last of the ninth. If the Yanks could just get some men on base . . .

I didn't have to finish the thought. In fact, I couldn't. I was in pain. I was hopping from one foot to the other, bending at the waist, rolling my eyes, bobbing my head, trying to contain my discomfort and, concurrently, impart some movement to the line.

The top of the ninth ended as we advanced to the outer reaches of the men's room, but there was still a line leading in the door. Relief seemed a long way off. As we inched along, a roar went up from the crowd. Seconds later the news rippled through the line that the first Yankee batter had reached base. Then we heard that the next batter had made out. And the next. Two outs. Sweat was dripping down my forehead. By now I was jumping up and down. These days someone would have noticed and cleared a path to a urinal for a child in the situation I clearly was in. Back then, kids were kids. They waited their turn.

Another roar—a second Yankee had reached base.

"Bobby, Bobby," my father said, excitedly. "Hendrich's up. He's gonna hit a homer and win the game."

I looked at my father, aghast. Didn't he know you never said anything like that, that predicting some heroic feat on the part of a favorite player was all it took to ensure it wouldn't happen? I didn't have time to explain to my father that he had jinxed Old Reliable because just then two urinals opened up. We rushed to them. Tommy was up, the crowd was cheering madly, I was relieving myself with as much dispatch as possible. As I finished, the stadium exploded. The crowd's roar blasted into the men's room. Tommy had done something, something great I was sure. I flipped and zipped, at the same time turning away from the urinal when the pain grabbed me. I started screaming just as the news of Tommy's game-winning three-run homer made its way to us. I had snagged myself in my zipper, a small piece of skin. Agony.

"Bobby, Bobby, what the hell happened?" asked my father, who always said my name twice in moments of excitement, confusion, or panic.

I didn't know what to say. I didn't have the words. I was too old to use the child's term employed within our family for that part of my anatomy and I may not have known the grown-up word. Even if I had known it, I don't think it had ever issued from my lips. I just stood there, mortified. Finally, tears coating my face, I pointed and said, "I'm caught."

I now had the attention of the other men.

"Kid, kid, how the hell did you do that?"

"Jesus, kid."

Men were squatting in a circle around me, telling me not to cry, as the cheers continued for Old Reliable. I noticed a few guys trying not to laugh.

My dad was patting me on the back, but offering nothing in the way of practical advice. Finally, someone said, "Son, just try to ease it out slowly. Take your time."

I tried. It didn't work. Then a man who may have said he was a doctor came over. He looked closely at my predicament. I was growing uneasy. Then he said, "Son, this is going to hurt a little." He reached for the zipper and pulled it down. I screamed. But I was free. No blood. Not much pain, either. The man told me to wash "the area" when I got home and put some peroxide on it.

"Let's go," I said to my dad, running out, hoping to plug into the fading excitement of the game's spectacular finish.

As we neared Baltimore, I was still thinking about that game and my dad and the city I was leaving. Life had been crazy, but I had had a lot of fun there. I also realized that I had missed a great deal. I had never been to the top of the Empire State Building or gotten to the Statue of Liberty. I had never been to Chinatown or Little Italy. I had never been to Greenwich Village or Wall Street. It seemed there would always be time. But now time had run out.

There was another reason. My life had been led on the fly, as if I were always just two steps ahead of the law. Sure, sports helped me fit in, but moving every few months for years at a time had taken a toll. You know, I said to myself, I guess I love New York, but I was never able to catch my breath there. And I sat back in my seat, put my hands behind my head and inhaled deeply as I hurtled clackety-clack into my future.

19

Flying Tiger

*F*or Bernadette Bushman's third Christmas, her parents gave her a tricycle. Because she was a small girl, her father put blocks on the pedals so she could reach them. Two days after Christmas, her seven-year-old brother, Bob, was playing in front of the family's house on Courtney Street in Flushing when he noticed Bernie's tricycle sitting by itself two doors down. Bob was his sister's unofficial guardian when they were outside, so he stormed down the street to scold her for being careless with her expensive new toy. He saw the two little boys Bernie had been playing with, but not Bernie. And then he saw his sister's legs protruding from beneath a baby grand piano that lay ingloriously on a concrete driveway. Bob tried to lift the piano. He couldn't budge it. He ran back up the street, screaming for his mother.

The piano, as events were later reconstructed, had been leaning on its side against a garage, awaiting pickup by a junk dealer. The legs had been removed. The boys had wedged themselves behind it so that they could pound on the keys. Bernie was standing in front of the piano when it toppled over. She was killed instantly.

All the Christmas decorations in the neighborhood were down by nightfall. As was the custom, the wake was held in the Bushmans' home, Bernie's tiny white casket resting where a gaily lit Christmas tree had stood the day before. The newspaper ran a short story of the tragedy, along with a picture of Bernie holding a teddy bear. The Bushmans moved away two months later. The parents separated within a year. A reconciliation failed, divorce followed, and Bob, by then nine, went to live in the Cypress Hills section of Brooklyn with his mother and grandmother. His father soon remarried and moved to Colorado, and Bob lost contact with him. His mother, who worked as a telephone operator, started drinking heavily after the second breakup. When she was at her worst, she cried uncontrollably for Bernie. The caretaker at St. John's cemetery once found her in the snow at her daughter's grave. Bob still has a little gold cross that belonged to his sister: It bears the imprint of a tiny tooth. And to this day he thinks about Bernie and the piano he was not strong enough to lift.

Bob Bushman's youth was no less difficult than Larry Kelly's or most other Lynvets. In many ways it was harder. But he didn't let it show. He was cool and controlled, rarely letting his emotions get the better of him. He came from Irish and German stock, but with his high cheekbones, smooth skin, and mildly olive complexion he bore a faint resemblance to an American Indian. His powerful upper body seemed a shade too heavy for his less-impressive lower torso, unless you had the misfortune of encountering his driving legs on the football field. He was also as tough as they come, but if you didn't have a need to know that, you never would.

Ask any Lynvet about Bushman and the response rarely varies. A class act. As offensive coach, he was soft-spoken and unfailingly polite, a quite presence who seemed content to do his job in Larry Kelly's ever-expanding shadow. No less than Larry, he lived and breathed Lynvet football. But Bob, unlike Larry, had another life.

His football exploits at St. John's Prep and above-average academic standing earned Bob scholarship offers from Bucknell and the University of Richmond, but his mother's drinking problem made him feel he couldn't leave home. Instead, in the fall of 1953 he enrolled at Fordham, commuting daily by subway, an hour and a half each way. Fordham didn't offer any scholarship money, but it had a football team. Bob figured he'd play his way onto the freshman squad and earn a scholarship the following year. Instead, an ankle injury at an early practice finished him for the season.

He worked at a variety of meaningless jobs during the school year—mailboy, stockboy, messenger, filling in graves. But working after school hurt him academically. And he had no sense of direction, no idea of what he wanted to do with his life. He gradually lost interest in school. At the end of his freshman year, he dropped out. His mother made him promise that he would go back to college, though he was careful not to say when he planned to do so. In truth, he had no idea.

He found the Lynvets that fall, introduced to them by some guys he played baseball with that summer. He arrived at his first practice much as I did a few years later, expecting little besides a crew of paunchy older guys who liked to screw around on weekends. He was stunned to see a team with some of the best ballplayers in the area—guys like him who had made All-City in either the public or Catholic high school leagues—and a coach, Charlie Fitzgerald, who ran an organized, disciplined practice and talked of nothing but winning.

The following spring, on Good Friday, he almost died in a motorcycle accident, suffering broken cheekbones, a smashed nose, a cracked jaw, a severe concussion, and enormous blood loss.

"You know, he was fifteen minutes from bleeding to death," a doctor told a friend who rushed him to the emergency room.

Bob spent three weeks in the hospital. With time to think, he asked himself a question: What the hell am I doing with my life? Watching the doctors go about their rounds, he decided he wanted to be a doctor, too. That fall, the fall of 1955, Fordham dropped intercollegiate football, but Bob returned to the school, determined to enter the pre-med program. But his grades as a freshman had been so lackluster that he had to repeat the year—in effect, start all over. The Jesuits didn't mess around. It didn't matter. What counted was that he was back in school after losing his way and spending a year in aimless, at times perilous, drifting.

He wrote a letter to himself shortly after starting school again. It said: *You can quit any time you want. There's nothing holding you here. But if you do quit, you will probably never come back.* He read and reread the letter many times over the next four years. He thought of it as giving himself permission to quit, but understood that it was a warning not to. And he didn't. Pre-med didn't work for him—the labs made him queasy—so he switched to economics and did fine.

A few months after he returned to college, Bob took a job as a cargo handler for Seaboard and Western Airlines at Idlewild. Seaboard was a young, aggressive freight carrier whose fortunes had been jump-started by the 1948 Berlin Airlift, in which the practicality of moving cargo by air was established. Bob's job was to load, unload, and clean the planes. It was not a part-time job. He was going full-time to Fordham and working from 5:00 p.m. to 2:00 a.m. five nights a week at the airport. He did it his entire final four years at Fordham.

It helped that he loved planes. As far back as 1945, as a nine-year-old, he wrote a letter to Claire Chennault, the legendary leader of the Flying Tigers, the elite group of American aviators who fought for the Chinese against the Japanese during the early days of World War II. Chennault responded with a personal note and a Flying Tiger patch. Bob immediately felt at home in the Seaboard hangar, surrounded by old bomber and fighter pilots, dashing figures who told thrilling tales of air battles with a bravado that made the stories sound as if the aviators had just returned from a mission deep behind enemy lines. He sensed that first night on the job that something new and important had entered his life.

Bob was twenty in 1955 when he started at Seaboard and, like most Lynvets, he had seen little of the world beyond Brooklyn and Queens. By the time he graduated Fordham four years later, he had, thanks to Seaboard and his own curiosity and wanderlust, acquired the ability to handle himself anywhere in the world. Seaboard employees could hitchhike on flights, and Bob took full advantage of his opportunities. Jack Bassano, an engaging and high-spirited coworker, was his frequent traveling companion. Together they traveled to the great cities of Europe—Paris, Rome, London, Hamburg, Stockholm, Copenhagen, Milan, Lisbon—as well as to India and the Philippines. Some trips lasted only a few days, others as long as two weeks. On their first trip to Paris they were at an after-hours bar when three prostitutes came in, their night's labors behind them. Bob and Jack invited them to breakfast. The women asked where they were staying. They had no idea. They had arrived a few hours earlier, with twenty-five dollars between them. Come with us, the women said. They brought Bob and Jack to the building where they lived and plied their trade, a brothel on the Left Bank. You can stay here, the women said, we always have a few rooms that are not in use. Bob and Jack and the three prostitutes became friends. The Americans also became friends with the prostitutes' friends. Over the next three or four years, they figured, they probably met every hooker in the French capital. And they always had a place to stay in Paris.

His first year back at Fordham pushed Bob to the limit. School most of the day, the job at Seaboard most of the night. He did his homework in the Quonset hut between servicing planes. He bought a '38 Chevy from a friend for five dollars and used it to commute from his home in Brooklyn, to school in the Bronx, to the job in Queens. The car threw out brake fluid, which he could not afford to replace. Instead, he used water, which was definitely not recommended but actually worked. Driving along, he would open a hatch in the floor and pour in the water. But he knew winter would be a problem since the water would freeze. He had a case of Beefeater's Gin, obtained duty-free in Ireland. He brought it to Old Joe at the Imperial.

"I'll trade you this case of Beefeater's for two cases of wine," said Bob.

"What kinda wine you want?" asked Old Joe, suspicious as always.

Replied Bob, "Any kind, Joe. Cheap wine."

Because of its alcohol content, wine has a lower freezing temperature than water. As the winter chill set in, Bob poured the wine into the hatch. That worked, too, except that the fumes from the brakes were so strong that he was invariably woozy by the time he reached school.

In June 1959, as his graduation day approached, IBM offered him a job. He was ready to take it when a Seaboard executive called and said, "Why not stay with us? Go into sales?" He accepted.

His decision to stay with Seaboard was rooted in his first night on the job, when he had thrilled to the stories told by the pilots. But that night was memorable for another reason. The Salk polio vaccine, introduced a few years earlier, depended on an extract from Rhesus monkeys. Seaboard had the contract for hauling the monkeys from India to Idlewild. They carried sixteen hundred of the animals at a time. The cages, piled two high, ten monkeys to a cage, were stacked on the tarmac in two long rows separated by what amounted to an aisle between them. Jack Bassano, a practical joker, told the new guy that it was time to feed the monkeys. He gave Bob a sack of corn kernels, told him to walk down the aisle throwing the kernels left and right into the cages.

Bob stepped off briskly, forgetting that monkeys, including Rhesus monkeys, were famous for copying the actions of others—other monkeys or, in this case, the young man who was throwing something at them. Halfway down the aisle, Bob found himself in the midst of a shitstorm as hundreds of monkeys responded by scooping up the accumulated excrement from a fifteen-hour, eight-thousand-mile journey and pelting him with it.

It was a rough initiation. Bob had to burn his clothes. But before the night was over, he said to himself, "I want to be the president of this company."

20

Anchors Aweigh

*N*othing prepares you for your first year at the Naval Academy, but informed advice can help. Most of my classmates had it. Many came from military families. A lot of them had fathers and grandfathers who had gone to Annapolis. A decent percentage had been enlisted men in the Navy or the Marines and had spent a year at the Naval Academy Prep School in Bainbridge, Maryland, fleshing out their academic backgrounds and picking up pointers on what awaited them forty-five miles to the south. Even those who came from non-military backgrounds as I did had enough sense to do some research on the place where they were getting ready to spend the next four years of their lives.

I didn't. To me, Annapolis was to be my safe harbor, the end of a long, hard journey, not the beginning of one. I had it backward. I reported to the Naval Academy completely unprepared. I had never even met anyone who had gone to a service academy. I knew there was something called Plebe Year, but I thought of it as good-natured, often madcap hazing in which everyone was in on the joke. I thus violated a central tenet of survival in unfamiliar circumstances, which might be stated thus:

Never wander into a strange cave until you've checked out the eating habits of those who dwell within.

I was being eaten alive by the cave dwellers. My head had been shaved, I was frazzled, and I had been pronounced a sorry sack of shit more times than I could count. And that was just the first day. Early on, I was treated to a description of the Academy as a place where you would get a forty-thousand-dollar education crammed up your ass a nickel at a time. Or a place where they take away the basic rights of man and give them back to you one by one as privileges. Or a four-year breaststroke through a pool of shit.

I was swimming against the tide without a nickel to my name. We were told that the juniors, or second classmen, who were our sherpas for Plebe Summer training, were among the Academy's best. To me they seemed devoid of humor, warmth, or pity.

"Who the fuck you looking at, maggot?" an upperclassman roared as I made the mistake of letting my eyes momentarily meet his.

That was one of the rules. In Bancroft Hall plebes were to keep their eyes "in the boat," meaning straight ahead, except when they were in their rooms, unless of course a commissioned officer or upperclassman walked in. That meant "bracing up"—snapping to attention so forcefully that your eyes bulged and the veins in your neck resembled a series of levees—and sounding off as follows: "Midshipman Timberg, Fourth Class, Sir!" Bancroft Hall, which had so impressed me when I had visited with my father, was said to be the world's largest dormitory. It was also the answer to the riddle "What has six wings, 360 heads, and sucks?"

We had to learn a new language, Navy lingo. Floors were decks, walls were bulkheads, ceilings were overheads, bathrooms were heads, beds were racks, stairs were ladders. This was shipboard terminology, and it drove me crazy since we were in a gigantic stone building, not a vessel on the high seas, and it reinforced my sense that I was living an Orwellian nightmare: War is peace. Freedom is slavery. Ignorance is strength.

Reveille was at six-fifteen, unless you had to get up earlier to run extra duty because you had been put on report for something like failing to slide a toothbrush laden with polish through the groove between the sole and the upper part of your shoes. A screaming electronic bell awakened us, thirty seconds of ear-splitting hell, followed by thirty more seconds of short, piercing blasts. By then you had to be out of your rack with all your bedding piled in the middle so that you could make the bed from scratch five minutes later.

I thought, briefly, that football might be my salvation. Navy was a big-time power in those days, and Joe Bellino, an All-American halfback and Heisman Trophy candidate, was returning that year. The school recruited heavily. Still, the freshman team was open to walk-ons, and I decided to try out even though my knee still felt fragile. The moment of truth came when a coach put two tires about eight yards apart and positioned backs on one side, linemen on the other. A one-on-one drill, the back was supposed to get by the lineman. I drew a fellow plebe named Mike Chumer, who seemed to fill the entire space between the tires. I faked right, faked left, never seemed to get outside his wingspan. So I put my head down and barreled right into him, with predictable results—a Lenny Rochester moment. I was not, it was clear, Navy football material. I tried for a time to convince myself that my size had done me in, but others no bigger than I, among them Bob Sutton, a kid from Florida, were clearly destined for the varsity. The truth was, I was not good enough.

Soon I was asking myself if I was good enough for the Academy. I could, it seemed, do nothing right, a point the second classmen training us reaffirmed for me twenty times a day. More than once, braced up along a bulkhead, eyes in the boat, sweat streaming down my face, I'd hear the words, delivered either angrily or sadly, in a southern drawl or a Texas twang or flat midwestern tones, "Timberg, you're just so fucked up."

And I was. My roommates—Mike Hewitt from St. Paul, Bob Woodruff from Michigan, Bill McClure from a small town in West Virginia, none from Idaho—had their own problems with the second classmen, but they seemed less rattled by them than me. In the evenings, at our desks, we compared notes as we spit-shined our shoes, each with a tin of black Kiwi polish in front of us, a damp cloth wrapped around our index and middle fingers making small circles on the leather. Mike, the youngest but the most mature, would often say, "They're just trying to see if we can take it." He was having a hard time, too, but he seemed to have made his peace with it.

In late August, we had Parents Weekend. My mother came down, as did Pat and Rosemarie, along with Joe Aragona and Larry Sifert, my friend from Kew Gardens with whom I used to lift weights and drink vanilla milk shakes, now playing with the Lynvet Seniors. Pat was miserable. All these great-looking guys in starched white uniforms and she had braces, so she curled her lips over her teeth when she smiled. That made it even worse. Everyone was impressed with the school. I confessed that I was not happy. Joe couldn't believe it. "Bob, golly, look at this place," he said. "Are you kidding me?"

Just before Labor Day the plebe class was reshuffled. I went to the Seventh Company and got three new roommates, Tom Richman, an Air Force brat who had lived everywhere, Dave Ahern, from West Hartford, Connecticut, and Frank Spangenberg, from a town outside Buffalo. The three upper classes returned from summer leave and training cruises a few days later, a reassembling of the clan that we had been warned about throughout the previous two months. Suddenly we were vastly outnumbered by guys who were carbon copies of our summer mentors, but without the charm.

To this day, the names send a chill through me. John Sullivan, John Morris, Bill Gage, Jim Miller—all Marines before entering the Academy and committed to returning to the Corps when they graduated. All four seemed decked out in dress blues even in their skivvies, at attention even when taking a leak. On the parade ground, one of them, usually Sullivan or Morris, would offer a running commentary of my failings in the manly art of marching. "Timberg, you're bouncing up and down," or (shades of my dad and Oliver McCool), "Timberg, you're out of step. Listen to the god-damn drum. Boom. Boom. Boom. Boom. Every time you hear the boom your left foot's supposed to hit the ground, you spastic little twerp."

In addition to the intensified hazing, the return of the Brigade signaled the commencement of the academic year. We plebes had English, foreign language, math, chemistry, engineering drawing, and seamanship, not to mention physical training. All but seamanship and PT involved homework, which ranked behind researching the so-called professional questions that the upperclassmen peppered us with in the Mess Hall. The questions were worse than the physical hazing, and we had to find the answers by the next meal, unless they were in "Reef Points," the two-hundred-page plebe handbook, in which case we were expected to know them because we had supposedly committed it to memory. For example, the response to the question "Why didn't you say 'sir'?" was:

Sir, sir is a subservient word surviving from the surly days of old Serbia, when certain serfs, too ignorant to remember their lords' name, yet too servile to blaspheme them, circumvented the situation by surrogating the subservient word sir, by which I now belatedly address a certain senior cirroped who correctly surmised that I was syrupy enough to say sir after every word I said, sir.

Some of the professional questions were serious. *What's a bangalore torpedo* or *Describe the use of mortars in the Tarawa campaign.* Others were impossible until your realized how simple they were. *Q: How many bricks did it take to complete Tecumseh Court? A: One.* Nearly all of them required enormous investments of time, a plebe's most precious commodity.

Plebes were also expected to be well informed. We could not watch television or listen to the radio, but we were supposed to read one of two newspapers, the *Baltimore Sun* or the *Washington Post,* prior to the 6:45 morning meal.

"Tell me about the debate, Timberg."

I am in the Mess Hall, shoved out, that is, in a sitting position but without a chair under me. My chin is rammed into the back of my head, my eyes, of course, are in the boat.

"The debate, sir?"

"The debate, Timberg."

"Sir?"

"Nixon? Kennedy? Ring any bells, Timberg?"

"Yes, sir."

"So tell me about last night's debate. You read the paper, right?

"No, sir."

"Why not?"

The truthful answer was—

I didn't read the paper because I had been in this guy's room braced up, seated on air, a ten-pound M-1 rifle resting on my outstretched arms, listening to him reel off a litany of my failings from ten minutes after reveille until five minutes before morning meal formation, time I had used futilely trying to deal with a string of stupid questions his asshole roommate had asked me at evening meal the night before.

The correct answer, was—

"No excuse, sir."

Some of the hazing was funny, if at times perilous. One evening my Seventh Company classmate Hank Salerno, an Italian kid from the Bronx, found himself standing on his head on a Bancroft Hall window ledge singing "Volare." Every now and then a plebe showed some chutzpah. One afternoon a first classman dragged the brash Sandy Coward to the window. "Look at her, Coward, isn't she beautiful?" said the firstie, pointing to his girlfriend, who was waiting for him on Tecumseh Court, her dog on a leash.

"Which one?" Sandy deadpanned.

He paid a price, but he became a hero to the rest of us.

Since we routinely had a quiz in each class every day, we were always playing catch-up. The professors seemed oblivious to the antics in Bancroft Hall. The upperclassmen, so far as I could tell, could not have cared less about our academic travails. In military terms, we were in the killing ground in a maneuver that the infantry whimsically calls The Hammer and The Anvil.

I began to think about quitting the day I arrived, and I thought about it every day through the summer and into the fall. I couldn't pick up the rhythm of the Academy. Each day seemed more ragged than the last. I had pictured Annapolis as my salvation, viewing it through a gauzy, flattering, thoroughly uncritical filter. Up close I found it intolerable. There was something else. I was horribly homesick. I missed my parents, with all their faults, and my sisters. And I missed the Lynvets, who were enjoying a marvelous season in that autumn of 1960, tearing up the league the same way we had in 1958. I didn't know which was worse, the Academy or the homesickness. Only occasionally did I regain a sense of proportion, and then not for long, realizing that what my classmates and I were going through was nothing compared to the pain and suffering afflicting much of the world beyond the Academy gate. Or that I was well on my way to becoming a poster boy for the manly art of pussying out.

I decided to quit. I told my parents. My mother, who never sounded drunk when I called home, listened to my story, seemed to see the reasonableness in my decision, but urged me not to act on it too quickly.

"You can't leave now," she said. "You've got to get through the first year. Do that, show everyone that you can take it. Then you can walk away with your head held high." That was always a big deal to her. I tried my father, from whom I expected a more sympathetic response.

"Bobby, Bobby, how can you quit, you just got there?" he asked. "What are you going to do? What are people going to think?"

"I don't give a shit what people think, Dad," I replied.

"Bobby, you're a tough kid. You don't want to look like you're running away."

He was right. So was she. More time passed. Things didn't get any better. I was ready to quit again, having neutralized my parents' words by telling myself that only an idiot takes the advice of two people who had already wrecked their own lives.

I thought about talking to our company officer, a rotund Navy lieutenant who wore aviator wings and whom the upperclassmen had nicknamed TF Squared—Too Fat To Fly. I decided not to.

Word about my misery drifted back to the Lynvets, probably through my sister Pat, who had become a cheerleader for the Junior team. Bob Bushman wrote me a seven-page letter. He said he and Larry Kelly were worried about me.

"People will form opinions of you by looking at your actions, but most important of all will be the opinion you have of yourself," he wrote. "If you believe in yourself you will radiate this trust to others. At this point in your life it is extremely important that you do not let things beat you that you know in your heart you can overcome if you try."

He talked about the 1959 season, of the adversity we had to face down before winning the championship, and what he said was my contribution to that sweet victory over Rockaway.

"Maybe you didn't score the winning touchdown but more important you earned the deep respect of those who perhaps because of your effort were able to wear the title of champions. The game itself and even the championship is not as important to us as watching a boy become a man, as watching a group form an undying respect for each other and friendships that will endure for a lifetime. This supersedes the football victories, for after the memory of the games grow dim, the marks of self-confidence and faith in your friend and the ability to say 'I will not lose' remains. This is in some way the Lynvet tradition in which you will always share because you have helped to make it."

And then, without elaboration, he added: "Remember, if you fail, we fail with you."

I responded to Bob's letter with a defiant, if mawkish, defense of my decision. Or what I thought of as my decision even though I had not yet done anything about it. It all seemed so terribly unfair. I was a good kid who had grappled with hard times. Now it seemed that in my determination to get out of one bad situation I had blundered into another. I blamed my parents. My mother, who had created an environment that had become unbearable. My father, whose weakness had propelled me into a setting for which I was totally unprepared and hated in the bargain. Time to move on, try something else. All I had to do was write a letter. I quit, Robert R. Timberg, Midshipman Fourth Class. That would do it. I would write it today.

I thought of Bob Bushman's letter: *If you fail, we fail with you.*
I thought of my Lynvet teammates: Joe Aragona and his undiluted
pride in me, who in some half-assed way seemed to see me as blaz-
ing a path for him. Chipper Dombo bobbing his head and glaring
at me, silently telling me I was letting the team down. Peter Connor, slapping my helmet, telling me to do it for Father Lynch.
Hughie Mulligan and the look of dismay he couldn't conceal when
I fumbled in the first game against Rockaway. John Faulkner,
coolly ripping the ball from Tommy Chapman's fingers after
Chapman had given me the slip, thus preserving our great victory.
Eddie Steffens and Herb Tortolani, whom you could always count
on when it mattered. Kenny Rudzewick, genial and generous, unless you were across the line of scrimmage from him. And I
thought of Larry Kelly, in whose eyes I always seemed to come up
short and whom I now was about to disappoint again.

For some reason, I had been handed an opportunity that none
of my Lynvet friends would ever have. But not one of them be-
grudged me the chance or envied my apparent good fortune. They
would all, I was sure, welcome me back. But I knew that I would be
a diminished figure, and that in some odd way they would feel diminished, too.

As Bob Bushman had said, without flatly saying it, I represented all my Lynvet teammates at Annapolis. And I was disgrac-
ing them.

I finally understood the rest of what Bob was trying to tell me.
It wasn't my mother who was to blame for my dismal performance
at the Academy, it was me. It wasn't my father who had folded in
a matter of weeks, it was me. It wasn't the upperclassmen, who
were asking of me no more than had been asked of them, it was me.
It wasn't always me, but it was me now. And there was no going
back.

I decided to hold off writing my letter of resignation for another day.

On November 4, John Kennedy was elected president. Three
weeks later Joe Bellino led Navy to a 17–12 win over Army and
walked away with the Heisman Trophy. The next day the Lyn-

vets—led by Bob Ferriola, Peter Connor, Joe Aragona, John Faulkner, and newcomers Teddy Horoshak and Danny Carro—captured their third consecutive Senior Division crown. Only a single touchdown had been scored against them all year. Tommy Wall and Mike Montore had arrived, too, Tommy ably backing up Ferriola, Mike taking my old spot in the defensive backfield.

By tradition, a Navy victory in the Army-Navy game meant the plebes were given "carry-on" till Christmas. That meant the upper-classmen were supposed to leave us alone. For the most part they did. Occasionally, in fact, they exchanged a few civilized words with us, asked us how we were doing, talked about their girlfriends and their postgraduation plans. John Bender, a sophomore from the state of Washington, sensed my difficulties and asked me to stop by his room one evening after dinner. Smart and soft-spoken, John was just months removed from his own plebe days. "You know, Timberg, this year really does end," he said. Not long after, he spooned me, meaning he offered his hand in friendship, dissolving the plebe–upperclassman divide.

In December, I went home for Christmas, the first time I had been out of the Academy's clutches in nearly six months. Two of my roommates, Tom Richman and Dave Ahern, came to New York for a couple of days. We saw Chubby Checker perform at the Peppermint Lounge. Sammy Davis Jr. and his Swedish wife, May Britt, were in the audience. Afterward we went to the Hickory House to see Marian McPartland. Seated at the bar, Dave ordered a scotch and soda.

"What kind of scotch?" asked the bartender.

"Canadian Club," replied Dave, at eighteen the soul of suave.

The bartender just stared, then gently informed Dave that Canadian Club, as it happened, was not a scotch.

"Oh," said Dave.

Duke Ellington sat down next to us. We recognized him, introduced ourselves. We called him Mr. Ellington, and he bought us a round of drinks when he learned we were midshipmen.

Classes resumed right after New Year's, and the upperclassmen reverted to the assholes they were. On January 20, the Brigade of

Midshipmen, thirty-eight-hundred-men strong, marched in President Kennedy's inaugural parade.

"Company—Eyes—Left!" our company commander bellowed as we passed the reviewing stand. For a split second I caught a glimpse of the new commander in chief, coatless, hatless, brimming with youthful confidence in the winter's chill.

By then I was no longer talking about quitting.

21

The Loner

*A*t first it looked like the Army was going to work for Mike Montore. He did well in boot camp at Fort Dix, completing his time there as the colonel's orderly, and at predeployment training at Fort Leonard Wood in Missouri, where he was tapped for squad leader. He managed to keep a smile on his face even though he was still aching from his crumbled romance. On the troopship that deposited him in Germany in late July 1959, he and his fellow soldiers talked excitedly about traveling around Europe on their leaves.

The situation started to sour his first night with his new unit. A couple of guys from the New York area, one from Brooklyn, the other from Jersey City, invited him to join them for a night on the town. Mike was alone at the table when another soldier came up and told him he was in his seat. Mike, who had been in the same seat all evening, told him he was mistaken. The soldier wouldn't back off. Finally Mike stood up, swung, and flattened the guy, knocking out one of his teeth. He turned out to be a corporal in Mike's new outfit.

The word quickly got around that the boot from New York was

a wiseass. Soon he was being baited into fights. He never lost, even though he was often fighting men much larger, but each victory seemed to incite someone else to take him on. One night he went out for a drink with a noncommissioned officer he considered a friend. He had met the man's wife and kids, thought of him as his sole connection to family and nonmilitary life. Trusting him, Mike revealed a side of himself he had kept carefully hidden, his softer, more vulnerable side. A mistake. After a few beers the NCO said, "You know, I don't think you're so tough."

Mike tried to talk him down. No luck. Finally, Mike said, "Okay, that's it." They went outside. Within a couple of minutes the NCO realized that Mike was as tough as the barracks talk made him out to be.

"Okay, okay, I quit," said the NCO.

Mike didn't take prisoners, not in those days. "No, you're not quitting now," he said.

Before long, he found himself at odds with a lieutenant in his company, then the company commander, a captain. He sensed they had singled him out as a troublemaker and were determined to bring him into line. The lieutenant, who seemed to take Mike's independent streak as a personal insult, perhaps even a threat to his authority, delighted in assigning him endless KP and other mindless, demeaning tasks. The lieutenant, Mike decided, was trying to break his will. Mike knew it was a battle he could not win. But he convinced himself that he would not lose if he refused to complain or otherwise reveal the toll the treatment was taking on him. So he settled for that.

Sometimes he fought back in subtle ways. On bivouac at four in the morning, the lieutenant ordered him to dig a hole for the garbage from the mess hall. He started digging. No one told him to stop, so he didn't. He was still digging at nightfall. By then the hole was so deep he couldn't throw the dirt out of it. Nor could he get out. They dropped a rope to him, but his arms were so tired he couldn't pull himself up. Finally they had to lower another soldier into the hole to retrieve him. At that point, to annoy the lieutenant, he acted fresh as a daisy. He had been reading Gandhi, thought of the episode as passive resistance.

Another time, he and the lieutenant were alone in the field.

"I heard your wife just had a baby," said Mike.

"Yeah," said the lieutenant.

"Any idea whose it is?"

Mike later said, "I did what I could do to maintain my self-respect. But I was insane. There's no doubt I was insane."

In the midst of the madness, he was offered the opportunity to apply to officer candidate school. He had, it seemed, scored highly on Army aptitude tests. But it was too late. An opportunity he would have leaped at a few months earlier now seemed like a sentence of servitude in what he viewed as a mindless hierarchical nightmare. Or, as he put it to his company commander, "I'd rather be a pimple on a dog's dick than a lieutenant in the Army." There followed more fights, more run-ins with his seniors, finally a court-martial. They threw the book at him—disobedience, disrespect, dereliction of duty.

Mannheim Prison was as bleak as it sounded, a feudal stone fortress with cellblocks, gun towers, and armed guards. He was eighteen and incarcerated with hardened criminals. On movie night, they saw training films. They booed the American troops, cheered the enemy. He read Caryl Chessman. You can endure anything if your hate is strong enough, the doomed author wrote. Mike took it to heart, cultivated his hate for the Army in general and prison in particular.

"I had gone from feeling vaguely alone in the world, believing that I must be wrong, to being starkly alone and knowing I was brutally right," he later said. At about that same time, he came up with what became his mantra in prison and beyond: "If you don't have it when you're naked and alone, it ain't yours."

His cell mate was a guy who spent most of his time detailing his philosophy of bowel movements and how they were the key to good health. He delivered his lectures astride the toilet in their cell, on which he regularly camped.

"If you ever convince me," said Mike, "we're going to need two toilets."

In a stroke of luck, Mike was assigned to the prison library. He rarely had any customers, so he read most of the time. One day he found a picture of a typewriter keyboard and set it on a table to teach himself to touch-type.

"You can't learn to type like that," scoffed one of his few visitors.

"Oh, yeah?" said Mike. "I haven't made a mistake in three days."

Two months into his six-month sentence he was offered a general discharge under honorable conditions. He would be eligible for GI benefits. He took it.

Back home, out of the service, he didn't trust anyone. He always had a good sense of humor and he still occasionally said something funny, but now he delivered his lines joylessly, with an edge and barely a grin. Mostly he kept to himself, carried a chip on his shoulder, came across as mean and angry. And the external toughness was no pose.

Soon he was working construction, framing houses six days a week. One Saturday night in the spring of 1960, he and three other guys ran into Peter Connor at a bar in North Baldwin. Peter suggested they go down the next day to Cross Bay Oval, where the Lynvets were having a spring practice session.

Mike and the others showed up in street clothes only to discover the Lynvets engaged in a full-scale scrimmage. They had no equipment, so Larry Kelly told them to stand on the sidelines and observe. After a few minutes, Mike said to the coach, "So when do we play? I didn't drive all the way here to watch."

Kelly figured what the hell and sent them in on defense without pads or helmets. They proceeded to intercept a couple of passes, run them back for scores, and put on a clinic on downfield blocking.

By the time the 1960 season began in the fall, Mike had established himself in the defensive backfield with John Faulkner and Eddie Steffens. Mike had hoped to play offense, too, but because of his grueling work schedule he almost never came to practice so he couldn't run through plays. That first season, though, met one of Mike's most fundamental needs: he wanted to hit someone.

Everyone in the league understood there was little to be gained by throwing into Faulkner's or Steffens's areas of responsibility. They had been around a long time and opponents knew what they could do. That left the new guy, Montore or whatever his name was, so they passed into Mike's zone. He loved it. He was getting all the action, at least at first, before they realized he was as quick as Steffens and hit nearly as hard as Faulkner. After a few games, though, the word got out. Fewer passes meant fewer collisions, which left Mike frustrated. He started playing possum, laying off receivers so they looked like they were open, then—as the ball arrived—taking them out with tackles that sounded like lightning striking the face of a mountain.

A new kid came down to practice one day. There was an intrasquad scrimmage. Everyone was going at three-quarters speed, careful to avoid injuries. The guy caught a pass, started streaking down the field. Mike raced over and shoved him toward the sideline. By the informal rules of the scrimmage, the play was over and the runner should have broken stride. Instead, he lowered his head and shoulders and drove his helmet into Mike's chest. Enraged, Mike flung him to the turf, pinned him, and knelt on his throat.

"Lighten up," said Mike. "It's a scrimmage."

"I'm trying to make this team," the guy sputtered.

"You have to be alive to make this team," said Mike.

Mike quickly realized the Lynvets were special. "Nobody had an ulterior motive," he said. "I knew that people were not there to get anything out of it. There was nothing to get. So that glory-boy stuff was impossible. There was no glory. There were no girls. There was nothing to be gained. You didn't even change indoors, for Christ's sake. There was no place to strut your stuff on Monday and Tuesday if you had a good game. You just went back to work."

There was more to it.

"I was going nowhere. I was, and felt like, a loser, unsure of the future, maybe even afraid. Getting on the field set me free. I needed a place in my life where I felt good about myself. Against the backdrop of my non-Lynvet life, the Lynvets were an oasis for my soul."

Like a Spartan, Mike as a defensive back was indifferent to the makeup and capabilities of the enemy, which was how he thought of the Lynvets' rivals. He pointedly ignored scouting reports, so the names of opposing players—Moran, Wickers, Chapman, D'Amato—meant nothing to him.

"I don't want to know anybody's name," he told the coaches. "Don't tell me anybody's number. I don't want a scouting report. To me, they're all garbage."

He played with an attitude—angry, relentless, and immutable—a legacy of the Army and a lost love. "It is impossible to score on me," he told himself. "It just can't happen. There's nobody in the world good enough to score on me." No one ever did.

Like Faulkner and Steffens, his mates in the defensive backfield, Montore was impervious to Kelly's mind games. That first year, Kelly and Montore connected only on their mutual love of football. "He needed the game," said Mike. "I understood that because I needed it, too." Kelly, in fact, relaxed for Mike the long-standing Lynvet rule that you don't play if you don't come to practice. He worked exceedingly long hours and lived too far away to make practice with any regularity. Kelly understood, and privately he admired the lengths to which Mike went to play ball.

To Tommy Wall, Mike seemed older and more mature than the other Lynvets, though in fact he was younger than most. He was friendly and approachable, but only up to a point. Mike, for his part, marveled at how his teammates welcomed him into their world. They all seemed to understand why he couldn't make practice and no one seemed to hold it against him. At a barely conscious level, he sensed that they genuinely liked him. But he didn't care. That first year he just wanted to play ball. He wasn't looking for friends.

22

April Is Over

During the first week of June 1961, the period they called June Week at the Naval Academy, I was sitting in my room on the fourth deck of Bancroft Hall slowly peeling off my sweat-soaked dress-blue uniform after the final parade of the year. Plebes could date for the first time during June Week, and my roommates had already showered, changed into summer whites, and raced off to find their girlfriends. Our days as plebes were numbered. To be exact, there was one day to go, the same number left for the first classmen until graduation and commissioning. President Kennedy was to give the commencement address the next day. He had just gotten back to Washington after a weekend summit in Vienna with Nikita Khrushchev.

Behind me, the door swung open.

"Midshipman Timberg, Fourth Class, sir!" I shouted, leaping to my feet, bracing up, eyes in the boat.

"Siddown, siddown, carry on, how you doin'?" said a stumpy, dark-complected figure about my height. He shook my hand. "Joe Bellino," he said.

Of course I recognized him, a rugged-looking Italian guy with an infectious grin who had dominated college football the previous fall. He dropped into the chair across from me, flung his feet up on the double desk, smiled. His thighs were so thick that the athletic shorts he was wearing required little nicks in the seams to accommodate them.

"I was just walking by and remembered this was my plebe summer room," he said, Massachusetts roots evident in his words. "I just wanted to take a look. I graduate tomorrow, you know."

"Yes, sir," I said. "I know."

"Hey," he said, laughing, "don't call me sir. Didn't I just spoon you?"

"Yes, sir, I mean, yes . . . Joe."

"Better. Better."

He didn't stay long. Maybe he would have lingered if I hadn't been there. We didn't talk much. Mostly his eyes surveyed the room, taking it in. Then he walked to the window, looked out onto the practice field below, gazed beyond that to the Severn, which sprouted billowing, gaily colored sails.

"Hey, take care," he said as he left. "It's almost over, right?"

I guess he meant Plebe Year, but maybe he was talking about himself, his four years at Annapolis and the glory that had been his for most of that time. I wondered if that day would ever come for me. Not the football stardom, but making it through to graduation, hurling my cap in the air, snapping on brand-new ensign's shoulder boards, handing a silver dollar to the first man, woman, or child to salute me.

I now thought that it might. In the second half of my plebe year, I had regained my footing. I was still mildly disoriented, but I had learned to deal with the daily chaos, sort of understood what it was all about. A few exceptional midshipmen prospered during plebe year. The rest of us survived—or didn't. I had survived, a little worse for wear, though still pretty much the same person I had always been. But not quite.

If I was a little different, the world around our tiny island of pomp and madness was changing at an ever-accelerating pace. You saw it mostly in the Deep South, where black people were demanding the right to vote and challenging a system that controlled where they could go to school, dine, sit on a bus, drink from a fountain, and relieve themselves. I and most of the people I knew thought of it as a southern problem. My meandering school days had regularly brought me into close contact with black people. I went to school with them, played baseball, basketball, and football with them. When I was in grade school, I saw an ad on the subway. It showed three kids, two white and one black, with baseball gloves and bats. One white kid was saying to the other one, "What's it matter if he's black or white? He can pitch." For me, at a young age and for years after, that covered the ground. Had I been more aware, I would have realized the issues were vastly more complicated and noticed the fallout from events in Alabama and Mississippi drifting north.

One day when I was going to Shimer Junior High School in South Ozone Park I was talking with my friend John Wider, an introspective black kid. He often called me "son," and on this day I did the same to him. I thought of it as a term of fondness. John, normally soft-spoken, bristled.

"You shouldn't call me that," he said.

"What? Why not? You call me that all the time," I said.

He tried to explain without really explaining, and I sensed that I had blundered into some murky area having to do with race.

"John, what the hell are you talking about?" I asked.

"Okay," he said, looking at me like I was hopeless. "Haven't you ever heard someone say, 'I don't call you son because you're mine, I call you son because you shine?' "

"No," I said. I still didn't get it. I asked him if it had something to do with colored people shining shoes. No, he said.

"Do people think colored people shine?" I asked.

"Yes," replied John, patiently leading me through a conversation that clearly made him uncomfortable.

I had never thought about that, and even after I did think about it, it still didn't make sense. But I stopped calling him son.

Soon there were more chilling echoes out of the South. One

night in the winter of 1955, I was playing a club league basketball game at Shimer, from which I had graduated a few months earlier. Both teams had a few fans, no more than a dozen each. We didn't even have a coach. Midway through the second half, the doors to the gym swung open and about seven or eight black kids stormed in and started swinging at players and spectators alike.

The fight was over as quickly as it started. I can't remember if the cops came or the intruders expected them to and fled after bloodying a few noses. I've never forgotten what they shouted as they waded into us.

"Remember Emmett Till!"

I knew instantly what had triggered the attack. A few weeks earlier, two white men had gone on trial in a segregated courthouse in Sumner, Mississippi, for the murder of Emmett Till, a fourteen-year-old black youth from Chicago. Emmett had been visiting a great-uncle, an elderly sharecropper named Moses Wright, near the steamy Delta town of Money that August. It seemed like an open-and-shut case. Emmett, a high-spirited youth who had been warned by his mother that rural Mississippi was not Chicago, had gone into a small country store and either whistled or said something to a white woman, the wife of the proprietor, that offended her.

A few nights later, Emmett was kidnapped by two white men. His body was found several days later. He had been brutally beaten, shot in the head, and thrown in the Tallahatchie River. A 150-pound fan from a cotton gin had been tied around his neck with barbed wire. When he was returned to his mother in Chicago, he was nearly unrecognizable. Rejecting the urgings of the funeral director, Emmett's mother demanded an open casket, and thousands of mourners from across the nation filed past the lifeless body of her horribly disfigured son.

Lynchings had been part of life in the South for decades, but this time, in the wake of the Supreme Court's 1954 *Brown v. Board of Education* ruling, the national press paid attention, descending in force on the courthouse in Sumner. Moses Wright offered eyewitness testimony that the abductors had been two white men, Roy

Bryant, the husband of the woman whom Emmett had supposedly offended, and J. W. Milam, Bryant's half brother. In doing so, Wright had done the unthinkable for a black man in Mississippi, accusing whites of crimes. Other blacks, buoyed by his courage, also came forward and provided further damaging testimony against Bryant and Milam. The all-white jury deliberated for just over an hour before acquitting them.

I had followed the case and my Stuyvesant friends and I discussed it a lot, both in and out of class. We were, of course, horrified. We ascribed it to the South, a place we thought of as not just fraught with bigotry but another world. Nothing like that could happen in the North, and certainly not in New York City, we assured each other.

The Lynvets for the most part took a live-and-let-live attitude toward black people without really knowing what that meant in terms of education, job opportunities, or housing patterns. But while I was battling my way through the difficult early months of Plebe Year, Larry Kelly had to contend with a sticky racial incident, one that showed that the Lynvets learned a few things from the coach other than football.

As preparations for the 1960 season began, a black kid, Jim Hawkins, tried out for the team. Hawkins wasn't very good, but he worked hard. That was enough for Kelly. He gave Hawkins a uniform and the Lynvets had their first black player.

Hawkins didn't play much and didn't make close friends on the team, but he got along with everyone and seemed to enjoy himself. Kelly kidded him about being the team's intimidator, telling him to get off the bus first at a preseason game against a black team so the opponents would "see that we've got a colored guy playing for us, too." At a postgame team party at the Imperial near the end of the season, though, Kelly was tested.

Hawkins, who had not gone to earlier parties, arrived with his date, an elegant black woman, along with another black couple. They were dressed well, better than most of the other Lynvets. Kelly, who was at the bar with Tommy Vaughan, Chipper Dombo, Peter Connor, and Tommy Wall, greeted them.

"What'll you have?" asked Kelly, shaking hands with Jim and his friends.

Hawkins ordered a gin and tonic. So did the others. Behind the bar, Old Joe stared.

To Hawkins, in a tone that suggested he was doing nothing more than giving directions to the nearest gas station, Old Joe said that he did not serve black people.

Kelly stepped in. "You have to serve him, Joe. He's a member of the team."

Old Joe, all earnestness and sincerity, the soul of reasonableness, turned to Kelly and explained, as if Larry had missed the point, that men and women of Hawkins's skin color were not welcome in his establishment.

Said Kelly, "If you don't serve him, Joe, I'm taking the team out of here and we're not coming back."

"But Larry. . . ."

Kelly held his ground, again threatened to march the team out. Finally, Old Joe turned to Hawkins and his friends. "Whaddya want?" he asked. They repeated their order. As the bartender turned to get them, Connor said to Hawkins, "He's a stupid old fuck."

Old Joe slammed the drinks on the bar. Hawkins and his friends, along with the rest of the Lynvets, drank quickly, then headed for the back room where the party was already under way. As they did so, Old Joe snatched up the four glasses and hurled them into the metal garbage can he kept behind the bar, smashing them to bits.

When I later spoke to Kelly about the incident, he took little pride in having taken a tough position and making it stand up. Instead, he lamented the unpleasantness that had befallen Jim Hawkins and his friends. He also understood the complexities of the situation. "He's an old guy and a nice man," Larry said of Old Joe. "He grew up with those attitudes. Things aren't going to change overnight."

But change of all kinds, excitement as well, was in the air during those first few months of 1961 as our Plebe Year wound down, and much of it seemed to date from John Kennedy's inauguration. The president issued an executive order establishing the Peace Corps on March 1. Two months later, on May 5, an Annapolis man, Alan Shepard, Class of 1944, became the first American in space, flying in the *Freedom 7* Mercury capsule on a fifteen-minute suborbital flight. Before the month was out, Kennedy, addressing a joint session of Congress, set the nation on course to landing a man on the moon by the end of the decade.

Not everything Kennedy did was so uplifting. An attempt by Cuban refugees to oust Fidel Castro was thwarted in April under confusing circumstances in which it seemed Kennedy had promised air support for the ragtag invading force, then reneged at the last minute. In a speech not long after what came to be called the Bay of Pigs fiasco, he talked of Cuba as an example of the Soviet Union employing guerrilla forces to subvert friendly governments. The other example he used was a place called South Vietnam.

Women were changing, too, more open, or more independent, or perhaps more available in a way they hadn't been before. They smoked, they drank, and, if they didn't go all the way, they went far enough for those of us who wouldn't have known quite what to do if they had been willing to do so.

Late in Plebe Year, I met a girl. Her name was Jane Benson, she was from Baltimore, and everyone called her Janie. We met at a tea fight, one of those dismal Sunday afternoon dances that the Academy sponsored for plebes to teach them various forms of social etiquette, such as politely asking a girl to dance, offering her your arm as you led her to the dance floor, and then dancing in a way that did not involve the touching of parts of hopefully mutual interest. You didn't have a choice of partner at the beginning of tea fights. Midshipmen and girls queued up separately, and you got whoever was next in line, as did the girl. You might be five foot seven, and she might be six foot one. Too bad. After the first couple of tea fights, my friends and I worked out a system. If a friend got stuck with an unattractive or inappropriate girl, we took turns cutting in until somehow we spun her off into space in a terpsichorean variation on centrifugal force. It wasn't nice, and the more sensitive among us considered it beastly, including me and I was present at the creation and may have had a hand in inventing it. Plebe Year could do that to you. At any rate, Janie was cute. All the other girls were dressed up. She was dressed down.

"Do you want to dance?" I asked her.

"No," she said.

"Then what are you doing here?" I asked.

"My friends told me it would be fun and dragged me along," she said.

"Then you may as well as dance," I said.

"No," she said, walking away.

That was it; I was smitten.

Janie wasn't my date for June Week. It was taking us a while to connect. But I did have a date, and as I concluded the musings that followed Joe Bellino's surprise visit I realized she was probably wondering what had happened to me.

President Kennedy, in his commencement address the next morning, talked of the broader responsibilities that would be expected of military officers in the years ahead. "You must be more than the servants of national policy," he said. "You must be prepared to play a constructive role in the development of national policy." He said nothing of his talks in Vienna with Khrushchev, which had focused on the mounting crisis in Berlin. The night before, however, in a televised report to the nation that we all missed because we were celebrating and getting into as much trouble as we could, he called the meeting "a very sober two days."

A summer training cruise followed June Week, the first extended reentry into the real world for the Class of 1964 in nearly a year. For me, that meant six weeks on the USS *Independence,* an aircraft carrier out of Portsmouth, Virginia. At sea we worked as enlisted men, much of the time in the ship's sweltering boiler room, which was presided over by a gruff chief petty officer and enlisted men known as snipes. In port we were welcomed to the officers' club and dated nurses stationed at the Portsmouth Naval Hospital.

In July, we steamed into New York harbor and up the East River. The *Independence,* the length of three and a half football fields, seemed to fill the whole river. I watched our passage from the bridge, the soaring skyscrapers of Manhattan to port, to starboard the dreary industrialized shoreline of Brooklyn and Queens. In August, after turning loose the midshipmen contingent, the ship would set sail for the Mediterranean, making port calls in Spain, the French and Italian Rivieras, and Lebanon. My imagination went into overdrive as I listened to the announcement of the post-cruise itinerary.

By then, the Lynvets had begun summer practice. The season of 1961 would be a true test of the team's resilience. The Lynvets had just concluded the first decade of their existence with three consecutive championships, but now many of the players who had powered the team during those glorious seasons were on the sidelines, casualties of the league's age limit. A few veterans were still around. In the main, though, the old guard had been relieved by younger, fresher, hungrier troops, much as John Kennedy and his new generation of leaders—"born in this century, tempered by war, disciplined by a hard and bitter peace"—had earlier in the year assumed the torch from men who had led the nation to victory in World War II and guided it into the postwar era.

In a way, I wanted to be with my old team. My two years with the Lynvets had been happy ones, and I doubted that I would ever find better friends. But I suspected that for me, and maybe not only for me, those days had come and gone.

I knew by then that I would not be going back. Whatever life had in store for me, good or bad, I sensed that it would not play out in Queens. April was over. Time to pass the Lynvets on to Tommy Wall and Mike Montore and the rest of the new guard and let them lead the team into the Sixties, a decade that dawned as the body double of the one that preceded it, that would end as anything but.

Over the next few years, I would lose touch with most of my Lynvet teammates, partly because of the demands of the Naval Academy, partly because of simple geography, but also because, it seemed to me then, we had less in common when football was removed from the equation. On that last point, I was wrong, though

it would take me a long time to realize it. As it turned out, the Lynvets and I were taking different paths to the same destination, a
new America in which those things we prized, that in many ways
defined us, were devalued and often ridiculed. The season of 1961
would serve as a prelude to the arduous and painful journey that
awaited us.

23

The Alumni Game

All the legends are here, Tommy Wall murmured to himself as he peered across the ragged dust-glazed clumps of grass at the Woodrow Wilson Vocational High School field on an unseasonably warm Sunday afternoon in the autumn of 1961. His eyes flicking from player to player, settling on one, moving on to the next, he grudgingly allowed himself to complete the thought. *Too bad all of them are on the far sideline.*

Glancing at the stands, the Lynvet quarterback smiled as he watched the fans climbing up to their seats. Always a good crowd for the Alumni Game. Big bragging rights at stake today. Lots of Schaefers and Rheingolds and Seven-and-Sevens, too.

Tommy would be starting his second Alumni Game this day. The year before, his first with the team, Bob Ferriola had been injured in the preseason and Tommy had been rushed into the lineup against the Alumni. On the Friday night before the game, a group of Alumni and some of the current players, Tommy among them, were drinking at the Imperial. There was the usual pregame banter, though Tommy hung back. He was new to the team and didn't know the older guys. He did not like what he was hearing, mostly juiced-up Alumni boasting that they were going to murder the Seniors, beat them by maybe three touchdowns. Why so confident? Ferriola was hurt, and there was no one to fill in for him except some young guy whose name no one even knew. Said one alum, "You really think you're going to beat us with that kid quarterback?" Tommy couldn't believe it. They were talking about him as if he wasn't there.

That year, he answered them on the field, smoothly guiding the Seniors to an 8–6 win. Afterward, Joe Aragona pounded him on the back and said, "Wow, you've got some future with this team." But that was Ferriola's team, as he proved when he returned from his injury and led the Lynvets to perhaps their finest season ever. Today, Tommy knew, the Seniors would be looking to him, not Ferriola, for leadership. They also needed him to perform at a very high level, not just in this game, but throughout the season. For Tommy, the question was "Am I good enough?"

Tommy's survey of the Alumni's ranks took in a daunting sight. Bob Ferriola, his fabulous predecessor whose passing and running had earned him two of the past three Most Valuable Player awards. Peter Connor and John Faulkner, the captains of last year's team, the two toughest players Tommy had ever played with or against. And there were others from that 1960 team as well, players Tommy would have been only too happy to have in his huddle today. *Well, shit, I beat them last year,* he told himself, *I can do it again.* A moment later, he conceded the obvious:

Last year I beat them with them.

The Alumni Game, begun as a tribute to Father Lynch, had by now established itself as an annual preseason ritual. In the three years they had been playing the game, the Seniors had won twice, the Alumni once, all the contests decided by a touchdown or less. And no one had ever accused either side of pulling its punches. Many of the Alumni had been out of organized football for five years or less, so they were older and possibly a step slower. But they were just as tough as they had ever been, maybe tougher since it seemed that half of them were now firemen or cops or had just gotten out of the Marines, the service to which Lynvets gravitated. And these were guys who had led previous Senior teams to seven championships in ten years. In the days leading up to this game, Larry Kelly had repeatedly told his players that the Alumni would probably be the strongest team they played all season. "There's no better way to start than against the best," he said.

None of the Lynvets doubted that, which said a lot about the respect the team had for the Alumni and hinted at the mild disdain the Seniors had for their opponents in the Pop Warner Conference, which would begin regular-season play in two weeks. In the three previous Alumni Games the Lynvets had faced one, at most two, standout players from the year before. This year was different. The ranks of the Alumni had been replenished, reinforced, and rejuvenated by no less than a half dozen players who had led the Seniors to the past three Pop Warner championships.

Like Tommy Wall, Kelly was troubled. He had enjoyed the weeks leading up to the game. In the summer Del Shannon had followed his smash single "Runaway" with a second hit, "Hats Off to Larry." It was on the jukeboxes at all the bars where Kelly hung out. When he heard it, he'd bat his blue eyes and say, "They're playing my song, boys."

The boys, a coterie that usually included Ferriola, Connor, Chipper Dombo, and a few others who would be suiting up for the Alumni in September, would tell Kelly he was nuts. Not only that, they were going to beat his Senior team so badly that they would even figure a way for Richie Brady to score. Richie was not a joke as a person, but he was close to that as a football player, at least in the past couple of years since returning from a hitch in the Marines. A Lynvet through and through, he was well liked by everyone, but his talents lay beyond the gridiron. He suited up for every game but spent most of his time on the bench, his athletic talents unaccountably diminished, so much so that he sometimes missed his hands when doing jumping jacks. His real position was social director. Handsome, funny, with blond curly hair and a mischievous smile that stopped just short of a leer, Richie arranged the weekly Lynvet parties at the Imperial, hiring the band, rounding up the girls, act-

ing as emcee. When Kelly was still coaching Richie, he ended one
pregame pep talk by saying, "Let's get so far ahead I won't be afraid
to put Brady in."

Kelly knew it was bar talk. Richie Brady might, just might, get
into the game, but there was no way he was going to score against
the Seniors. But Kelly also knew that this year's Alumni team was
the best he had ever faced. More to the point, his Senior team was
untested. Tommy Wall was a savvy quarterback and a strong leader,
but he was no Bob Ferriola. And pound for pound little Jackie
Meyer was probably the fiercest defensive player Kelly had ever
coached. With one exception, Peter Connor, who weighed forty
pounds more and would be on the other side of the ball in the
Alumni Game after three years of terrorizing opponents and occasionally his own teammates. If Kelly could admit that anyone was
irreplaceable other than himself, it would be Peter. Of course, Kelly
still had Joe Aragona, the league high scorer in 1960 and by now
arguably the best Lynvet running back ever, along with two other
terrific backs, big Teddy Horoshak, who tore up the league the previous year, and the loner, Mike Montore, who was finally going to
get some time on offense. Larry was also keeping his eye on Mike
Faulkner, a fullback up from the Junior team and the younger
brother of two Lynvet stars, John Faulkner and Paul Faulker.

Yet Kelly had not been pleased with what he had seen so far. At
the urging of Paul Frey, he had installed a new offense that held the
promise of enhancing the running game, in part to compensate for
the loss of Ferriola and his magnificent passing arm. But the team
had not taken to it and it showed. Fumbles, blown assignments,
even some grumbling at practice. On at least two occasions in the
past three weeks Kelly had angrily warned the team that they were
taking the Alumni too lightly.

"You guys better wake up," he shouted in frustration at one
practice. "You're gonna get killed if you don't."

The Lynvet universe, past and present, was centered that day
on a high school football field across the street from Baisley Park in
the Jamaica section of Queens, but the wider world had other con-
cerns, some most serious, others less so. In Jerusalem, Adolf Eich-

mann, charged with crimes against humanity, was awaiting the verdict of the court after a trial that had lasted four months and riveted the world. In Cuba, a cocksure and defiant Fidel Castro was emptying his island of priests and marching his few remaining foes before firing squads.

East-West tensions were high. In August, the Berlin Wall went up, exacerbating the Berlin Crisis amid international saber rattling, though in this case the sabers had nuclear tips. With little fanfare, President Kennedy had given the order for an upgrading of the American commitment to embattled South Vietnam, a blip on the horizon in a region of the world that many Americans still called French Indo-China even though France had been booted out seven years earlier by a fierce and committed guerrilla army.

As that Sunday dawned, the New York Yankees seemed assured of still another pennant, their eleventh in the past thirteen years and their first under Ralph Houk, who had relieved Casey Stengel, the "Old Perfessor," as manager before the season started. Lefty Whitey Ford had just won his twenty-fourth game, but Roger Maris's assault on Babe Ruth's record of sixty homers in a single season had been stalled at fifty-six for a week. An unhappy Maris, before a doubleheader in Detroit, complained to the press that he was "being ripped by writers in every city," who seemed to feel that he lacked the heroic dimensions to challenge the immortal Babe. After the twin bill, in which he produced only a single in nine times at bat, Maris avoided reporters completely, choosing to remain in the trainer's room and sulk, as one scribe portrayed his demeanor.

As for me, I was a long way away that Sunday, in more ways than one. Even without the pressures of Plebe Year, the Naval Academy was proving to be an all-consuming experience. The Yard, as the walled campus was known, defined our lives. As sophomores, we had expanded privileges, but they didn't amount to much. The academic year had begun a couple of weeks earlier and we were still feeling our way, not quite sure where we fit into the Academy system. We weren't plebes, but we didn't feel like upperclassmen, either. For the most part, sophomore year seemed like a time for consolidating our gains, for me the most notable being that I was still at the Academy rather than explaining to people why I wasn't. Given the choice, I would have loved lining up in the backfield with Joe Aragona against the Alumni that Sunday, the Gold Dust Twins together again. But there was no choice. Joe's gold would always gleam. Mine, had I quit the Academy, would have been forever dulled.

The game went much as Kelly had feared, thanks to Ferriola, who picked apart the Lynvet defense, completing fifteen of twenty-two passes. By halftime, the Alumni seemed to have the game well in hand, except on the scoreboard, the first thirty minutes ending with the teams deadlocked 0–0. The third quarter was barely under way when the Alumni mounted a drive deep into the Seniors' territory. From the eighteen-yard line, Ferriola hit Herb Tortolani, the tall, stylish receiver who had caught so many of his passes in traffic during the 1958 season, with a short pass over the middle. Tortolani gathered it in, dodged a succession of tacklers, and carried the ball into the end zone. After a two-point conversion, the Alumni were up 8–0.

The Seniors, meanwhile, sputtered under Tommy Wall. They'd get a drive going, pick up a couple of first downs, then run out of gas. The offensive line slowed Peter Connor, but it could not stop him. As usual, he was everywhere and let you know it. "Nothing here! Nothing here!" he shouted before almost every play. Tommy called a swing pass to Mike Montore, which required Mike to drift out toward the right sideline, turn back toward the quarterback, and take the pass. No sooner had the Seniors broken the huddle than Connor jabbed his finger at Montore and shouted, "I got you, Mikey, I got you."

Christ, thought Montore, it's not bad enough that he's the best player on the field, he even knows what play we're gonna run.

And he did. As Montore turned toward Wall, he could hear Peter's clomping strides, closing on him, shouting, "I'm coming, Mikey." Montore caught the pass a split second before Conner drove his shoulder into the small of his back, flattening him. Mike could not remember a clean hit that ever hurt so much. Picking himself up, acting like he hadn't felt a thing, Mike congratulated himself on not fumbling. Then he congratulated himself for not crying.

In the fourth quarter, Ferriola took off on one of his signature jaunts around right end. Fifteen yards later he was in the end zone. The conversion failed, but the Alumni led 14–0. All that was left was Richie Brady.

Somehow, some way, Brady entered the game unnoticed at left end late in the fourth quarter, then managed to get loose in the end zone. Ferriola lofted one of his picture-perfect passes, the kind defenders are tempted to admire rather than knock down. Just as it was about to settle in his hands, though, Brady stumbled and the ball bounced off his chest.

For the Seniors, avoiding the humiliation of a Brady touchdown was the only satisfaction they could take from the game. Tommy Wall, who had struggled to move his team on the ground or in the air that day, was angry that the Alumni had even tried to carry out their threat. "They were goofing on us," he groused.

No one panicked. Lynvets had beaten Lynvets. The Alumni were kin, the game a celebration of the extended Lynvet family. The Seniors had two weeks to prepare for their first Pop Warner game. Plenty of time to energize the offense and fine-tune the pass defense. Nothing, really, had changed.

24

Ring of Valor

*F*or me, everything had changed. Reports reached me in Annapolis that the Lynvets were struggling in the early weeks of the 1961 season, but 250 miles to the south, I wasn't. That fall was proving a far cry from my rocky Plebe Year. We youngsters, as sophomores were called, walked on eggshells for a day or two after returning to the Academy from our cruise and summer leave. We quickly realized, though, that no one was going to brace us up or bombard us with professional questions and we settled into a routine that, though rigorous, made no outlandish demands on us. We had next to no authority, which meant leaving plebe indoctrination to the upper two classes, but no responsibilities, either, other than keeping ourselves out of trouble and academically solvent.

I had three roommates, Tom Richman and Dave Ahern from the previous year, and a new one, Dave Wilshin, a lacrosse player who came from the Baltimore suburbs. We were a compatible crew, at least as compatible as four guys can be living together in a small room with two bunk beds, one shower, and a single sink. As youngsters we were permitted a radio and a record player, but televisions were authorized only in company wardrooms, the preserve of first classmen. Our album collection was eclectic without being interesting. We had a Ray Conniff that I started off hating because it seemed so uncool, but actually came to like. Tom, a jazz fan, contributed a Dave Brubeck and a Mose Allison. Someone chipped in the theme from *The Sundowners*. My contributions were two Frank Sinatra albums, *In the Wee Small Hours* and *Come Fly with Me*, and one by Johnny Mathis, *Open Fire, Two Guitars*. The Johnny Mathis was my favorite, slow and easy, a reflection of the early weeks of youngster year when plebe memories were fading and no one seemed to expect much of me and my classmates.

Those days afforded me a broader view of the Academy system, which made more sense to me than it had only months earlier. Plebe Year had been a trial by fire and we were the survivors. Had we lost classmates who would have proven fine midshipmen and, more important, superior naval officers? Probably, though in many cases I was convinced that the Academy, the Navy, and my erstwhile classmates were better off. One thing seemed sure, the system had been administered equitably, if ruthlessly. Joe McCain, the son and grandson of admirals, the scion of a family whose naval service dated back to the turn of the century, had flunked out even though he was more committed to a career in the Navy than his older brother John, a future senator and war hero whose wildman antics as a midshipman were still talked about and had led to his graduating fifth from the bottom of the Class of 1958.

In those early weeks as a third classman it became evident that once beyond Plebe Year coasting was possible, that if you stayed out of trouble and could handle the academics you were going to graduate and get your commission. The alternative was competing within the system, working for good grades, and trying to excel in those nonacademic areas known officially as leadership, informally as grease, to some as bullshit. Grease involved several factors, some concrete like personal appearance, grades, conduct. Other qualities were less tangible like personality, bearing, even the snappiness of your salute. Some of my classmates in the Seventh Company like Jerry Welch never bought into the system but were among the leaders despite average grease grades. Ron Benigo, like Jerry a Marine enlisted man before entering the Academy, blended a Buddha-like demeanor with a sly sense of humor and a stunning academic prowess that belied his roots in a blue-collar section of Detroit. Without trying, Ron rose to the top of the class in grease. The rest of us had to work at it.

A year earlier, the idea that I'd even be at the Academy the following fall seemed implausible. Now it slowly dawned on me that with some extra effort I could do well there, perhaps excel. Academically, I was doing fine. I had made the Superintendent's List at the end of plebe year and, assuming I could figure out what the hell was going on in a course called Strength of Materials, I would make it again this semester. So I had a choice: coast or compete. I thought about my Lynvet teammates, many of whom with the right breaks could have been there with me. What would Joe Aragona have done? Or Tommy Vaughan or Bob Ferriola or Hughie Mulligan? They would have done what Lynvets had always done—play to win. So I would, too.

Personal appearance was important to your standing on the class leadership ladder. The hundreds of tourists who saw us on the streets of Annapolis on weekends and jammed the Yard for Wednesday parades probably thought we all looked terrific in our white caps and navy blue uniforms. Within Bancroft Hall, though, subtle distinctions could be enormous, reflecting an attention to detail that bordered on the insane. Mercifully, as a sophomore my Plebe-Year roommate Frank Spangenberg dispensed with his over-the-top penchant for spit-shining his slide rule case, but we still spent a lot of time with tins of Kiwi. Was it possible that one pair of shoes spit-shined to a mirror finish could look appreciably better than another pair? Yes, if you spent a half hour on them each day instead of the usual fifteen minutes and picked up a few tricks from old salts. From his days in the Corps, Jerry Welch knew how to work with marching boots, which resisted a bright shine. He put on the black Kiwi, held the boots over a lighter to soften the polish, then worked it in by rubbing it with the side of a bottle. But footwear was just the beginning. The wire device called a Spiffy that we wore under the collars of our blue work shirts to hold down the points had to be completely out of sight. Sometimes, if you weren't careful, the Spiffy peeked out. Brass belt buckles had to blind the inspector—Brasso was the polish of choice—and line up precisely with the shirt and fly. The dimples in our ties had to be centered and well defined. Doug Peterson's was the best. Once he got it tied right, he wore the same tie all year, running a toothbrush over the half-Windsor knot once a week to raise some nap and make it look freshly tied. The tucks in the backs of our shirts had to overlap equally on both sides. Roommates took turns giving each other tucks. God forbid that an errant piece of thread, known as an Irish pennant, should alight on our uniforms. And those of us in the game routinely spent at least half an hour before the weekly command inspection at Saturday noon meal formation brushing our blue dress uniforms to remove the faintest trace of lint. If you did all these things and more, including handle the academics, you earned a reputation as "squared away." The opposite was "fucked up." Some midshipmen were said to be "nonsweat," meaning they played along with the system but refused to take it seriously. If they got put on report for something, like room in disorder—or worse, room in gross disorder—they laughed it off. Others of us brooded about it.

Occasionally I would wander alone along the tree-lined paths of the Yard, where I could briefly lose myself in the peace and serenity of the grounds, to forget that the Academy saw itself first and foremost as a crucible for warriors. Then I would come upon statuary, perhaps the twenty-one-foot-tall marble obelisk known as Herndon Monument, named for the sea captain who in 1857, amid a ferocious hurricane, transferred 152 passengers and crewmen to a rescue vessel, then went to his quarters, changed into a full dress uniform, and returned to the bridge suitably attired to go down with his ship. Or the memorial to four midshipmen—Clemson, Hynson, Pillsbury, and Shubrick—who died at Vera Cruz in the Mexican War. Along the catwalk of the armory known as Dahlgren Hall, which housed naval guns two stories high and the M-1 rifles we carried in parades, but also did double duty as a ballroom for formal dances, I saw walls lined with tributes to fallen classmates. The plaque for the Class of 1932 listed the names of the thirty-eight classmates killed in World War II. To the left and right, other classes remembered comrades lost in that war. In all, members of fifty-four Academy classes, all the way back to the Class of 1892, fought in World War II. Twenty-seven graduates won the Congressional Medal of Honor, the nation's highest award for gallantry, fourteen of them posthumously. They won three more in Korea, two by Marine lieutenants who were not around to collect them.

The Brigade of Midshipmen had a sense of humor. How else to explain the June Week tradition in which plebes clambered up the grease-slathered memorial to Captain Herndon's terminal bravado to place atop it a midshipman's cap and punctuate the end of their yearlong travails? Or the life-sized, cast-bronze mountain goat, representing Bill the Goat, the Academy mascot, that the Class of 1915 had bequeathed to the Brigade? If you looked closely, and you would only do so if you were perversely curious or in on the joke, you'd see that the goat was anatomically correct. You would also notice that his impressive set of testicles, and just the testicles, had been Brasso-ed to a gleaming gold finish.

A sense of humor, yes, and a sense of fun, but no sense of irony. We knew that we were involved in serious business and that at the end of our four years at Annapolis a good deal was expected of us, that we would be given a stunning privilege, the privilege of commanding other men in combat, where the leadership we displayed and the decisions we made could mean the difference between life and death, theirs and ours.

I thought from time to time of a movie that we were shown shortly after we arrived at the Academy, a black-and-white film in which the Academy ring served as the device to tell the story of the school. The film opened with a close-up of a heavy gold class ring as the unseen narrator, the actor Robert Taylor, said, "This ring is worn proudly by every officer who has been graduated from the United States Naval Academy. It is truly a ring of valor." The ring was shown on the hand of a submarine officer as he raised a periscope, a deck officer peering through binoculars, a midshipman holding the white-gloved hand of a fetching young woman. No surprise, the film was called *Ring of Valor*, and because we were still young and earnest we did not laugh where others may have. Midshipmen were forbidden from wearing the ring until June Week of their second class year, days before they became first classmen and took over the leadership of the Brigade. As plebes, we understood how far away we were from that day, if it ever came, and what would be required to earn the ring. And I think we sensed that in years to come the ring, if it were ever to grace our hands, would be on our fingers in situations we could only begin to imagine. So, no, we didn't laugh.

The film dwelled at length on the Ring Ceremony, which takes place at the Ring Dance, the high point of June Week for the junior class. During the dance, a midshipman's date wears the ring on a ribbon around her neck. At a certain point, the couple enters a large replica of the ring. The young lady takes the ring and dips it in a binnacle containing waters from the seven seas. She then places it on the finger of her midshipman escort. If the couple is to be engaged, he slips a smaller, more delicate version of his ring onto her finger. And then they kiss, the moment recorded for posterity by a nearby photographer.

Many years later, in the 1980s, a friend two decades younger remarked on my ring. One thing led to another, and I found myself telling her about the ring ceremony. She managed to keep a straight face as I described the binnacle with the waters of the seven seas, and she even asked, in a tone of genuine curiosity, what the seven seas were (I had to guess), but she started to lose it when I told her about stepping into the giant ring. Really, she was trying not to laugh, and I was trying not to get angry, but soon I started laughing, too. By then, I guess, I had discovered irony.

But not at the Academy. There were too many reminders of what the ring meant and on my solitary walks through the Yard I thought about myself and my classmates, so young and strong and filled with such promise, and wondered how our lives would play out. I never guessed that one would become Secretary of the Navy, another Commandant of the Marine Corps, a third ambassador to

China. That the class would produce twenty-three Navy admirals and Marine generals. Or that a war that barely anyone smelled in those days would in a few years time cost the lives of 122 Academy men, many of whom were at Annapolis with me, ten of them my classmates.

There is a ceremonial peroration to every Navy football game that moved me the first time I participated in it and moves me more deeply today. Moments after the gun sounds, the cheering stops and a curious silence takes hold on the Navy side of stadium. The midshipmen in the stands rise to their feet and remove their caps, as do Navy and Marine officers in the crowd. Alumni, those not in uniform, stand at attention, along with their spouses. The players on the field suspend the postgame handshakes, take off their helmets, and face the Navy fans. Voices on and off the field then join in singing the academy's hymnlike anthem, "Navy Blue and Gold":

> *Now college men from sea to sea*
>   *May sing of colors true.*
> *But who has better right than we*
>   *To hoist a symbol hue.*
> *For sailor men in battle fair*
>   *Since fighting days of old*
> *Have proved the sailor's right to wear*
>   *the Navy Blue and Gold.*

As the final notes fade, the midshipmen raise their caps skyward and shout as one, "Beat Army!" That final burst of school spirit seems to some unnecessary, a trivialization of the intense bonding that precedes it. For others, that cry is needed to break the mood, to shift their thoughts away from battles fought, friends and classmates lost, long-ago wars, today's wars, and wars still to come.

25

The Season of '61

*I*n early October, two weeks after the Alumni Game and midway through the Lynvets' first game of the 1961 Pop Warner season, the team was driving toward a touchdown when the referee abruptly stopped play.

"Who called a time-out?" asked a nonplussed Tommy Wall, who was bringing his team to the line of scrimmage when the whistle blew. Across the line, the opposition, old rival Greenpoint, seemed equally perplexed.

Over the loudspeaker, the referee said: "Ladies and gentlemen, I just wanted to announce that Roger Maris has just hit his sixty-first home run and broken Babe Ruth's record."

The crowd applauded, respectfully but not enthusiastically. There were even a few boos. The Babe's record had been a constant in the lives of most of the men in the crowd for over three decades, threatened now and then, but never bested. More than a few felt a kind of wistful sadness, some confusion as well, as if realizing, however vaguely, that one of the fixtures in a world they knew was no more. But Tommy Wall was having none of it. "You're kidding me," he muttered to himself. To his team, in the huddle, he snapped, "Fuck Roger Maris. Fuck Babe Ruth. We're playing football here." Then he called the next play.

The game ended 26–0. The Lynvets had dominated, affirming their belief that the loss to the Alumni had changed nothing, that they were, as they had been for the past three seasons, the class of the Pop Warner Senior Division. But any thought that the Tommy Wall–led Lynvets were going to fire out of the Alumni Game defeat and rampage through the conference as they had in 1958 and again in 1960 was exposed as a delusion when the Rego Park Crusaders beat them 26–12 in the second game of the season, manhandling them in the second half.

The game highlighted the Lynvets' personnel losses. But for Larry Kelly, lamenting the absence of a player, no matter how gifted, was not in the Lynvet playbook. It was an article of faith dating back to the beginning in 1950 that no single player carried the team. Kelly had taken that credo a step further. He looked at each new team the way a sculptor surveys a block of marble, as raw material to be shaped into something glorious. Rather than being intimidated by the labors ahead of him in the wake of the Rego Park defeat, Kelly was invigorated by the challenge and confident of the result, at least outwardly. Did he, in moments of solitude, long for a Ferriola or a Connor or a John Faulkner? Who knows? Those who asked him about such things received a cold stare, then a curt, dismissive response: "The uniforms don't say Ferriola, they say Lynvets."

The Lynvets rebounded from the Rego Park debacle by winning the two games that followed, against the Garity Knights and the Marine Park Uniques, by lopsided margins. The next game, against the Rockaway Knights, their most persistent challenger during the previous two years and currently leading the league with a 4–0 record, would tell them if they had actually righted themselves. Not only were the Knights undefeated but no one had even scored on them. And, in contrast to the Lynvets, Rockaway, though losing John Hourican to the league's age limit two years earlier, had held on to most of its other key players, including

Tommy Chapman and several they picked up when the Baisley
Park Bombers folded after the 1959 season.

Baisley's contribution to the Rockaway Knights was a big one.
Woody Wickers was now in the Knights' backfield. His mother,
the redoubtable Mrs. Wickers, was of course part of the package.
But that wasn't all. Tagging along with Woody was his best friend,
a young giant named Mike D'Amato.

In many ways, D'Amato was the point man for a new breed of
Pop Warner players—bigger, faster, stronger. He represented the
generation then coming of age, a player of the 1960s rather than of
the 1950s. In his day, Bob Ferriola may well have been the best
player in Pop Warner, but his skill level remained within the range
of what might be expected of a great athlete of a certain era. D'Amato bumped that up a notch or two. He could run, pass, catch, kick.
On defense, he was a monster, making as many tackles from his defensive halfback position as the linebackers did. Kelly had made a
furious effort to recruit him, but Richie Knott, the Rockaway
coach, reeled him in.

The game was at Far Rockaway High School, from which
Knott had recruited most of his players. The Lynvets hated the
field—no grass, dirt like gravel that tore up arms and legs. They
found the setting depressing, too, almost forbidding. Chain-link
fences jutted out from the corners of the school, enclosing the field
so that it resembled nothing so much as the exercise yard of a state
penitentiary. And the air was heavy, a dreary mist from the ocean
coating players and spectators alike. The huge crowd that day consisted mostly of Rockaway fans, who were emotional and often
rowdy. The previous year a Rockaway partisan had burst from the
sideline to tackle a Greenpoint defensive back who had intercepted
a Rockaway pass and was racing toward the goal line. Getting to
the field was difficult without a car (and even then it was a long
trip), which accounted for the routinely poor attendance by fans of
Rockaway's opponents at the Knights' home games, a classic
home-field advantage.

The play of the day came early. In the first quarter, D'Amato
crashed through the Lynvet line and blocked a punt deep in Lynvet

territory. Rockaway recovered. A few plays later, D'Amato took a handoff, tore over the left guard, and powered into the end zone. Then, punctuating his presence, he gathered in a pass for the two-point conversion.

The first half ended with Rockaway leading 8–0. Both teams moved the ball effectively in the second half, but neither could put it across the goal line. In the fourth quarter, a final indignity. Tommy Wall, fading back to pass, was sacked in his own end zone for a two-point safety. The game ended 10–0. Rockaway, still unscored on, was flying high at 5–0. The Lynvets' record stood at a solidly mediocre 3–2.

A week later the Lynvets, beginning their second run through the division, again rolled over Greenpoint. No one went crazy. They had hammered Greenpoint in the first game of the season, only to lose to Rego Park by two touchdowns the following week. But Rego Park was next, and this time the Lynvets were determined to be ready. They were, winning 14–6. Joe Aragona scored the first touchdown, taking a pitchout from Tommy Wall going to the right, then completely reversing his field and scooting around left end and over the goal line from ten yards out. Before the half ended, Tommy hit flanker and ex-quarterback Bobby Schmitt with a forty-yard touchdown pass. Even so, Rego Park refused to fold, scoring on a forty-five-yard touchdown pass to claim second-half bragging rights—and sending the message that they had no intention of backing down if the two teams met for a third time, in the playoffs, a wrinkle added to the Senior Division the year before.

The Lynvets got even better news the next week. The plucky Garity Knights ended Rockaway's undefeated and unscored-on streak, upsetting them 8–0. Garity, coached by a savvy, red-haired firebrand named Torchy Smith, was well drilled and disciplined, but it was the youngest team in the league. The year before, the Knights had moved up together from the Junior ranks, meaning that all but a handful of players were just eighteen, the league minimum. They had learned a lot that year, but they had paid for their education, losing to the Lynvets 55–0. This season, a few weeks back, the Lynvets clobbered them 30–0. And these guys beat

D'Amato, Tommy Chapman, Wickers, and all the other Rockaway hotshots? For the Lynvets, the world was finally starting to fall into place.

Or was it? Eddie Keane, a Lynvet co-captain, sensed something was off, not terribly off, but off nonetheless, like a piece of meat that has an odd odor that no one else notices. He and Teddy Spiess, the other co-captain, worked to keep the team together, but Eddie detected a difference between this team and those that preceded it. Some of the guys no longer seemed to recognize what had made the Lynvets near invincible all those years. Talent and coaching were important ingredients. More than anything, though, it was their willingness to practice harder and longer than any of their rivals, then take the field on Sunday determined not simply to win but to break the will of their opponents. The league was changing, just as the world was. No longer could the Lynvets throw their helmets on the field and expect to win, any more than the United States had been able to stop the Russians a few months earlier from throwing up a concrete wall layered with barbed wire in Berlin.

There were still great, crazy times. One evening after practice, Jackie Meyer and Danny Gersbeck stole Eddie Keane's car. Actually, they stole a car, but they didn't know it was Eddie's. In fact, it wasn't. It belonged to Eddie's brother-in-law, who had loaned it to Eddie. Eddie had stayed behind for a few minutes to talk to the coaches, and when he headed off he discovered the car was gone.

Jackie and Danny had been stealing cars regularly for a couple of years. Their M.O. was to take a car, drive it around for a few days, and then abandon it in the general vicinity of where they had found it.

The following Monday, at a team meeting at the Imperial, Eddie walked in and announced that his brother-in-law's car, the one he had been driving the previous week, had been stolen. Uh-oh, thought Jackie.

"Where'd this happen?" Jackie asked Eddie.

"At practice," Eddie replied.

"What kind of car was it?" Jackie asked.

"A Chevy," said Eddie.

At that point, Jackie and Danny came clean. They told him they had taken the car and informed him where he could find it. They had been driving it to practice when it ran out of gas, so they pulled over to the curb and left it. It's only a few blocks away, they told Eddie.

Eddie, flaring, hollered, "You assholes stole my brother-in-law's car?" He was enraged and indignant. Jackie and Danny understood his consternation and took his angry words as their due. Up to a point.

"There was no fucking sign on it, Eddie," said Jackie. "We didn't know it was your car."

Eddie, who was starting to cool down, erupted again. Jackie and Danny were now getting angry themselves. Didn't Eddie see that it was an honest mistake? And they were returning it, after a fashion, in good condition. "We didn't wreck the fucking thing, Eddie," they protested.

By now, the rest of the team was taking sides. Eddie realized he would get the car back, but little else in the way of satisfaction. "You idiots," he said. Then he dropped it.

The rematch with Rockaway came the first Sunday in December. By then, the Lynvets had won two more games after holding on to beat Rego Park. They handled the Marine Park Uniques easily, but Torchy Smith's youthful Garity Knights were growing up fast and surprised Kelly's team by playing them even for most of the game before losing 8–0.

Both Rockaway, with a record of six wins and one loss, and the Lynvets, at five and two, were assured berths in the playoffs. Neither team relaxed. A victory would give Rockaway the undisputed regular-season title. The teams would share the honor if the Lynvets won. More to the point, both teams were intent on establishing dominance going into the playoffs, in which the only championship anyone cared about would be decided.

The game came down to one play. With less than two minutes left on the clock and the Lynvets leading 8–6, Rockaway took over near midfield. Three plays gained only a few yards. On fourth down Coach Richie Knott sent in a play from the sideline. The

Lynvets figured that Knott wanted a first down and four more chances to pierce the Lynvet defense. That meant a short-possession pass.

But Knott was a gambler, and he went for it all. On the snap, the quarterback flipped the ball to Mike D'Amato running left as Rockaway's big wide receiver, Don Moran, sped through the drawn-up Lynvet defenders. As the Lynvets closed on D'Amato, he raised his right arm and hurled the ball in Moran's direction. Moran made a diving catch in the end zone. The pass covered fifty-two yards. Adding insult to injury, D'Amato skirted left end for the two-point conversion, putting the Knights up 14–8. The game ended that way. Trudging off the field, Eddie Keane recalled, not for the last time, something Larry Kelly had once told the team: Never let the outcome of a game depend on an official's call or a last-minute miracle.

By then, the Lynvets knew their opponent for the first round of the play-offs. Rego Park, a rubber match. They also knew that they were not the 1958 or 1960 powerhouse Lynvets. Their model was the 1959 team, which had stumbled badly but had finally managed to drive a stake through the heart of John Hourican. Now they had to find a way to do the same thing to Mike D'Amato.

26

A Date with Judi

*H*e was at the 1890 Club on Grand Avenue, the Baldwin crowd's singles bar of choice in that late winter of 1960–61, when Carol Weaver brought her over.

"Mike, you remember Judi," said Carol.

Jesus, thought Montore, Judi Dunham. He didn't recognize her. What the hell happened? A lifetime ago at Baldwin High he had singled her out as the best all-around girl in the school. Not necessarily the prettiest or the smartest or the sexiest, just the all-around best—bouncy, popular, wholesome, her dirty-blond hair trailing behind her in a pony tail, always at the top of her game. They hardly ever talked. The exception was each February 1, when they'd wish each other happy birthday, about all Mike figured they had in common. He thought of her as a snob, but when he was honest with himself he admitted he disliked her because he was not in her league. Now he tried to connect the Judi Dunham he remembered with the frosted hair, the sickly thin figure, the strained, heavily made-up features of the woman standing before him.

He couldn't. As Carol moved off to join her date, Bob Levy, Mike murmured, "You look as bad as I feel."

Judi, her words barely audible against the sounds of the band, replied, "That may be. I haven't had a real good time."

Even after a season with the Lynvets, Mike was where he had been since the service—angry, bruised, directionless, interested in neither friendships with men nor relationships with women, other than those he met at the bar who liked to squirm around with him between sets in the backseat of his latest forty-dollar jalopy. But he sensed that Judi needed something else. For once, Mike told himself, be a gentleman, not a jerk.

And he was. Judi had a story to tell and she needed to tell it. She had married five months after she and Mike graduated in June 1958. It had been a whirlwind courtship, one that Judi's mother had strongly encouraged. Judi's husband had matinee-idol good looks and, it seemed, rich professional prospects. They were married that fall. Within months, Judi was pregnant. Donna was born in October 1959. Soon Judi began to suspect that her husband was a wanderer. Before long, a series of events convinced her that her suspicions were accurate. She wanted to leave him. Her mother argued against it. So did the local minister. Divorce was still frowned on, and there was the child to consider. One day, on a hunch, Judi drove to Uniondale, about five miles from Baldwin, and peered in the window of a bar her husband liked to frequent. She went home, called the minister, and told him to go to the bar, look in the window, and call her back if he still thought the marriage was worth saving. She never heard from the minister again.

She and Donna moved in with her parents. She was barely twenty, separated from her husband, and the mother of an infant. Mike had misread her in high school. Despite a facade of self-confidence, she was shy and critical of herself. Now those qualities tumbled into depression and a pernicious anxiety, a sense that she had somehow squandered her youth and that her life was over before it had really begun. She took a part-time job making sandwiches for high school kids who couldn't handle the lunches in the school cafeteria. Donna sat in a kiddie seat on the floor beside her.

She lived like that for about a year. Slim but with an appealing figure before, she lost weight. For months her friend Carol Weaver had been telling her she had to get out, meet people again, reclaim her life. By the time Carol persuaded her to go to the 1890 Club with Bob Levy and her on that Friday night, Judi was down to ninety pounds, twenty-five under her playing weight, drawn, fragile, lifeless, almost bereft of hope.

Judi was still recounting her tale when Carol and Bob, one of Mike's few friends, and not a close one at that, suggested they go to quieter bar. Mike and Judi looked at each other.

"I guess we're together," said Judi.

For the next several weeks they double-dated with Bob and Carol. For Judi and Mike, each battered in a different way, it was a time for healing more than passion. If Bob and Carol were going somewhere, they included Mike and Judi, who enjoyed essentially pressure-free dates since neither had instigated them. During that period Judi and her mother climbed aboard a Greyhound bus and headed off to Montgomery, Alabama, where divorces were quick and cheap.

After a time Bob and Carol broke up, depriving Judi and Mike of a ready excuse for being together. They kept on dating, however, sensing they were good for each other, neither having a clear idea of where the relationship was leading. Mike was stretched thin. He was taking courses at Nassau Community College during the day, working construction at night, and answering the phone (and doing his homework) at a Jewish funeral home in Glen Cove on weekends.

Still, he and Judi managed to find time for each other. Now, though, more and more, there were three of them. Judi's mother detested Mike. He had a hard edge, no education to speak of, and a future clouded by an erratic past. Judi had already been hurt once, and her mother saw more trouble in store for her if she kept hanging around with Mike. So she wouldn't babysit for Donna, which meant the little girl, by now a toddler just beginning to form words, went almost everywhere Judi and Mike went. Their dates were parks, playgrounds, occasionally Jones Beach. Mike thought

Donna was terrific. She had shiny blond hair cut Prince Valiant style and a cute little pigeon-toed walk. Mike could tell she really liked him. More than that, he felt needed and began to wonder if maybe the time had come to clean up his act.

He was not quite there. One day, after an afternoon of drinking, he was cruising along Grand Avenue in still another forty-dollar special when a driver stopped at a stop sign suddenly gunned the engine of his red-and-white '56 Ford and tried to beat Mike through the intersection. Mike, who had the right of way, snapped. Instead of easing off the gas, he depressed the accelerator and rammed the guy's left rear fender. He drove off, but two police cars were on him in seconds. The cops accused him of leaving the scene of an accident.

"That was no accident," he told the cops. "I hit the fuck on purpose."

That cost him his license for ninety days, which explains why he, Judi, and Donna were in Judi's father's car when a wonderful thing happened. They were heading for the beach. Donna, who was developing a vocabulary, said something to Mike, then added a word: Daddy.

Judi stiffened, horrified that Mike might think she had put Donna up to it. She started to correct Donna, but Mike said, "Leave her alone. She doesn't know any better."

And then he smiled.

Not long after, the 1961 season began and the Lynvets began to notice a difference in Mike Montore. He still had an edge, and his ferociousness on the football field had not diminished. But the anger that had always seemed to be lurking just below the surface became less evident, as if a fire was being brought under control. Not quickly, with the immediacy of a clump of snow falling on the flames, but gradually, like glowing embers slowly giving way to a soft spring rain.

The Lynvets noticed something else. Mike had started showing up for games with a cute blonde and a shiny-haired little girl. They looked like a family.

27

Knight of the Open Road

I was playing football that autumn of 1961, too. Not varsity football, but intramurals, which was a full-equipment, full-contact sport at Navy. By midseason, though, I was in the naval hospital on the Academy grounds because of a recurrence of the knee injury from Lynvet days. My father came down to visit and handed me a paperback book.

"Someone gave me this. He thought it would make a great musical comedy," my dad said. "The writer's a little crazy, though, and I don't think anybody can get the rights. But I thought you'd like it—it has lots of dirty words in it."

It was the only book my father ever gave me, and I'm at a loss to explain why he thought my taste in books ran to those rife with expletives. Doesn't matter. *The Catcher in the Rye* jumped me as no book ever had before. I realized that many of the things that drove Holden Caulfield crazy did the same to me. Right at the beginning, as he stands on a hill watching a Pencey Prep football game, he says, *The game with Saxon Hall was supposed to be a very big deal around Pencey. It was the last game of the year, and you were supposed to commit suicide or something if old Pencey didn't win.* I felt the same way about Navy football, a very big deal at Annapolis, not because I didn't care about the team, but because I wasn't good enough to be on it. I cheered like a madman, but my heart wasn't really in it, and I felt disloyal. Through Holden, I realized that such unworthy emotions were not confined to failed Navy running backs.

By then I had begun an intense correspondence with Janie Benson, whom had I met at the plebe tea fight the previous spring. Actually, the intensity was all on my part. Janie, who had grown up in Baltimore, was in her freshman year at Lake Erie College, a women's liberal arts school in Painesville, Ohio, and having a great time as the target of feral men from nearby colleges, or so I imagined. I wasn't even in the hunt. As youngsters, although we were allowed to date on weekends in Annapolis, our liberty was not much better than when we were plebes, in that we could not leave the Academy until Christmas. Not a single weekend off. Would I have driven the three hundred miles to Painesville to see her on a weekend, even a weekend that began after noon meal inspection on Saturday and ended at evening meal formation on Sunday? In a minute. But there was no way, not with mandatory bed checks on Saturday night and compulsory chapel on Sunday morning.

Actually, driving was problematic. I couldn't exactly drive, though I had learned enough at a driving school during my postcruise summer leave to get my license. Everyone I knew had one, including Janie. I stopped off in Baltimore to see her on my return to the Academy from summer leave. The visit set up a driving fiasco that rivaled my boyhood problems at Yankee Stadium. Her parents, no doubt with Janie mouthing "No! No!" as they talked to me on the phone, invited me to spend the night at their home, in a leafy suburb north of downtown, before I reported back to the Academy. Janie's world was very different from mine. She lived in a freestanding house surrounded by trees. She rode horses. She had married parents, Protestant ones at that. I think that until I went to the Academy I knew a total of two white people who weren't Catholic or Jewish.

That evening, Janie drove me to Washington in the family's

second car, a Renault. I would have driven, or at least tried to drive even though I had never been on the road without an instructor by my side in a dual-control vehicle. But it turned out the Renault had a manual transmission, on which I had received just a single lesson. Janie drove fast, with flair, shifting gears smoothly.

"What'd you just do?" I asked.

"Downshifted," she said.

"Oh, yeah, downshift, right, I remember that."

I felt diminished, a kid in a grown-up world, for the first time sensing the allure of the automobile and the freedom it conferred.

We had dinner at a fashionable but modestly priced restaurant that Janie knew about. The vibes were not good. The hour drive from Baltimore in the passenger seat had left me feeling awkward, insubstantial, as if I'd been neutered. As we left the restaurant and headed for the car, I said, "I'll drive." Janie protested, pointing out the obvious, that I had said earlier that I hadn't mastered a stick shift. "Don't worry," I said. "I know what I'm doing."

I didn't have a clue. Somehow I got the car out of the parking lot, but before I knew it we were on Dupont Circle, in the heart of Washington, and I just fell apart. We'd lurch forward. Then I'd stall.

"Bob," said Janie, cool and calm, "first you depress the clutch, then you put the car in gear, and slowly let up on the clutch."

Lurch, stall, squeal—the last from cars veering away after coming on us sitting dead in the middle of one of the city's busiest traffic circles late at night. More lurching. Another stall. More squeals and the grinding of gears. Horns blasting. Angry shouts.

"Bob, do you want me to drive?"

"No! I'm getting it."

"Okay, let's try again. Just do what I tell you. Press the clutch down with . . . No! No! Not the gas pedal!"

"Don't panic. I can do this."

"Hey, shithead! Get that fucking thing moving!" This from a fellow knight of the open road, not Janie.

A police car pulled up behind us. The cop, a young guy, got out and came to the driver's side.

"Having a problem?"

"Uh . . ."

"He's just a little new to a stick shift," said Janie. "Bob, why don't you let me take over?"

"Sure," I said, smiling at the cop, opening the door, holding it for Janie as she slid behind the wheel. I thanked the cop for his interest, walked around to the other side, and climbed in as Janie expertly put the car in gear. The cop was biting his lip.

Trapped in Annapolis, I poured out my frustrations to Janie in long, anguished letters, to which she replied, when she got around to it, with smart-ass college-girl tales of drinking bouts with men from Kenyon College or with some guys from the University of Virginia, a legendary party school, who just happened to show up on campus. Or of spending a weekend partying in nearby Cleveland. I detected a dismissive tone to her letters, as if she were writing back merely out of politeness. Still, I begged her to come for a weekend. She finally agreed.

It was not a great weekend. Annapolis has a rich colonial history—for a brief time, in fact, it was the nation's capital—but beyond that the city seemed little more than a sleepy fishing village. Midshipmen, moreover, were forbidden by state law from drinking within a seven-mile limit measured from the dome of the Academy chapel. Closing the loop, Academy regulations prohibited midshipmen from venturing beyond seven miles. There were a couple of pricey restaurants, but just a handful that could accommodate the limited budgets of most of us. The Little Campus Inn on Main Street, a brightly lit soda fountain with a few booths, was where my friends and I usually wound up after going to the movies on Saturdays. So that's where I took Janie for dinner. Janie, her perkiness laced with a hint of untapped sexual friskiness, was fun to be with, but it's fair to say that romance did not blossom at the Little Campus as we chatted across the white Formica table.

Women who dated midshipmen were known in Academy slang as drags, and those who were not local stayed at what were called draghouses. These were two- and three-story homes just outside the Yard on King George Street or Duke of Gloucester

Street or across Main Street leading down to Spa Creek. Today, after gentrification, those houses are probably each worth more than a million dollars. Most draghouses were owned and run by elderly women, usually widows or spinsters, who were sweet and kind and, for the most part, understanding. On almost any weekend, as many as a dozen girls would be put up in a single draghouse, often sharing rooms. On Saturday night, starting at midnight, liberty expired for the three upper classes in fifteen-minute increments. Thus the Flying Squadron.

Midshipmen knew to the minute how long it would take them on a dead run to get from their favorite draghouse to Bancroft Hall, where an officer, a ceremonial sword dangling from his hip, stood solemnly on the steps alternately checking his watch and eyeing the Flying Squadron as it strained to close the distance. One minute Annapolis was quiet, as you would expect of a small town late at night, the next minute the streets were alive with the sound of leather slapping pavement as midshipmen ripped themselves away from whatever they were up to and dashed from darkened draghouses near and far, ties askew, caps in hand, eyes like saucers. Those midshipmen closer to the Academy fell in with those from more distant draghouses, the herd swelling, the noise intensifying, thundering through Gate One or Gate Three or Gate Eight, breaking into a sprint as the lights of Bancroft came into view.

After a few minutes, the sounds faded and nighttime silence returned, an uneasy one. Fifteen minutes later the racket erupted all over again. And again fifteen minutes after that. Then, and only then, the good citizens of Annapolis could sleep, while in Bancroft Hall midshipmen in pain stared at ceilings or the bottom of a roommate's bunk. Sadly, for me, the only thing I had in common with members of the Flying Squadron was the pain. I said goodnight to Janie at the draghouse door and had plenty of time to stroll back to Bancroft.

Janie and I were headed in different directions. She was intent on shaking off tradition, especially as it related to a woman's place in the world, and she had no patience for convention. Those qualities had been among the ones that had first attracted me to her, along with a refreshing openness and her strong resemblance, in appearance and style, to Audrey Hepburn, with whom I had fallen in love a few months earlier when I saw *Breakfast at Tiffany's*. Compared to the girls I had known prior to the Academy, Janie just seemed more independent, in an exciting way. One of the first things she told me was that she had no intention of getting married, but that if she ever did it would not be to someone in the service. She was not, she insisted, going to be a military wife under any circumstances. A philosophical line in the sand, she explained, nothing personal. She talked of joining the Peace Corps when she graduated.

In addition to her evolving feminism, Janie responded to other forces of change that were building in America. She participated in civil rights demonstrations, at least once getting arrested and hauled off to the pokey. I cheered her on but saw no place for myself on the civil rights ramparts even though signs of discrimination flickered on the periphery of my consciousness. Our class of about one thousand included only a handful of black guys. In Annapolis, there were four movie theaters, but blacks were welcome at just one, the Star. Seven years after *Brown v. Board of Education* many school districts in Maryland were just starting to desegregate.

I was in a different place from Janie in more ways than one. At Annapolis I was embedded in the tradition and convention that she found oppressive. Some of my nonsweat classmates dealt with the dating problem by pooling their cash and renting apartments in town, known within the Yard as snake ranches, so they could drink and otherwise relax with their dates on weekends. I didn't. Though I called some of the regulations horseshit, notably the limits on weekend liberty, I abided by them. I had worked too hard to get to the Academy and to make it through Plebe Year to chance endangering my place in the Brigade of Midshipmen.

There was something else. I liked the tradition and conventions of the Academy, which translated for me as stability and order, qualities that had been missing in my life up to then. And I was proud to be a midshipman, each day walking in the footsteps of men who had served America with gallantry and daring since 1845. As for the social and cultural rumblings I sensed building in the world beyond the Yard, I saw my role and that of my fellow Academy men in that autumn of 1961 as protecting the nation as it sought to come to grips with its problems.

Janie and I continued to correspond. She wrote that I was taking our relationship, such as it was, too seriously, that I was making her uncomfortable, that I seemed to want an exclusivity that she was not nearly ready for. Reading between the lines, I guessed that she also was saying that even when she was ready, it wouldn't be with me.

I was getting the picture. Without flatly saying so, she was telling me I was boring, a hard label to shake. But I kept writing and, oddly enough, she kept writing back.

28

The Princess and the Shoes

*E*ven as he quarterbacked the up-and-down Lynvets toward the playoffs, Tommy Wall was coaching a Woodside Chiefs Peewee team made up of kids ten to thirteen. He had put the team together that spring. With a pot of flour and water, he pasted posters on the walls of schools and other buildings, delivered flyers to bars to attract the notice of fathers.

Forty kids showed up for the first practice. The kids, strong and eager, loved it, couldn't get enough. Neither could Tommy. The Peewees seemed to think of nothing but football, unlike the older kids he had coached, who were more interested in girls and impressing their friends. He put in a highly sophisticated double-wing T offense, with traps, pulling guards, reverses, and audibles. He drilled the team endlessly. They practiced two hours a day, five days a week, running every play a hundred times.

The team had talent, but he had to mold it. His fullback, Skippy Gleason, was destined for the priesthood. Skippy ran with power but lacked aggressiveness, didn't like to hurt opponents. "Skippy, this is not a nice-guy game," said Tommy. "Run over people." He warned the kids to keep their parents away from him; he didn't want any politicking for positions or playing time. "I'm not Ozzie Nelson," he told the team, which needed no such disclaimer.

He was not above some Kelly-style psychology. Minutes before the Chiefs took the field against Marine Park, he confided to them a distressing experience earlier in the week at a league meeting. The Marine Park coaches, he said, had complained long and loud about the Chiefs' home field in Woodside, where the game was to be played.

"They said it was a slum, it was shabby, and that our neighborhood was shit," said Tommy, his tone matching his sorrowful eyes. He added, "You know how I feel. Just because your father is a bricklayer or truck driver or a bus driver, that doesn't mean you don't have a right to compete with lawyers' kids and doctors' kids."

None of it was true—Marine Park was hardly the silk-stocking neighborhood that Tommy had made it out to be—but it worked. The Chiefs, breathing fire, won 44–0. Three members of the Marine Park team, none the offspring of doctors or lawyers, wound up in the hospital.

The Chiefs won the first five games of the season, then grew cocky. Greenpoint pounded them 25–6. In December, a week after the Lynvet Seniors lost to Rockaway for the second time and eight days before the Seniors were to begin the playoffs against Rego Park, Greenpoint and the Chiefs met in a rematch for the Peewee Division championship. Tommy punctuated the importance of the game by hiring a bus to take the Chiefs to the field, paid for by the patrons of bars where he had placed jelly jars. "It's the championship game," he told the kids. "We're going in style."

It was Greenpoint's turn to be cocky, but that didn't last long. The Chiefs scored on their first play from scrimmage, going seventy yards on a slant pass. Greenpoint tried to recover on their first series, only to have the Chiefs intercept a pass and drive for a second touchdown, taking control of the game early.

Late in the second half, Tommy called a play the Chiefs had never used but had been practicing for weeks, a pass off a triple reverse. Greenpoint was dazzled by the slick ball handling, frozen by the sleight of hand. The fans were flabbergasted. They'd seen college and pro teams routinely screw up a single reverse, couldn't imagine a team of kids thirteen and under executing such a complicated sequence of handoffs and fakes. The play went for twenty yards, putting the Chiefs on the threshold of a third touchdown.

The game ended 20–6. The Greenpoint coach, congratulating Tommy, was glassy-eyed, close to tears. "I can't believe this," he said.

Later, Tommy assembled the players, shook their hands, then read out the names of those who had made the all-star team. Everyone was surprised when Mike Savage didn't make it. Mike, a good kid who played a terrific tackle and had been a leader on the field, began sobbing when his name was not called. Tommy—privately sympathetic, publicly anything but—turned on him. "The all-star stuff is bullshit," he said. "We won the championship today. That was our goal. This is a day of joy for the team. Cut the shit. Grow up."

Tommy's words hit home when I heard the story. With admirable economy of phrasing, he had boiled down the message Bob Bushman had conveyed to me in his letter a year earlier when I was struggling with the rigors of Plebe Year at Annapolis. It had taken Bob seven pages. Tommy had delivered the same sermon in two crisp sentences, totaling five words.

I had grown up, at least I was getting there. I kept in touch with the Lynvets, after a fashion, through my sister Pat, who was a cheerleader for the Junior team but friends with a number of Seniors who had moved up over the previous two years. Pat joined the cheerleaders after passing muster with those who controlled membership—the City Line crowd, led by Margie Lyons, the captain.

Pat, the embodiment of perkiness and a true innocent of fifteen who did not smoke, drink, curse, or, so far as I knew, make out, began her audition at the local teen hangout, Dodegge Brothers Ice Cream Parlor. Larry Sifert, the most gentlemanly of the Lynvets though built like a brick that had sprouted legs, escorted her to the Pahlah, as it was known. The neighborhood was mildly threatening to Pat. The three highways that intersected near our aparment building provided a sense of openness, whatever its other drawbacks. City Line seemed cramped, with small homes attached to one another, narrow streets, and a rougher crowd than Pat was used to.

Larry led her past the soda fountain to the seating section in back. Five girls in Lynvet jackets, all smoking, were jammed in a booth. Pat thought they were older than her, though they were all about her age. Addressing Margie, one of the prettiest, Larry said, "This is Pat Timberg. I told you about her." Margie, her command authority barely softened by her youthful good looks, said nothing, turned to the other girls, and nodded. They scrambled out of the booth. "Sit," she said to Pat, gesturing to the seat across from her with one hand, dismissing Larry with an airy wave of the other. Pat felt as if she had been dropped into a scene from *West Side Story*.

Margie stubbed out one cigarette and lit another as Pat settled into the red plastic booth. "Do any cheerleading before?" asked Margie, smoke streaming from her nose and mouth. Pat was entranced by Margie's smoking skills. God, she really knows how to smoke, Pat marveled. Then, realizing she had been asked a question, she replied, cheerily, "No, but I like to dance." Margie stared as if she had never seen anyone quite like Pat, took another drag, finally said, "We're gonna practice now. C'mon with us." They practiced for two hours on a patch of grass on North Conduit Avenue, the service road for the Belt Parkway. The cars that sped past coated them with exhaust fumes. Afterward, Pat asked if she had made the team. Ignoring the question, Margie told her when the next practice would be and walked off. Pat thought Margie was the coolest kid she had ever met.

Just as the Lynvets provided a sanctuary for me during difficult times, the cheerleaders and the Junior team itself cushioned Pat's life for a few years. She even managed to persuade Margie to install Rosemarie, who was ten, as the team mascot. The boys on the team, easily as rough-and-tumble as Margie, treated the cheerleaders—especially the nondrinking, nonsmoking City Line outsiders like Pat and her friends Lyn Wheeler and Mary Pesce—with deference and respect, perhaps more than they wanted. There were parties, usually involving drinking, but no matter how late they ran one or more Lynvets would ride buses and subways with Pat, Lyn, and Mary to make sure they made it home safely.

Most of the parties were held in wood-paneled basements in City Line. But Pat and Lyn decided to throw a party at Lyn's apartment in Kew Gardens one Saturday night. Lyn didn't tell her parents, who were away for the weekend. About two dozen Lynvets, players and cheerleaders, showed up. Lyn, wary that smudges on the carpet would tip off her parents when they returned, told everyone to take off their shoes and leave them at the door. Around midnight, with the party still going strong, one of the guys stumbled on a handgun Lyn's father kept in the apartment and accidently fired it out the window. The shot scared everyone; they knew it would bring the cops. The partygoers ran for the door only to discover that their shoes had disappeared. After a few moments of consternation and frantic searching, they blew out of the apartment in their socks. Pat and Lyn waited for the police to arrive, but they never did. Finally, the two girls climbed into Lyn's bed, chatted a bit, and fell asleep. Lyn woke up after a couple of hours, awakened Pat out of a deep sleep, and complained that her whole body ached. Something's wrong with this mattress, Lyn said. That's when they found the shoes. All of them, including two pairs of combat boots. Before the gun incident that caused their guests to run for the hills, someone had stashed them under the mattress as a practical joke.

"I guess I'm not a princess," said Pat.

As I kept my head down at Annapolis in that fall of 1961, I also kept it in the sand as far as the home front was concerned. My parents and sisters wrote often, their letters invariably upbeat. I called home every couple of weeks, waiting out the long lines for the few phone booths available to midshipmen in Bancroft Hall.

"How are things going?" I'd ask Pat, offering her an opening to fill me in on the situation with my mother.

"You know, the same," she'd reply, hesitantly, waiting to see if I'd pursue the issue, willing to drop it if I didn't. I rarely pressed for details.

I was only too glad not to be home that Thanksgiving. When my mother put her mind to it, she was a wonderful cook, her signature dish roast leg of lamb, though she was often drunk by the time the food was ready. She could cook a great turkey, too, as she did for Thanksgiving, along with mashed potatoes, candied sweet potatoes, turnips, and giblet gravy. That evening, though, shortly after the turkey came from the oven, crisp and golden brown, she became angry at Pat and Rosemarie and in a drunken rage threw it out the window.

The Brigade spent Thanksgiving in Annapolis, so I didn't hear what happened that night until a week later. It wasn't so bad, said Pat. To make herself feel better, she said, she imagined that a poor man was walking under the window when a beautiful turkey fell from the sky into his arms.

I winced when I heard the story. Then I put it behind me. There was nothing I could do about it, I told myself, as long as I was at Annapolis and not in Kew Gardens. And how would my being there change anything? I lived each day with a low level of anxiety and guilt, but I kept it under control and did not let it immobilize me. If things got really bad at home, I knew Pat would tell me. Then I would react, one way or another. Until then . . .

I was holding my breath, but at the same time I was distancing myself from my family. Pat was sixteen, I told myself, her watch now.

29

Crunch Time

*T*welve weeks into the season and it had come to this: The Lynvets had lost three games and now, as the play-offs began a week before Christmas, they had to beat a tough Rego Park team that had beaten them once if they were to make it into the championship game against Rockaway, which had beaten them twice. As the players arrived at the field, they saw what the coaches already realized. Their star performer, Joe Aragona, had been reduced to a bit player. Joe glided, sprinted, twirled like a leaf in a stiff wind. But he was not going to be able to do any of those things today. Not on this field.

The snow had fallen earlier in the week, seven inches of it. Since then the thermometer had hovered around the freezing point, which meant the snow on top melted during the day, then refroze at night, a pattern that had repeated itself for the past three days. Now, two hours before game time, four inches of snow still covered the field, but it had a glassy veneer, as though someone had coated it with shellac. In truth, the snow was topped by a sheet of ice a half-inch thick, making the field more suitable to the clomping strides of a Clydesdale than the stylish meanderings of a head-strong thoroughbred like Aragona.

Mike Faulkner was starting at fullback because Teddy Horo-shak, a bruising runner, was hurt. "You're gonna have to do the job today," Bob Bushman told Mike when he delivered the news. "You and Montore. We can't run Joe."

Mike smiled. "Okay."

He knew what Bushman meant. Power running. Nothing fancy. Montore was perfect for that kind of game. He had nearly as many moves as Aragona, but he liked to run over opponents, not dance away from them like Joe. "Yeah, it was fun," Montore once told his teammates after darting through the line and sprinting un-touched into the end zone, "but, shit, there was no collision."

Mike Faulkner felt no sense of dread on hearing Bushman's words, as he might have earlier in the season. He had made a frag-ile peace with constantly being compared to his older brothers, John and Paul, both of whom had starred for the Lynvets, and never quite measuring up. And he was beginning to believe that over the course of the season he had proved to his coaches and teammates that he was every inch a Faulkner. Now, having been told the game might hinge on his performance, he accepted the challenge, knew he could meet it.

The field was perfect for him. He was strong and ran with power, as long as he was going straight ahead. On a rainy day, with a muddy field, he was the equal of anyone. In the snow and ice, he might even be better.

Larry Kelly had not made it easy on Mike. The coach had never been able to play mind games with John and Paul Faulkner, but he quickly saw that Mike was vulnerable. In fact, he was not as good as either of his brothers, but he was very good, a hard-running full-back on offense and a tough linebacker on defense. But Kelly sensed Mike's feeling of inferiority and used it to motivate him. To an extent it worked, but Mike Faulkner did not need a lot of out-side motivation, and it came at a price. When Larry said to him, as he often did, "Okay, John, I mean Paul, I mean Mike . . . ," Mike was mortified.

Part of the problem was Mike himself. He was not John or Paul and never would be, but he couldn't keep from comparing himself to them. If he did something well, which he often did, and you said, "Hey, Mike, nice job," he would respond by finding some fault in his performance totally unnoticeable to anyone else.

Mike Montore thought Mike Faulkner was a terrific kid. With the exception of his constant self-criticism. When that started, he could be a pain in the ass. But over the course of the season he had come a long way. A couple of weeks earlier Montore had put the finishing touches on his education. The team was practicing at Victory Field. A cold night, but a good practice, one that left the team invigorated and confident. Montore had especially liked the way Faulkner had played, and as he walked to his car he told him so. Faulkner, to Montore's surprise, seemed down, said he didn't feel he had performed well at all. He then began to enumerate what he saw as his deficiencies.

Montore had had enough. As Faulkner started to move off, Montore flung him against a car. Before Faulkner had time to react, Montore's hands were on his throat, squeezing, raising him onto his toes.

"Mike," said Montore, his fingers tightening, his voice low and laden with menace, "*This* is a real problem. This is going to be death if it lasts long enough. Everything else is not a problem. You've got to learn the difference."

Faulkner stared at Montore, dancing on his toes, barely able to draw a breath. Montore increased the pressure. Faulkner's eyes bulged. His voice still low, Montore asked again, "Do you understand, Mike?" Faulkner managed to nod. Montore released his grip, walked to his car cursing to himself, and drove away.

The officials looked over the field and discussed postponing the game. The coaches, however, wanted to play. Both teams were ready. A plow had cleared the sidelines, end zones, and yard lines.

The refs said they'd make do. The teams raced onto the field, crunching through the crust of ice that covered it.

The game was bruising. Neither team could pass or run to the outside. It was trench warfare, a lot of action, little to show for it. To the few spectators, the game looked like a tug-of-war, not football. The field was pounded into shards of ice. The snow was smeared with blood as the ice sliced, ripped, and tore arms, legs, and occasionally faces unprotected by masks.

Mike Montore was hitting someone on every play, as either ball carrier, blocker, or defender. Punchy, he grew restive in the huddle, couldn't wait to fire out of his stance and drive into the line still again. Like the seasoned battlefield commander who can step back and make sense of the chaos around him, he saw the game as shorn of all but the essentials. Most games featured elaborate pass patterns, razzle-dazzle ball handling, fancy sweeps, and complicated reverses. This game had none of those things. What was transpiring on that frozen field was pure football—blocking, tackling, power running—the soul of the game. By the fourth quarter, the strength draining out of him, his head cleared momentarily and he had a thought:

I never want this game to end.

Mike Faulkner, no less groggy, felt like he had carried the ball on every play. Though there was not a lot of evidence, he tried to convince himself that Rego Park was wearing down, that his and Montore's punishing runs were on the verge of breaking the will of their rival. One problem: the game was nearly over and Rego Park led 8–6. Everyone was worried, except Montore, who was in his own world and may have known something no one else did.

The clock was winding down and, with it, the season. With less than ten minutes to play, the Lynvets began a drive. Guided by Tommy Wall, they moved across midfield, then deep into Rego Park territory. The drive looked like it was about to stall, fourth and five on Rego Park's thirteen-yard line. Kelly signaled Wall to go for the first down, as if there were any question, but he had faith in Tommy's field generalship and left it up to him to call the play.

Tommy, who had not thrown a pass all day, was ready. He called Eddie Keane's number.

"Strong right, tight end opposite, pass blocking," said Tommy.

Even Montore reacted. A pass on this field with the game on the line? The team broke the huddle. This is it, Tommy murmured to himself as he moved behind the little center, Al Schneeberg.

"Ready. Set. Blue twenty-four. Hut one, hut two, hut three . . ."

The ball smacked into his hands. A sound like a five-car pileup erupted from the clash of bodies. Keane faked a block on the left tackle, then cut across the middle. Tommy, shielded by the two Mikes, dropped back gingerly because of the treacherous footing and planted himself. From Rego Park, surprised cries of "Pass! Pass!" Coolly, Tommy laid the ball into Keane's hands. Eddie pulled it in and put a death grip on it as two defenders leveled him. "First down," shouted the referee. The Lynvets were on the six-yard line with less than a minute left in the game.

In the huddle, Tommy called the play: C-6 dive, wedge blocking, Faulkner up the gut behind Schneeberg and right guard John Schmauser. Tommy shifted his eyes to Keane and Teddy Spiess, the right tackle. "Eddie, you take the tackle high. Teddy, you clear him out." To flanker Bobby Schmitt, Tommy said with a wink, "Bobby, you've got the linebacker." Schmitt smiled. "I've got him, Tommy." It was a joke. No one on the team was less likely to forget his assignment, or fail to execute it, than the one-time quarterback, but Tommy loved to hear Bobby's confident, no-nonsense response. Finally, to Faulkner: "Mike, six yards to the championship game. Six yards to glory." The team was holding hands in the huddle, the first time they had ever done so.

Tommy called the signals. Blue, fifty-four, hut, hut, hut, hut-hut! A reverse spin, then a handoff to Faulkner, who tucked the ball into his right arm and headed to where the hole was supposed to be. It wasn't there, but a fraction of a second later the wall of bodies abruptly dematerialized, as if someone had just slipped a fresh slide into the projector. Mike charged through the hole, was met by two guys about three yards from the goal line. He threw both arms around the ball, lowered his head, and barreled into them. Legs churning, he tried to maintain his momentum as the defenders fought to stop him, force him back. He twisted his body, drove his legs, took short, choppy, battering steps. The Rego Park defenders gave ground and lost their footing as Mike careened through them and into the end zone.

The Lynvets piled on Mike, cheering, screaming his name. Montore, on the ground a few yards away, was staring into space. As Faulkner got to his feet, he saw the fans on the sidelines going crazy, his brother John among them.

Mike's touchdown made the score 12–8. The conversion attempt failed, so Rego Park could still win the game with a touchdown even though there was next to no time left. Rego Park got a good return on the kickoff, taking the ball to midfield. Time for one last play. The Lynvet defenders knew it had to be a pass, but they were fooled by the target, not one of Rego Park's fleet receivers, but the big fullback. Larry Kelly wasn't the only coach that day who understood that the field conditions favored a power runner, even if he was not that fast. It was a daring play. The whole team swung to the left, drawing the Lynvet defense with them, while the fullback drifted out to the right. Suddenly the ball was in his hands, a perfect swing pass, and he was tearing for the goal line. The only Lynvet defender not completely fooled was Mike Faulkner, who gave chase, his pursuit intensified by his realization that his moment of glory, the greatest day he had ever had, was about to be eclipsed by another frog trying to become a prince on a sloppy field.

But Mike was closing on his prey. As the ball carrier crossed the ten-yard line, Mike launched himself, felt the fullback break stride, stagger, then crumple to the ground. Time expired. Final score: Lynvets 12, Rego Park 8. John Faulkner raced from the sidelines, swept Mike into his arms, and carried him off the field.

Teammates and fans slapped Mike Montore on the back, told him he played a terrific game. He mumbled "Thanks," but never looked at anyone as he clumped toward the locker room. Inside, he took off his helmet, leaned back against the wall, lifted the toes of his low-cuts, and slowly slid on his back cleats to the cold concrete floor. He had never been happier. He had given everything he had, and it had turned out well. He was staring straight ahead, his legs stretched out in front of him. The moment was like a dream, and he knew that the only way you can hang on to a dream is to keep your head still so you don't dislodge the images. To himself, he said, *This is it. This is as good as it's ever going to be.*

On the other side of the locker room, Mike Faulkner was accepting congratulations, a beaming John by his side. Mike knew that John, after Mike himself, was the happiest man there. Larry Kelly walked up. To Mike: "Great game." To John: "Oh, I know you. You're Mike Faulkner's brother."

Outside, the fans chanted, "We want Rockaway! We want Rockaway!"

30

The Catch

*O*n the day of the Lynvet-Rockaway showdown, December 31, 1961, America was suspended in perilous equilibrium, a nation at the angle of repose. The Fifties had ended, but the Sixties, as we would come to know them had not yet begun except on the calendar. The new president was completing his first year in office. He had stumbled at times. Even so, he had tapped a vein of idealism in the young and imparted a refreshing vitality to the nation. No one had heard of Lee Harvey Oswald, who at about game time was partying with friends in Minsk and preparing to return to the United States after two years in the Soviet Union. The civil rights movement had become a formidable force, and there was a sense of progress toward a truly just society. And no American cities had burned. Americans were not at war, at least not many of them, though there seemed to be an upsurge in the number of military men—advisers they were called—drifting into South Vietnam. Whatever that meant. Nothing good, said some of the few who noticed. Young men, on reaching their eighteenth birthday, still signed up for the draft and did their service time when called. People picked them up when they hitchhiked in uniform, wouldn't let them pay for their drinks at any hometown bar worthy of the name. In California, Richard Nixon, defeated in his quest for the presidency a year earlier, plotted a comeback, starting with a run for governor of his home state in the new year. The Pill was on the market, but its full impact had not yet been felt. Crooners Perry Como and Eddie Fisher and songstress Patti Page were still popular even though rock had been a staple of the music charts for six or seven years and Elvis was king. Bob Dylan was performing in Greenwich Village coffeehouses and folk clubs and preparing for the release of his first album. And Kris Kristofferson, his words delivered by an exuberant Janis Joplin, had not yet explained to us that freedom was just another word for nothing left to lose.

As the regular-season champion, Rockaway enjoyed home-field advantage. That meant the game would be played at Far Rockaway High School, the Lynvets' least favorite field—dreary, mist-shrouded, hard for their fans to get to. To make matters worse, it was an icy day, with a killing wind. Looking at the sparse crowd on their side of the field, the Lynvets wondered how many of their fans had awakened that morning, checked out the weather, and decided they needed to save their strength for the New Year's Eve festivities that evening. Rockaway, by contrast, had at least two thousands fans, along with two costumed, thoroughly oiled knights prancing around on horseback.

Snow from a recent storm was piled along the fences. Once white and cheery, the snow had taken on a dirty brown glaze. As the two o'clock game time approached, the field was frozen and uneven, studded with pockets of ice. Mud had frozen in jagged peaks, jutting like crude spearheads from the rock-hard ground. It was so cold that the football felt like a brick to Tommy Wall, his fingers skimming clumsily over the pebble grain as they sought purchase on the pigskin.

The Lynvets had practiced every night the previous week at Pal's Oval, adjacent to Cross Bay Oval in Woodhaven. For illumination, they plugged the portable lights that they stored in the basement of McLaughlin's bar into the city electric line. They also practiced Saturday morning. Tommy Wall thought the practices had been good ones, crisp and efficient. Larry Kelly and Bob Bushman, huddling on the sidelines as the team warmed up, felt differently. They were proud of their team. It had played well, if not brilliantly, during the season and bravely fought back from near extinction. There was no question they could win this day, turn the tables on Rockaway just as the Lynvets had in 1959. But unlike the nights of practice leading up to that championship game two years earlier, culminating in the boozy sing-along at the Flora Dora and Peter Connor's rousing impersonation of George M. Cohan, last week's practices had seemed flat, emotionless.

The weather—frigid temperatures and a flaying wind—was a big part of the problem. Lynvet practices were usually fun. Not these practices. It was so miserable that no one wanted to be there. There was something else. Neither Kelly nor Bushman gave voice to it, but both realized how much the team missed Peter. Not so much his play-making ability, but the emotion that he generated, a refuse-to-lose attitude that swept through his wide-eyed teammates like a contagion, that grabbed them and shook them and battered them and flung them from side to side and left them believing that nothing in their life would be as emotionally crippling as walking off the field on a championship Sunday as losers. After Friday night's practice, a number of the Lynvets had gone barhopping, hoping to re-create the spirit of the Flora Dora. But the occasion seemed forced and didn't quite come off, and the players who participated arrived at practice the next morning with little to show for the evening's revelries except beery breath and mild hangovers.

The bleakness of the day cast a primordial mist over the field, as if rival tribes on an isolated plain were about to engage in a struggle of interest to no one but themselves, with implications that would extend no further than the next few hours. Really, who cared if the era of Lynvet dominance continued another year or two or three? I would have, I guess, had I known the game was going to be played that day, but I didn't, and I had other things on my mind. I was up in Connecticut with one of my Annapolis roommates, Dave

Ahern, thinking about the Holly Ball, which we were going to attend in our dress uniforms that night.

The Lynvets, on their first possession, got the ball on their own thirty-yard line and commenced a signature Lynvet drive. No big plays, but sustained progress—Aragona and Montore off tackle, around end; Mike Faulkner up the middle; Wall completing short, ball-control passes. It was as perfect a drive as the Lynvets had mounted all year. Tommy could feel the excitement in the huddle, the faces of his teammates looking expectantly at him, trusting him, knowing that this sequence of plays, and the touchdown sure to conclude it, would be a statement, a line in the sand, letting Rockaway know that the good times were over. Disbelieving silence from the Rockaway fans as the Lynvets ground out first down after first down.

Suddenly Joe Aragona burst over right tackle, shook off two defenders and drove toward the end zone. From where Tommy stood, it looked close. But no, Joe had been brought down short of the goal line. Tommy trotted over and checked to see where the refs had spotted the ball. Great, he thought, the one-yard line. We're going in on the next play. He turned and looked for Al Schneeberg, around whom the huddle would form. Then he saw him. The little center was on the ground, his helmet off, wincing in pain, rubbing his leg. Al had been hit on the play and his leg had cramped up. The players gathered around Schneeberg, waiting for the pain to subside. But it wasn't easing. Al would have to go out, at least for a few plays. Kelly sent in Ronnie Grier, a defensive standout who rarely played center, to replace him.

Tommy had never become comfortable taking the snap from Ronnie. With Al, the snap was automatic, as it should be. Now, as the injury time-out ended and Ronnie jogged onto the field, Tommy called another time-out, this time to take some practice snaps from the backup center.

Quarterback and center moved to the sideline. Eight snaps executed satisfactorily, though Tommy was still troubled. He knew himself. He practiced so hard, committed so much to muscle memory, that he could feel any hitch in the rhythm of the snap.

Back on the field, Tommy called Mike Faulkner's number, but the moment the ball smacked into his hands, Tommy knew he didn't quite have it. He spun to his right as Faulkner closed on him, eyes fixed on the hole, arms moving into position to take the hand-off, right arm up across his chest, left arm down across his midriff, forming a pocket for Tommy to slip the ball into. And Tommy did, but not smoothly, more of a lunge, because he didn't have full control of the ball. And because Tommy never had full control, Mike had even less when he tried to close his arms over it. And then Mike didn't have the ball at all, Rockaway did, a seventy-yard drive wasted.

Rockaway's defense, little short of impregnable all year, had felt an all-too-familiar chill as the Lynvets glided effortlessly down the field to the threshold of their end zone. Now, after the fumble, Knight defenders seemed emboldened, back on their game, seeing the Lynvets as a good team but not an invincible one. Rockaway had gone into the game knowing that their two victories during the regular season meant nothing, that the Lynvets still thought of themselves as champions and—if the truth were known—that was how the Knights thought of them, too. Until the fumble. After that, the Lynvet luster was no longer blinding. Rockaway knew it could win.

The defensive struggle the coaches had anticipated now materialized. For Rockaway, Mike D'Amato was picking up hard yards. And though he was no John Hourican, their little quarterback, Ray Ortiz, was a cool, capable signal caller and an effective, if not terribly graceful, runner. Early in the second quarter, the Knights scored, converted, and went up 8–0.

The Rockaway touchdown roused the Lynvets out of the lethargy that had set in following the fumble. In the huddle, Tommy Wall sensed the team coming back to life. With a few minutes left in the half, the Lynvets began another drive. Aragona and Montore were getting outside, picking up good yardage on sweeps. Tommy completed short-possession passes to Eddie Keane and Bobby Schmitt. Throughout the half Tommy had been watching the Rockaway linebacker on the right side. He was aggressive, con-

stantly pinching in. On a couple of occasions he had crashed
through and leveled Tommy a split second after he had gotten off a
pass. "You no-face-mask mother fucker, I'm gonna fuck you up,"
the linebacker said after the second knockdown. *Time to pay,*
thought Tommy. He reached back into the Lynvet repertoire for a
Paul Frey special, a play they hadn't used in weeks, one where he
rode the fullback into the line, then pulled the ball out and pitched
it to Aragona coming around behind. The play depended on the
Rockaway linebacker allowing himself to be suckered by the fake,
and strong blocking by the Lynvet tackle, end, and flanker. Along
with a healthy dose of Aragona magic.

The linebacker bit, flattening Tommy just as he pitched the ball
to Joe, but taking himself out of the play as he did so. The blockers
did their job, and Aragona fought his way downfield, spinning
away from a defender and into the end zone just as he was buried
under a swarm of tacklers. The conversion attempt failed, leaving
the teams at 8–6 as the first half ended.

The schoolbus that had carried the Lynvets to the field doubled
as a locker room at halftime. The players called to the driver to turn
up the heat. Most of the uniforms had blood on them. The spikes
of frozen mud had taken their toll. Arms and legs sported long
gashes, bordered by diaphanous flaps of shredded skin. The
co-captains, Teddy Spiess and Eddie Keane, went from player to
player, smacking them on the back, telling them to just keep playing as they had been, but no more mistakes, and they would walk
off the field as Lynvets always did in big games, as winners. Jackie
Meyer, his eyes seeming to spin, was all over his fellow defensive
players. "Nothing! Nothing! They get nothing!"

Neither team could move the ball on their first two possessions
of the second half. Midway through the third quarter the Lynvets
began another drive. Again it was Aragona, Faulkner, and Montore
finding the holes the line kept opening for them, or sweeping the
ends. Tommy Wall could feel it. The team was in and out of the
huddle in a matter of seconds, making its way down the field. With
Schneeberg back at center, Tommy was confident there would be
no fumbles. Handoff, handoff, pitchout, handoff, pitchout. The

way the team was moving, Tommy felt he could have driven them into the icy surf a few blocks away. He almost felt cheated when they crossed the goal line and had to stop. Once again the conversion attempt failed, but now the score was 12–8 Lynvets.

Rockaway could do nothing with the kickoff, and the Lynvet defense led by Spiess and Meyer swarmed noisily back onto the field, as if they had been cheated of playing time because the offense had taken so long to score. The Rockaway fans tried to jump-start their offense, but it continued to stall. The sun was beginning to go down and the wind was whipping up, but the ground had given way here and there to pounding cleats and temperatures that had risen slightly above freezing by midafternoon. Most of the field remained like concrete, but patches of mud mottled the heavily trafficked portions of the field, making the footing uncertain.

As the fourth quarter began, the Lynvets began to move again, grinding it out, using up the clock. Then Joe Aragona took a swing pass from Tommy Wall that caught Rockaway off guard. Suddenly Joe was streaking down the left sideline all alone, only a single Knight defender in pursuit.

Then, unaccountably, or so it seemed to Larry Kelly and Bob Bushman, Joe cut back into the middle of the field in an effort to avoid his pursuer and ran into the arms of three Rockaway players.

"Shit!" shouted Kelly, slamming his clipboard to the ground. Bushman shook his head, a voice screaming in his brain: *There's no one in this league that can bring Joe down one-on-one. And he cuts back?*

Even so, Joe had taken the ball inside the twenty. But for the second time in the game, the Lynvets were unable to capitalize on exceptional field position. Little more than a minute after Aragona put the Lynvets in position to salt away the game, they were turning the ball over to Rockaway.

All afternoon long the Lynvets had kept Mike D'Amato under control. Now, though, with the game on the line, D'Amato took over—he and the little quarterback, Ray Ortiz. Neither was getting loose for long runs, and Ortiz was not connecting on his passes. But time and time again in what was clearly Rockaway's final drive, as their fans alternated between ear-splitting cheers and deathly silence when Ortiz called signals, the two backs picked up crucial first downs. The Lynvets consistently had them in long yardage situations, third and six, fourth and five. Each time, when giving up the ball meant an agonizing end to another season, D'Amato, with punishing runs, or Ortiz, with ugly scrambles, picked up the yardage for a first down. But the drive was eating up time.

Ten seconds left, Rockaway on the Lynvet eight-yard line. Slick ball, bad footing, it didn't matter, it had to be a pass. And the Lynvets knew what it was going to be, Rockaway's old standby, D'Amato through the line, then a sharp cut toward the right sideline. The Lynvets even had a name for the play: the D'Amato Special.

They were right. D'Amato burst through the line as Ortiz dropped back to pass. From their positions at the opposite ends of the defensive line, Eddie Keane and Bobby Schmitt broke toward the quarterback. Keane fought his way through the blockers to Ortiz and managed to snag a cleat as the quarterback tried to roll away from him.

D'Amato, meanwhile, lost his footing in the mud as he tried to make his cut and fell flat on his back in the end zone. Ortiz, unaware that D'Amato had taken a pratfall, tried to shake off Keane as he waited for his big receiver to break from the pack toward the sideline. Finally, on faith, he threw where he expected D'Amato to be.

Charging in from the opposite side from Keane, Schmitt leaped into the air, swatting at the ball as it left the quarterback's hand. A split second earlier and Schmitt would have batted the ball to the ground. A moment later he would have missed it completely. Either way, the Lynvet victory would have been sealed. Instead, Bobby just managed to tick the ball and knock it off course. That would have been fine if D'Amato had been in the right flat, where he was supposed to be and where Ortiz had aimed his pass, since the ball was definitely not headed in that direction. Now, though, it was floating straight ahead, fluttering really, a ruptured duck, a wounded sparrow, a piece of shit as passes go, except for one thing:

it was fluttering right toward the spot where D'Amato lay on the ground. Panicked Lynvet defenders dove for the ball.

No one could reach it. Instead, the ball settled in the lap of Mike D'Amato, who wrapped his arms around it and rolled to his left, cradling it to his chest.

"Touchdown!" shouted the ref. "Game over."

As the Lynvets walked off the field, they could hear horns blare. Some Rockaway players came over to shake hands, among them D'Amato, who did the same thing win or lose so there was no way you could accuse him of rubbing it in. He found Tommy Wall and told him he had played a great game.

"I was at the league meeting last week," Tommy told Mike. "They voted you MVP. You deserve it."

"Thank you," said Mike.

Kelly assembled the Lynvets in the stands as the raucous serenade of automobile horns intensified, as headlights flashed, as expletives from Rockaway's fans, though not from its players, rained down on them.

"You're champions," Kelly said. "Walk off this field like champions. Keep your heads up." He and Bushman sat together in the front of the bus on the ride back to the Imperial, where the team had dressed for the game. The closest of friends, they barely exchanged a word, as if they sensed that something had happened beyond the loss of a football game and they weren't ready to talk about it.

31

Distant Thunder

*L*arry Kelly dropped out of sight for the next three weeks. Some said he had gone on the drunk to end all drunks. When he finally surfaced, he rededicated himself to recruiting Mike D'Amato. It took another year, but he did it by telling Mike he had contacts at Hofstra College out on Long Island and might be able to swing a football scholarship for him if he played a season for the Lynvets. For years after Mike's defection, Tommy Chapman, Woody Wickers, and others of D'Amato's old teammates refused to talk to him. And they never forgave Kelly.

"If you can get the kid a scholarship, get it for him," fumed Richie Knott, the Rockaway coach. "Why hold him back a year? Just so your team can win? And the funny thing is, they didn't win with Mike."

The Lynvets did not even make it to the championship game in 1963, the one year D'Amato played for them. D'Amato was as good as he'd even been, but Rockaway beat them in the semifinals, only to lose the title to Torchy Smith's fully matured Garity Knights, who completed a second-straight undefeated season as they went about becoming the new Lynvets. Torchy was so thrilled after his first victory over the Lynvets that he raced across the field, embraced the flabbergasted Kelly, and kissed him.

But Larry Kelly came through for D'Amato. Through his friendship with Howdie Meyers, the Hofstra coach, Kelly helped secure a scholarship for Mike. It didn't hurt that Meyers had not seen too many ballplayers like D'Amato wander onto the Hempstead campus.

Judi Dunham and Mike Montore were married on a Monday in October 1962, the day after a Lynvet football game and just days before the Cuban Missile Crisis flared. As Judi left her parents' house that morning for the courthouse in Mineola, her mother hollered after her, "You'll be back in six months."

Mike and Judi thought they had made an appointment at the courthouse, but the judge was not expecting them.

"Where are your witnesses?" asked the judge, surveying the empty courtroom where the ceremony was to take place.

They told the judge they didn't know they needed any. Grumpily, the judge told them to stay where they were, went out in the corridor, collared two workmen, one white and one black, and began the ceremony.

"Do you, Mike Montrose, take this woman . . ."

Mike let the judge's mispronunciation slide, though for years after Judi would say, "Mike, do you really think we're married?" The ceremony took at most five minutes. Afterward, they stopped at Casey's, a bar where Mike could always get served when he was underage. Stash, the owner, bought them each a bottle of Champale and ceremoniously poured them into glasses normally reserved for fifteen-cent beers.

"Congratulations," said Stash.

The only other person there was a guy with throat cancer. "Congratulations," he croaked from the end of the bar.

The next year, Mike scraped together three hundred dollars and enrolled in a computer school on 42nd Street in Manhattan that was arguably a notch above the places that advertised on the inside of matchbook covers. He went there every Saturday for twenty weeks, he and Judi fretting each Friday about whether he would have enough money for train fare. Only three of the forty guys finished the course. Mike was one of them. His new credential as a programmer in his hip pocket, he set aside two weeks to find a job. He spent the first week getting laughed at. The second week he went to an employment agency on Wall Street. They had one posting for a programmer, at a bank. The agency told Mike he had no chance. They had sent fifteen applicants to the bank, most with college degrees, and hadn't placed a single one.

"So what do you have to lose if you send a sixteenth guy over there?" said Mike.

At the bank, the man who did the hiring drew on his pipe and began a well-rehearsed brush-off.

Mike stopped him. "Look, I know you've spoken to a lot of people, but you need to understand something. I'm not what you think. I'm not your average guy. I'm a guy that doesn't fail."

He got the job. A hundred and five dollars a week. He still had to work construction at night, but it was a start.

Things looked like they were working out for Larry Kelly, too. Not long after Mike D'Amato entered Hofstra, Kelly was named head coach of the football team at Manhattan College, in Riverdale, just north of the city. Manhattan had dropped football during World War II, but thanks to a student-driven organizing and fund-raising effort it was starting a club team, with the prospect of gaining varsity status a few years down the line. Kelly named Peter Connor and Chipper Dombo his assistant coaches. For Larry, it was the chance of a lifetime.

Through a friend, Tommy Wall made a connection with Mesa Junior College in Colorado and was offered a football scholarship. Lightning had struck the Hoople. To flesh out his academic background, he went to night school five nights a week, taking chemistry, math, and Latin. He passed them all.

He played football at Mesa and saw another part of the world. He knew now that he wanted to be a football coach, high school for sure, but who knew what might follow. He earned an associate's degree in physical education, then moved on to Colorado State College in Greeley. Nothing worked there.

Depressed, he left school, took off for Denver, and went to work for the railroad. By now he was drinking more than ever. After six months, he returned to Woodside and became a bartender.

"It was the ideal job for a drunk," he would later say. "You drink for free. You're around the love of your life."

At about the same time Mike D'Amato was starting his lone season with the Lynvets, I was beginning my senior year at the Naval Academy. My first class cruise had been aboard a destroyer, the USS *Barton*, in the Mediterranean. This time we were treated as junior officers both at sea and ashore. We picked up the ship in Malta, made port calls in Rappallo, on the Italian Riviera, Beirut, and Theoule, a small coastal town outside Cannes. The cruise ended there in late July. Those of us who wanted to spend more time in Europe were turned loose. I took the train to Rome and hooked up with a couple of Academy friends with whom I traveled for the next two weeks. I spent a third week on my own in Paris, checking into a small hotel on the Left Bank recommended by a stylish woman about my age whom I met on the Orient Express. She said she planned to stay there, too.

She was an American of Baltic descent with just the trace of an accent. For the first few days we went our own way even though the concierge, unbidden, had given us rooms on the same floor a few doors down from each other. One day we met in the small lobby and decided to go to dinner that night. After that we did other things together—strolled along the river, sipped cheap wine at sidewalk cafés in the afternoon, barhopped in the evening—returning to our separate rooms after midnight. I was in love with Janie, but this seemed different, something rooted in time and place. Paris, the Left Bank, a chance meeting on the Orient Express. There was something else. I was twenty-three and unpracticed and nervous as hell about it, so I was putting myself in what Catholics call the occasion of sin and rooting for Satan the way I used to root for Old Reliable.

My last night in Paris we returned to the hotel later than usual. I walked her to her door, kissed her goodnight, and went to my room. I climbed into bed but couldn't sleep. After about an hour, I got up, sat on the side of the bed, struggled lamely against a cascade of morose delectations. Eliot's lines from "Prufrock" flashed through my brain:

> *"That is not what I meant, at all.*
> *That is not it, at all."*

Well, I thought, we'll see. I grabbed a half-full bottle of wine, padded down the hall, knocked on her door. She smiled when she saw me. She didn't look like she had been sleeping, either.

"I thought you'd never come," she said, taking my hand, drawing me into the room.

In August of 1963, about a week after I returned from Paris, I received a call at home from Captain Roger McLain, who had relieved the overweight lieutenant we'd nicknamed TF Squared as the Seventh Company officer at the end of Plebe Year. McLain, an Air Force exchange officer for whom we would have stormed the gates of Hell, said he had selected me as company commander for the first three months of the academic year, up through the Army Game in late November. The company, the basic unit of the Brigade, numbered about 160 men.

I invited my father to Annapolis for the first football weekend. At Navy home games and a few away games, notably Army-Navy, each of the Academy's twenty-four companies marched onto the field, accompanied by the Naval Academy Band and the Drum and Bugle Corps. My father was in the stands as I led my company through the gates of the Navy-Marine Corps Memorial Stadium. The facing of the stands on both sides of the field were emblazoned with the names of famous Navy and Marine battles—Midway, Leyte Gulf, Guadalcanal, Iwo Jima, Inchon. As we passed through the gates of the stadium, the PA announcer said, "The Seventh Company, commanded by Midshipman Lieutenant Robert R. Timberg of Kew Gardens, New York." We executed a left turn that took us toward a spot facing the Navy fans. As I gave the order "Company . . . Halt!" I searched the stands for my dad, but I couldn't pick him out.

"Ladies and Gentlemen, the Brigade of Midshipmen," the announcer intoned when all twenty-four companies had arrayed themselves on the field. The crowd rose to its feet and cheered.

Midshipmen were required to sit together during the game, so I planned to meet my father when it was over. Moments after the kickoff an announcement came over the PA system: "Midshipman Timberg, report to the Officer of the Day." My friends looked at me. I shrugged. "No idea," I said.

The OD had a grave look on his face when I found him. "Your father collapsed in the stands right after the march-on," he said. "They took him in an ambulance to the emergency room at Anne Arundel General. We've got a car waiting to take you there."

I ran for the car. Christ, I thought, I can't remember my father having a sick day in his entire life. Speeding through the narrow streets of Annapolis, we reached the hospital in minutes. As we pulled up to the emergency room entrance, my father emerged with a man in a medical smock. They were laughing it up like old friends. I leaped from the car and hurried over.

"Dad, are you all right? What happened?"

"I'm fine, Bobby."

He looked fine. I turned to the doctor.

"Your father just had a little episode of vertigo up in the stands," he said. "It happens sometimes. The steps are steep, you're kind of high up. But, really, he's fine."

I gave him a look that said I was not convinced.

"We checked him out thoroughly," the doctor said, putting his arm around my father's shoulders. "I know what you're thinking. His heart's fine. Heart like a horse. Your dad's a great guy. He was just telling me about his days with the Marx Brothers."

My father had been trying to break into the conversation.

"Bobby, Bobby," he said, "I'm standing up there in the stands and they announce you as the commander and I'm all excited and you come marching onto the field and I hear the band and I'm watching your feet and the band goes boom and you're out of step. Your foot's supposed to hit the ground on the boom and your foot's up in the air. And I keep watching and thinking boom, step, but you're off. Can't you tell when you're out of step, for chrissakes? So I'm watching and all of a sudden I get dizzy and the next thing I know I'm on the ground."

What if he had hit his head on the concrete steps? I wondered. I might have killed my father because I can't keep a beat. I decided that he was wrong, that I was on the beat, but because light and sound travel at different speeds he saw my feet hitting before he heard the drum. In other words, the same thing would have happened if he had been watching some other guy. I tried to explain this to him, received a disbelieving stare for my trouble.

I was in sick bay in the basement of Bancroft Hall one afternoon in November undergoing my precommissioning physical. The television was tuned to a soap opera, *As the World Turns*. The hero was agonizing over whether he should remarry his ex-wife. Suddenly the screen flashed the word "Bulletin" and a jacketless Walter Cronkite appeared.

"In Dallas, Texas, three shots were fired at President Kennedy's motorcade. The first reports say the President was seriously wounded, that he slumped over in Mrs. Kennedy's lap, she cried out, 'Oh, no!' and the motorcade went on . . . The wounds perhaps could be fatal." There followed a string of details. Texas School Book Depository Building. Something about the Dallas Trade Mart. Governor Connally also hit. The open presidential limousine tearing off for the hospital. Cronkite passed on an unconfirmed report from an unfamiliar reporter named Dan Rather saying the president was dead.

The Army-Navy game, scheduled for that Saturday, was postponed a week. Janie, in college in Ohio, had final exams, so she couldn't make it to Philadelphia for the rescheduled contest. That meant she wouldn't see me leading the company into Municipal Stadium before a hundred thousand fans. I was disappointed, though it seemed a small thing with the country in agony, our national iris imprinted with images of a riderless horse, a woman in black, and a small boy saluting.

Navy beat Army 21–15. The team was led, as it had been for the past two years, by quarterback Roger Staubach, who though only a junior won the Heisman Trophy. My class, the Class of 1964, had thus beaten Army all four years we had been at the Academy. Heisman Trophy winners Bellino and Staubach served as bookends for our time at Annapolis. Navy ended the season ranked number two in the nation.

By then I had made a decision that meant I'd never snap on an ensign's shoulder boards. I decided I preferred the gold bars of a Marine second lieutenant. When pressed to explain my reasons, I facetiously replied that I wanted to sleep under the stars at Camp Pendleton, the giant Marine base south of Los Angeles, and date Hollywood starlets on the weekends. In fact, I wanted to command troops and I thought I'd get the chance sooner in the Marine Corps than in the Navy. There was another reason. Marshall. Weber. Finn. Dever. Kelly. Donelan. Gallagher. McLaughlin. Rooney. Mulligan. Dombo. Vaughan. Delahunty. Brady. Girolamo. Ferriola. Keane. It was what Lynvets did.

In the weeks after Christmas leave, our musical tastes abruptly changed as the sounds of a British pop group called the Beatles swept Bancroft Hall. "I Want to Hold Your Hand" and "Love Me Do" blasted from every upperclass room. We had never heard anything like it. Each night after evening meal and before study hour began, the first classmen in our company crammed into the room of Sandy Coward, a tall, blond, with-it classmate, the same one who as a plebe confused a firstie's girlfriend with her dog. Sandy, among the few midshipmen who knew how to dance to the new music, generously gave us lessons. I flunked. Problems with the beat.

Janie and I spent New Year's Eve together in New York. About three in the morning we wandered into a tavern off Times Square. Most of the crowd had cleared out, so it was easy to find a spot at the bar. An older guy, maybe thirty-five, trim, short hair, was sitting by himself. Janie and I were tipsy. He was a lot further along. A nice guy, but not much for small talk. He turned out to be a Marine major back in the States after several months as a military adviser in South Vietnam. He said things were not going well over there. I told him that I was a midshipman and would be commissioned in the Marine Corps in June. He smiled sadly and shook his head. I don't think we talked much after that. I didn't know a lot about Vietnam other than that we had a few thousand advisers in the country. Sure, I knew the French had lost a colonial war there, that they had been badly outmaneuvered at a place called Dien Bien Phu, and that guerrilla forces backed by communist North Vietnam were attempting to topple the shaky pro-American regime in the south. I figured the major had reasons for his distress, but, hey, it was New Year's and I was in love.

We graduated on June 3, 1964. Of the 1,258 young men who entered the Academy four years earlier, only 927 of us were left, a casualty rate of 26 percent, amazing when you consider the place is free—in fact, they pay you to go there. A month later, a freshly hatched second lieutenant, I reported to the Basic School in Quantico, Virginia. It was early July, and Vietnam still seemed a blip on the horizon.

Quantico was physically demanding. Long marches, night patrols in snake-infested woods, the obstacle course, the confidence course, the rifle range, hand-to-hand combat. We also had classes, mostly small unit tactics, and indoctrination into the history and traditions of the Corps that included tales of the fabled Chesty Puller, the greatest of all Marines, holder of five—five!—Navy Crosses and who said at the Chosin Reservoir, "They've got us surrounded. The bastards won't get away this time." But Quantico was not the Naval Academy. We worked hard during the day, but the evening, unless we had some night maneuver, was ours. Also, with a few exceptions, we were free on weekends.

My roommate at Quantico was Dave Wilshin, with whom I had lived for more than two years at the Academy. Janie, who was between her junior and senior year in college, was working as a waitress that summer at a mildly raunchy restaurant and bar called the Bottle & Cork in Dewey Beach on the Delaware shore, a few miles south of the more genteel coastal resort of Rehoboth Beach. Dave was dating a college friend of Janie's, so we made a run to Dewey Beach our first weekend at Quantico, a distance of about two hundred miles.

The owner of the Bottle & Cork, a rotund, saucy woman who wore ladybug pins all over her dress, turned out to be the aunt of a midshipman from our Academy company who had graduated a year ahead of Dave and me and had also gone into the Marines. She liked us and generously offered us jobs for Friday and Saturday nights, which would cover our expenses on weekends. Dave was a bartender. I would have been one, too, except I could not master drawing a draft. Instead I checked IDs. Every weekend Dave and I would make the four-hour drive to Dewey Beach, work in the evening, and play during the day. Janie and her friend were living in a small cottage behind a Chinese restaurant in Rehoboth called Bob Ching's, so that's where Dave and I stayed. Sunday night late we drove back to Quantico, usually arriving in time to get maybe two hours' sleep after listening to preachers and gospel music, the only thing on AM radio in the middle of the night. Invariably, our first class Monday morning was hand-to-hand combat. Dave and I, for obvious reasons, maneuvered to pair up with each other.

By then, Lyndon Johnson and Barry Goldwater had locked up the Democratic and Republican presidential nominations. Vietnam was an issue in the campaign; Goldwater was pressing for greater American support for the increasingly embattled South Vietnamese government, Johnson trying to display restraint while demonstrating that he was not soft on communism. He increased aid to Saigon but said he would not send American boys to fight a war that Asian boys should be fighting for themselves. That worked for me.

One Saturday night in late July, it must have been close to three in the morning, Janie and I were heading back to Rehoboth after finishing work at the Bottle & Cork. Our relationship was in one of its down periods. As she was prone to do from time to time, she was explaining to me, in a patient way that drove me crazy, that I was boring. I was getting angry.

"I have no idea what you're talking about," I said.

Just then the town water tower came into view on our right.

"Have you ever thought of climbing that?" she asked.

"Hell, no," I replied.

"See what I mean?" she said.

"Goddammit!" I said, stopping the car, climbing out, slamming the door behind me.

I was nearly to the top when I heard the sirens. Then a spotlight hit me, pinning me like a cat burglar trying to jimmy a tenth-story window. The cops told me to come down. I glanced toward the ground. The cops looked very small. Everything did. I didn't see Janie.

I made it down, far more slowly than I had gotten up. The cops asked me for identification. I passed them my driver's license and my military ID.

"You're a Marine?" one of them asked.

I said I was.

"An officer? You got to be kidding me."

I assured him that I was not.

"So what the hell were you doing up there? That's as fucking dumb as it gets."

I started to explain that my girlfriend had dared me to do it, but before I got more than one or two words out of my mouth I realized how stupid I sounded.

Instead, I said, "I'm a Marine."

The cops warned me to stay off the water tower, promised to throw me in jail if they caught me climbing it again. "Semper Fi," one of them shouted out the window of their squad car as they drove away. Janie came out from behind some trees a moment later.

"Sorry," she said, looking sheepish, an expression I had never seen on her face before.

In early August, there were reports that two American destroyers had been fired on by North Vietnamese vessels in a section of the South China Sea called the Tonkin Gulf. In Washington, President Johnson asked Congress for authority to respond. The so-called Tonkin Gulf Resolution granted him extraordinary powers. It passed the Senate with just two dissenting votes. The House of Representatives approved it unanimously. When the news reached Quantico, thirty miles to the south, one of my lieutenant friends said, gleefully, "We gonna go."

32

Mount Out

*W*e finished Quantico in December. I had asked for and been assigned to the infantry, my first duty station Camp Pendleton with the First Marine Division. I started the drive to California in late January 1965, taking the southern route along Interstate 40. As I passed through Nashville, there were radio reports of racial trouble in a small Alabama town about 250 miles to the south named Selma. Martin Luther King Jr. and nearly eight hundred others had been arrested when they marched on the courthouse to protest discrimination in voter registration.

I pulled into Camp Pendleton and discovered at FirstMarDiv headquarters that I had been assigned to an antitank battalion instead of an infantry unit. Technically, it was an infantry officer's billet, but I wanted to lead a rifle platoon. Instead I was being given a platoon of lightly armored tracked vehicles called Ontos that were armed with six recoilless cannon. Their mission was to take out enemy tanks and provide covering fire for ground troops. I checked around, determined that the three infantry officers at the bottom alphabetically of my Basic School class had been sent to antitanks instead of an infantry battalion.

I reported to my new commanding officer, a lieutenant colonel, and explained to him, politely but firmly, that I did not want to be in his battalion. Less politely, and more firmly, he explained to me where the desires of very junior second lieutenants fit into the battle plan of the Marine Corps. Not a good start.

I called Janie that night and told her how upset and frustrated I was. We had been engaged over Thanksgiving and were to be married in the summer. She was understanding until, under her gentle probing, I let slip that, yes, running an Ontos outfit was probably safer than leading a rifle platoon. Then she went berserk.

Janie and I were married under crossed swords at the Naval Academy chapel in July. My ushers included fellow Marine Dave Wilshin. Absent Academy friends included Ron Benigo, also a Marine, and Navy men Tom Richman and Dave Ahern. They were already overseas or in the final stages of predeployment training for Vietnam. The only nonmilitary male member of the wedding party was my best man, Joe Aragona, irrepressible as always, by then a graduate student at Adelphi College on Long Island.

Janie and I honeymooned in the Canadian Rockies, though the two weeks we planned on were scaled back to a week by the Marine Corps. Elements of the division had already departed for South Vietnam. The day after we returned from the honeymoon, a lieutenant in my battalion came by our little apartment in San Clemente just north of Pendleton to say we would be mounting out in a month.

Many of my fellow lieutenants couldn't wait to go, at least that's what they claimed, but maybe that was their way of steeling themselves for what lay ahead. I was in no hurry and was happy when our departure date was moved back to January. Those stolen months were wonderful ones for Janie and me. We moved from San Clemente to a small town about ten miles to the north called Laguna Beach, which had a lovely beach, cliffs that swelled high above the ocean, and a long-established colony of artists. Janie had taken a job teaching severely mentally retarded children in a public school in Garden Grove, which was even farther north, so our commutes were about the same, though in opposite directions. Our apartment was above a three-car garage on Thalia Street, two short blocks from the ocean, which we could see from our tiny porch.

I thought of those months as found time. I was happier than I had ever been. Though the war was waiting for me, I was finally able catch my breath, to reflect on the long journey that had taken me from West End Avenue and the Greystone Hotel and Brighton Beach and the madness of Kew Gardens to a place where I could sit on a rock with the woman I loved and watch the surf break gently over my feet. Occasionally, but only occasionally, I lifted my eyes to the horizon and wondered what lay in store for me beyond it.

I was a long way from the Lynvet practice field and, in ways I only dimly understood, so was my nation. A storm was gathering in America. The year just ended had seen lacerating clashes in the South between black Americans and the police. The Watts section of south central Los Angeles, about forty miles north of Camp Pendleton, burned for six days in August. Though most Americans supported the war, an antiwar movement was building, especially on college campuses. In April, twenty-five thousand people marched on Washington to protest the U.S. bombing of North Vietnam. Mid-October saw antiwar "Vietnam Day" rallies at forty colleges. The following month, a Baltimore Quaker, Norman Morrison, set himself on fire and died below the Pentagon office window of Robert McNamara, the secretary of defense.

A generation, my generation, was about to crack along a fault line called Vietnam, throwing my old Lynvet teammates and me together again, this time on the wrong side of history. The war would last ten long years and haunt the nation at least through the end of the century. We all made choices. Some of us went, some of us didn't, and a lot of us died. Those who didn't go had their reasons for deciding as they did. And amid their bluster, self-absorption, and insufferable pose of moral superiority, they raised troubling questions about the war that our leaders seemed at a loss to answer.

Did I ever consider not boarding that troop ship in Long Beach in January 1966? No, not once. I was a child of World War II and Korea. I came of age in the 1950s. I had marched in John Kennedy's inaugural parade. On that day the new president proclaimed that Americans were willing to "pay any price, bear any burden, meet any hardship to advance the cause of freedom in the world." I believed him.

We were both wrong, but I didn't know that then, and it probably wouldn't have mattered. I was a Lynvet. I knew what Lynvets did. Father Lynch had set the example. Larry Kelly had taught me well. And I believed in America.

On a brisk day in January, I climbed the gangway to the quarterdeck of the USS *Talladega*, snapped a crisp salute at the flag flying from the ship's fantail, turned, and saluted the officer of the deck.

"Request permission to come aboard, sir."

"Permission granted," the O.D. said, returning my salute.

I was no longer the awkward boy of Kew Gardens days, but I was not Chesty Puller, either. As the ship got under way, I waved so long to Janie, who looked scared and and small and very alone amid the wives, kids, parents, and girlfriends clustered on the dock. As for me, it was out to sea and off to war, steaming westward into the last lingering shadows of Twilight Time.

Epilogue

Mike D'Amato remembered his famous catch differently from the Lynvets across the line from him that long-ago day. In his version, the play went pretty much the way it had been drawn up. He blew past the center, cut toward the right sideline, never fell. Ortiz's pass was behind him, but he was able to reach back with his right hand, flip it over his head, then bring it in with both hands.

Either way, same result.

D'Amato fulfilled one of Larry Kelly's dreams, a Lynvet making it to the National Football League. Mike carried the dream even further. He played on the New York Jets team that improbably upset the heavily favored Baltimore Colts in Super Bowl III in 1969.

In that way in which our lives veer off in curious directions when we're not paying attention, Bob Bushman found his life's work not because of his studies at Fordham, but because of the after-hours

job he took to pay his way through school. At Seaboard and Western Airlines, he ran airlifts out of Vietnam, Biafra, and Idi Amin's
Uganda. Working with the Military Airlift Command, he held a
civilian rank equivalent to a four-star general.

He rose swiftly in the corporate world, as vice president of
Flying Tiger Airlines after that company, a spin-off of Claire
Chennault's old outfit, bought Seaboard, then as president of
Orion Air, the airline subsidiary of a New York Stock Exchange
company called the Aviation Group. By the following year he was
president and chief executive officer of the parent corporation. He
has served on prestigious corporate boards and is considered one of
the nation's leading experts on the handling of air and maritime
cargo.

On a breezy fall day a couple of years ago, Bob, Tommy Wall,
and I went down to Cross Bay Oval to check in on the latest incar-
nation of the Lynvets, a multiracial, multiethnic Peewee league
that provides a wholesome, if hard-hitting, outlet for about 250
neighborhood kids, many of whom would probably be called at risk
in today's environment. Larry Kelly started the league back in
1961. Bob was wearing an only slightly frayed maroon parka with
LYNVETS emblazoned in bold letters on the back and 1954 CHAM-
PIONS embroidered on the front.

"I still have my maroon number seventeen jersey, too, the last
one I ever wore," he smiled. "That's forty-five years ago. I'm a
grown man and I'm still acting like a kid when it comes to the
Lynvets."

Six years after Mike Montore started the job at the bank, he and
Judi were sitting on the patio of a hotel in San Diego, sipping
Bloody Marys, and marveling at the view of the water. Mike was
feeling pleased with himself. His employer, the Avis rental car
company, was holding its annual management conference there. By
then Mike was a supervisor in the Avis computer department. He
and Judi had four kids, a house on the water on Long Island, two

cars, and a small boat. They were not rich, they were not even well-off, but they were no longer barely getting by.

"What's wrong?" asked Mike, annoyed that Judi didn't seem to be sharing his feeling of contentment.

"I don't know, but I know that what we're doing isn't doing it for me," said Judi.

"If this isn't it, then what is?" asked Mike.

"I don't know," said Judi.

"Is it where we live or what we're doing?" asked Mike.

"I guess it's both," said Judi.

"Well, that about covers it, doesn't it?" said Mike.

For Mike, success had come at a cost. Long hours, little time for his kids, even less for Judi. Judi was not only feeling neglected, she was also losing her sense of herself again as she watched other women batter down barriers to personal and professional fulfillment. Mike did not try to explain away her frustration. Just like that, he accepted it. There were, he told her, two issues: Where do we go? What do we do?

That fall, Mike and Judi piled the kids into a nine-hundred-dollar truck with a snowplow on the front and set off for New Hampshire, a state they barely knew existed until a few months earlier, to take over a failing country store near Lake Winnipesaukee. They worked twelve hours a day, seven days a week. They lived in the back of the store. The customer was always right. A woman came in one night for lemon meringue mix. They didn't have it on the shelves, but Judy had some in her cupboard and gave it to the woman. In a year they doubled the business. Again, success came at a price. Mike had quit Avis so that the family could spend more time together, and this was even worse.

"Time to leave," Mike told Judi.

"But we planned to be here for five years," she replied.

"True," said Mike, "but we've done all we wanted to do in one year. If we stay, we'll just be doing penance for overachieving."

Mike and Judi were just getting started. They turned out to have a flair for entrepreneurship and a willingness to take risks. A passing thought from a long-ago football game had stayed with Mike:

Yes, you can get hurt, but you almost never die. And you recover from everything else.

When I met up with him years later, he and Judi were living in a two-hundred-year-old colonial farmhouse on fifty acres of land outside Concord, New Hampshire. The Merrimack River ran along the far border of their property. For ten years they also owned a home on Sanibel Island off the Gulf Coast of Florida, to which they could flee the harsh New England winters.

They owned commercial property in Concord and over the years ran a number of successful businesses. A beauty school. Two hair salons. A tanning salon. A sporting goods store. A sub shop. A Mailboxes Etc. Along the way, Mike earned a bachelor's degree in accounting from New Hampshire College in Manchester, getting straight A's in his final fifteen courses and graduating summa cum laude in June 1977. That fall he was teaching computer science at the school.

One day, after his and Judi's net worth had moved well into the seven-figure range, some odd event provoked a thought about his high school sweetheart and the disrespect shown him by her father. He briefly considered sending the father a golf ball, not a new one, but one that looked new because it had been scrubbed so thoroughly by the best damn golf ball washer around. He decided not to. When he thought of the success that he and Judi had made of their lives, and the deep love that had accompanied it, the idea just seemed stupid.

In the Army, Mike thought of himself as a loser. After four years with the Lynvets, he got it right. By then, as he told the man at the bank, he was a guy who didn't fail. Not himself. Not anyone. Not anymore. Larry Kelly and the Lynvets had been crucial. At a terrible time in his life, he later said, they gave him a place to heal.

I was at my desk in the basement of my home in Bethesda, Maryland, one day in 1989 when the phone rang.

"Hey, Bobby, it's Tommy Wall."

"Hi, Tommy," I said.

I don't think we had talked in twenty-five years, but there was no sense of time having passed. He told me that he and some other Lynvets were planning a reunion for the fall of 1990.

"We ran into each other at an AA meeting and decided to do it," said Tommy. I couldn't tell if he was joking. He was and he wasn't.

By the mid-1970s, Tommy was nearly down for the count, drinking around the clock. He needed seven or eight shots in the morning before he could even read the paper, which he always did in good times and bad. He did his drinking at different bars in the fanciful belief that no one would put together the reality of his life, that he was a pathetic drunk.

He took a few stabs at quitting, tried Alcoholics Anonymous, detox, even managed to stay sober a couple of times for several months. But he still hung out in bars, nursing Cokes, resisting the urge to drink until, each time, the temptation became too great. He became bloated. He was seeing things, hearing things, sweating almost all the time, sensed he was in danger of convulsing.

That's when he stopped. On his own, he went back to AA. "I had no choice and I knew it," he said.

For at least a quarter-century his life had been defined by alcohol. Everything he did had revolved around drinking—fishing, ball games, weddings, wakes. He and his friends went to ski lodges not to ski, but—as they put it—"to get fucked up." He once asked his friends what would happen if Hugh Hefner invited them to the Playboy Mansion, promised them two women apiece, but forbid drinking. Tommy answered his own question: No one would go. For Tommy and his drinking buddies, distances were not measured in miles. How far to the Hamptons? "A good six-pack." Montauk Point? "That's a case of beer for two guys. It's a long trip."

This time, armed with a new resolve to stay out of bars altogether, he succeeded at AA. As he put it, "A bar is no place for a drunk, even if he's drinking Coke." So Tommy saved himself and, in due time, he saved the Lynvets, ending their long diaspora by running them down from one end of the country to the other and bringing them back together in a series of triumphant reunions.

Along the way, Tommy became one of the steadiest, most reliable people in the world. When friends had problems, he was there, not just with a kind word, but with sustained involvement in their lives. He also became, if not rich, then something close to that. Injured in an industrial accident, he took his small settlement, read up on the stock market, did all his own investing, and wound up with an impressive nest egg. He stays out of bars, but he has not become warm and cuddly. His anger can still flare unexpectedly in response to what seems a minor provocation, much like Vietnam veterans I've known who claim to have put the war behind them, only to have their sense of betrayal blindside them at odd moments.

These days he lives with his wife, Kathleen, in a Forest Hills condo. Most afternoons you can find him in the Barnes & Noble on Austin Street reading the latest nonfiction. Either there or out on Jamaica Bay in his kayak.

One day not long ago he called me.

"Tennis isn't a game for people like us, right?" he said.

"Right," I said.

"Well, I'm really into tennis."

The first reunion was held in October 1990 at the Elks Club on Queens Boulevard in Elmhurst. Hughie Mulligan, newly retired from academia, along with Bob Ferriola, Tommy Vaughan, and Chipper Dombo, all retired firefighters, flew in from Florida. At least a dozen Lynvets had manned the firehoses, including steady Eddie Steffens, who would remain on the job into the new century. Larry Kelly arrived from Albuquerque, where he had been living for several years, sporting a western outfit and cowboy boots, but he looked thin and unhealthy and there were whispers that he had cancer. My sister Pat came from California and danced the Lindy with Mike Faulker and other old crushes from cheerleading days.

Peter Connor, a happily married father of three, drove from Cincinnati, where he was in the midst of a successful career as a salesman.

Richie Brady arrived in a van, from which he was lowered in a wheelchair. Though few of the Lynvets knew about it before that night, Richie had suffered from multiple sclerosis for decades, many of his friends believing that the first stirrings of the disease dated back to his playing days, when his coordination deserted him. Peter was standing with about a dozen others at the top of the broad bank of steps leading into the hall, not far from the majestic cast-iron elk that greets commuters streaming home from the city along Queens Boulevard. They all raced down and gathered around Richie. After they welcomed him, an embarrassed silence took hold. The hall had no wheelchair ramp. Everyone was growing uncomfortable, especially Richie. Peter said, "Come on, you guys, let's get Richie up the stairs." Then Peter and some of the others hoisted his wheelchair and, with Peter leading the cheers, carried him triumphantly into the hall as if he were riding the shoulders of exultant teammates after hauling in a pass from Ferriola for the game-winning touchdown.

Joe Aragona and his wife, Muriel, arrived in their new Infiniti Q45. Joe had graduated Adelphi as a theater major and for a time tried his hand at acting. He had several small roles in films and TV commercials and a bit part in *The Godfather*. He's the photographer whose camera Sonny Corleone destroys during the extended wedding scene at the beginning. Along the way, Joe married the daughter of Jack Somack, the wonderful character actor perhaps best remembered for Alka Seltzer's "spicy meatball" commercial in which he moans, "I can't believe I ate the whole thing."

Joe's acting career fizzled, and so did that first marriage. True to form, Joe kept his feet and built a lucrative career in the insurance business. His old teammates greeted him in the manner befitting one of their stars. Before long, though, he was over in a corner with Larry Kelly, explaining—or trying to explain—why he changed direction in the 1961 championship game against Rockaway. All those years later and Larry still wouldn't grant him absolution, rolling his eyes, shaking his head, giving the sputtering Aragona the tight smile that meant he was not convinced.

Mike D'Amato and Bobby Schmitt, meanwhile, found themselves in a shouting match about whose version of D'Amato's catch was the correct one. D'Amato was with the wrong crowd to make his case. Mike Faulkner overheard them. Amazing, Mike thought. This guy has a Super Bowl ring and he's still lying about a sandlot football game.

The evening ended with Peter rambling around the ballroom on someone's shoulders leading endless choruses of "Over There." His trousers were nowhere in sight.

Pat and Rosemarie moved out on my mother in the summer of 1966, shortly after Pat graduated from St. John's University, and took an apartment together a couple of miles away. Pat had a teaching job; Rosemarie was a senior in high school. The separation had a healthy effect on their relationship with my mother, who seemed to be drinking much less in their absence. Pat married her college beau a year later. My mother persuaded her to move back to the Kew Gardens apartment for the two weeks before the July wedding. Big mistake. My mother was drunk almost the entire time. On the day of the marriage, two AA people went to the apartment to try to sober her up, but they couldn't do it and she missed the wedding. I had been wounded in Vietnam that February and was recuperating in a San Diego hospital, so I didn't make the wedding, either. It was one of the best days of Pat's life and one of the most miserable.

But Pat is like Joe Aragona—you can't take her down. These days she's living in New York, teaching in a public high school in the Bronx and trying to put together a Broadway show built around our father's music. Rosemarie, no less resilient, is a therapist in Eugene, Oregon. She specializes in hypnosis, employing it to help people stop smoking, control their weight, manage stress, and overcome their fears, such as fear of failure.

My father died in the summer of 1992 in Scranton, he and his wife having moved there some thirty years earlier. His wife owned a lovely, comfortable home in the suburbs, but my father missed the sounds of a city, so they sold the house and moved to a suite in a downtown hotel that boasted a stunning crystal chandelier in the lobby and had once been something. He remained a minicelebrity there by virtue of his boffo run at the Europa Lounge in 1955. He became a boulevardier, Scranton-style, dropping in on most of the merchants in a four-block circuit he walked each day. Angelo Gallucci at the music store, Henry the barber, whom of course he called Hendry, the boys at Shookey's Deli, who knew he liked his toast "boined" and his soup scalding hot. In his later years, he ate almost every night at Preno's, an Italian restaurant where he was treated like a much-loved uncle. In the 1980s the mayor declared Sammy Timberg Day in Scranton. By then he was a widower, his wife having passed away a few years earlier. Because of her family's prominence, waitresses occasionally called him by her first husband's last name. It took my breath away—not that it happened, but that he found it amusing.

He had been a Christian Scientist for twenty years, which caused enormous tension in his life because he was also a hypochondriac. Rather than go to doctors, he befriended them as a device to keep them at bay, taking one or the other of the local physicians to dinner at least once every couple of weeks. The last decade of his life was colored by public service announcements that finally persuaded him to have his blood pressure checked. He learned his was slightly elevated, nothing serious, no need for medication. Every day after that he dropped in at the office of a doctor friend on Wyoming Avenue and had the nurse take his blood pressure. If you saw him on the street, he always looked like he was fiddling with his watch. Actually, he was checking his pulse.

His idiosyncracies, I now see, obscured his many accomplishments, at least from me, who remained wary of him to the end, as if I could still be infected by his weakness, or what I thought of as his weakness, even after I realized how much my mother had distorted my view of him. After he died, Pat researched his music at the Library of Congress and found a body of work that numbered hundreds of songs. The library staff, fascinated by the material she uncovered, gathered it together and established the Sammy Timberg Collection. Pat also learned that among animation enthusiasts he was something of a cult figure, the music he had written for the Superman and Betty Boop cartoons, among many others, considered classics of the genre.

None of this would have meant much to him. He never stopped practicing the piano and writing songs, and he wanted nothing less than to be the toast of Broadway, as his brother Herman had been for a time decades earlier. Because that never happened, he thought of himself as a failure. And because he thought that, I did, too.

But what did he fail? Certainly not his kids. He couldn't have loved us more. And he took care of us. We never seemed to have much money, but we always had enough, wherever it came from. And he didn't fail his talent. The work was there, and it kept coming, even if much of it in later years went unpublished. In addition to his music for cartoons and for Herman's shows, he wrote a ballet, a bolero, and a jazz rhapsody that explained the early comparisons to Gershwin. The rhapsody was performed once, by an orchestra he led at the Capitol Theater in New York around 1930, then kept under wraps because he feared he might not have the rights to it because of contractual issues.

He failed only as a salesman, as a marketer of his music. He could promote others, but not himself. Relying on his wife's money and his own music royalties, he wined and dined bigwigs in the music industry, but couldn't close the deal, say to them, I need your help, get this song to Frank. This didn't become clear to me until recently, when I thought of a comparable experience of my own. In November 1986, I was the White House correspondent for the *Baltimore Sun* when the Iran-Contra scandal blew up in Washington. By January, I was having vague thoughts about writing a book that used the scandal as a vehicle to explore the impact of the Vietnam War on the nation. Having never written a book, I had no idea how to set the process in motion. I called my friend Richard Ben Cramer, an old *Sun* colleague who I knew was working on a book of his own.

"Richard, I'm thinking there might be a book in all this stuff," I said. "What do I do?"

Without hesitation, Richard replied, "Call my agent." A moment later, he said, "Never mind, I'll call her for you."

Thus did Flip Brophy enter my life. Since then, she has done for me what my father couldn't do for himself and, truth to tell, I probably couldn't have done for myself: find a publisher, promote my credentials, negotiate contracts. She has freed me to do the only parts in the process for which I am qualified, the reporting and the writing. My father never had a Flip Brophy.

At the time of my father's death, my mother was living alone in an apartment building for senior citizens in Hollywood. She had pretty much stopped drinking, but she had fallen a few times before she did and now needed a walker and often a wheelchair. She told us on the phone she was coming to Scranton for the funeral. That meant getting to LAX, flying to New York, then catching another plane from there to Scranton, where the service was to be held, then back to New York, where he was to be buried near his mother and father. Not to mention getting around all those airports in a wheelchair. My sister Pat and I urged her, in fact ordered her, not to come, resorting to some hurtful declarations in our effort to discourage her. ("Listen, goddammit, it's his funeral, not one of your shows.") No surprise, she came anyway, looked smashing, and charmed everyone, as always the belle of the ball. My father, I'm sure, was happy she was there.

I gave the eulogy. "Anyone who does not understand what a kind, gentle, loving man my father was did not have their ears tuned to the right pitch," I said. My sisters thought I was talking to the children of his second wife, whom we always felt undervalued him. In truth, I was conducting a monologue with myself. As the service ended, the mourners filed out to the sounds of my father's rhapsody. Pat had a tape that he had made for her a few years earlier, just dad on the piano.

My mother died two years later on the Monday before Thanksgiving. She had cheered me on for years as I struggled with my first book, and I had put the finishing touches on it minutes before the doctor in Los Angeles called with the news. She had gone into the hospital over the weekend. It did not seem serious at first, then things changed quickly. I had been planning to fly out later that day to be with her. She was buried from St. Rose of Lima church in Flatbush, her childhood parish, near where her father's blacksmith shop had once stood.

From an early age, my mother flew head-on into circumstances that she never saw coming. If my sisters depended on me for guidance and emotional support, her whole family—widowed mother, six younger siblings—had depended on her, when she was barely more than a child, for the money to buy food and pay the rent. And, while she never yearned for a colorful life, she had lived one, mingling with the great and the near great, moving to the threshold of a stardom she never coveted, then pitching it all aside when she fell in love with my father. There's a cartoon that a friend drew of my parents back in the thirties that says a lot about their relationship. It shows my mother, blond, beautiful, confident, proudly displaying the cast on her leg as she returns by train after a skiing accident at Lake Placid. My father is waiting for her in the station, anxious, biting his nails, the shards flying left and right.

I never let my parents off the hook. I was a dutiful and loving son, but I never gave them the credit they deserved and I withheld from them my approval, which I knew they craved, even though by then I had stumbled enough times myself to understand that sometimes you do things that in your youth you think yourself incapable of. Now, I'm haunted by my refusal to give them the thing they wanted most from me. But I no longer toy with the idea that I was switched at birth. Not a chance. I'm glad I'm their kid.

One day in 1974, Peter Connor opened the door of his home outside Cincinnati to find Larry Kelly standing on his doorstep. Larry had a dog with him. Peter recognized the dog, Jasper, the Manhattan College mascot, a wirehaired terrier who lived with Kelly in a bungalow on campus.

"Hi," said Larry. "Got room for us?"

Larry's coaching job at Manhattan had gone well for several years. The glossy fifty-two-page program that heralded the return of football to the college after a twenty-three-year hiatus included his picture—a youthful, clean-cut, chubby-cheeked Irishman flashing a winning smile—and a gushy full-page article that described him as "just about the winning-est coach of amateur football extant." He quickly became a recognizable figure at the school. He contributed articles to the student newspaper, answered casting calls in the city as a lark, even did some modeling for an ad agency.

What he did not do was take advantage of his presence on the campus to work toward the degree that was all but a requirement for coaching in high school or college. This is a club team, Peter told him, there's lots of enthusiasm now, but the excitement can fade. And you can't count on the team becoming a full-fledged varsity sport anytime soon. Even if it does, there's no guarantee that you'll be the coach. Larry, said Peter, you've got to protect yourself, get a degree.

Larry, riding high, brushed aside Peter's warnings. A few years later, after Peter, newly married, moved to Cincinnati, Larry landed hard, lost the job, drinking at the heart of the trouble that cost him the chance of a lifetime.

Larry and Jasper moved in with Peter, stayed with him, his wife, Bobbi, and infant son, Kevin, for the next six months. A few years later, they took Larry in again, this time for two years. To neutral observers, Larry was down and out. Peter wasn't neutral, and he treated Larry with the deference Larry always seemed to see as his due.

Peter arranged jobs for him, one answering phones at the University of Cincinnati sports ticket office. But Larry was incorrigible, greeting callers with the words "O-and-7 Bearcats." Before the Bearcats could reach O-and-8, Larry was again out of a job.

Throughout the 1970s and '80s, there were occasional Larry sightings, none encouraging. He showed up in Florida, where Chipper Dombo and his wife Kathy were living outside Orlando. Chipper set him up for a time with a mobile hot-dog truck and canteen, but Larry couldn't make it work. Someone recalled seeing him washing dishes at a bar on Long Island. For one six-month period, he stayed with his sister and her husband, also on the Island. One day he put a note on the mirror—"I hate goodbyes. Take care. Love, Larry"—and vanished.

He stopped drinking in 1985 after a circulation problem in his foot was traced to alcohol and he feared amputation if the problem worsened. By the end of the decade he was living by himself in an apartment in Albuquerque, not far from his half sister, Muriel, and her husband, Tom. The whispers at the 1990 reunion proved accurate. He never smoked, a vice he had avoided, but he had throat cancer. On Christmas Day 1994, he hemorrhaged and a small hole was cut in his throat so he could breathe. To talk, he had to cover the hole with a finger.

The 1995 reunion, again at the Elks Hall in Elmhurst, was billed as "A Tribute to Larry Kelly." The physical deterioration, already evident five years earlier, was far more pronounced. He looked gaunt and moved gingerly in his western duds, which included a leather vest, but there was no gray in his hair, his eyes gleamed, and his bearing was so jaunty that it left no room for pity.

Just before the ceremony, Tommy Wall said to me, "You're it. You're the speaker. I need you to talk for at least fifteen minutes."

I don't remember much of what I said, but I do recall how my remarks ended: "During my first summer at Annapolis, Plebe Summer, I often thought about quitting and going home. But when I did, I thought about the Lynvets and what they would think of me. And in the years that followed, tough years at Annapolis, a tougher year in Vietnam, and the dark years that followed my time in Vietnam, when I needed strength, when I needed more than anything else not to feel sorry for myself, I would think of the Lynvets. And as the years passed, the Lynvets crystallized for me into the face of one man. And that man was Larry Kelly."

Larry took the microphone, claiming the spotlight like a seasoned performer. Gesturing with the mike in his right hand, he casually covered the hole in his throat with his left.

"I hope you can understand what I'm saying," he began. "Raise your hand if you can't understand me." No hands went up.

In truth, it was almost impossible to understand him, but his stage presence was so formidable that you knew what he was talking about. He'd mention a name, "Bobby Bushman," and point the mike at him, then twirl and aim it at Peter Connor, or Chipper. He no longer looked like the Larry Kelly I remembered, but there was no doubt that he was the same person who showed up at the Imperial in the midst of that dreadful run in 1959, said "Forget the losses, it's a new season," and made you believe it.

"I'm going to end with a tune that says everything I feel about the people in this room," he said, turning toward the bandstand where the disk jockey had queued a song.

Did you ever know that you're my hero . . .

Till then, "The Wind Beneath My Wings" was near the top of my list of sappiest songs of all time. Since then, I can't listen to it without tearing up.

As the song played, Larry moved back and forth across the floor scanning the crowd, like Ed Sullivan on *The Toast of the Town* searching out celebrities in the audience. His eyes flashed as he recognized someone, and he spoke the name and pointed the mike, as if it were a sword and he was bestowing knighthood.

Then the parade began. Peter was first. He came from stage left, threw his arms around Kelly, and hugged him. Mike Montore was next. "Thank you," said Mike as he embraced him. Larry looked surprised; he and Mike had never been friends, in fact had often clashed. Bob Bushman and Mike D'Amato followed. Everyone was standing and applauding now. Richie Brady climbed from his wheelchair, grasped his walker, and struggled over. Larry met him halfway, took his hand, and kissed him on the cheek.

After a while the applause stopped, but everyone remained

standing, transfixed as Lynvet after Lynvet came forward to embrace Larry, not streaming toward him in a line, but one at a time, out of the crowd, each approach a separate, distinct, and personal tribute. Kenny Rudzewick. Tommy Vaughan. Tommy Wall. Bob Lulley. Mike Faulkner. Bob Ferriola. Joe Aragona. Eddie Keane. Hugh Mulligan. Mike D'Amato. On and on and on. Almost to a man they had been more conventionally successful than Larry once their Lynvet days ended, but in those few minutes they all wanted his eyes to meet theirs, especially those he had coached, so that, like Mike Montore, they could thank him for what he had done for them and once more, or perhaps for the first time, they could feel his approval.

When the parade ended, the applause began again. For a moment Larry just stood there, then he threw up his arms in triumph, as if signaling a touchdown. Days later, flying back to Albuquerque, he wrote to Bob Bushman, "I never knew the boys felt that way about me."

Afterward, Hugh Mulligan said it best:

"If he has a legacy, it's not in the number of wins or the undefeated seasons, it's not that he was necessarily inspirational or brilliant, it's that under his tutelage a bunch of ordinary men rose to excellence and made it a part of their lives."

Larry died the following August. For the next couple of years various Lynvets, among them Tommy Wall and Chipper Dombo, talked about spreading his ashes at Cross Bay Oval. But no one took the lead to ensure that it happened. During this time, Larry's sister, Mary, on Long Island, kept the urn containing his ashes on the console above her TV and, because he loved country music, played Garth Brooks's greatest hits album over and over for him.

Larry's half sister Muriel in New Mexico eventually lost patience with what appeared to be dithering on the part of the Lynvets and told Mary to send the ashes to her. When the postman arrived, Muriel thought, "Here's Larry on my doorstep again."

Muriel had the ashes sealed in a crypt near her home in Rio Rancho, outside Albuquerque. The crypt looks out on a mountain. The urn is black. There is a gold plaque below it. The inscription reads:

LAWRENCE R. KELLY

THE COACH

"It was Rockaway's time," said Eddie Keane.

Four decades after Mike D'Amato's circus catch I was having dinner with Eddie, the co-captain of the 1961 Lynvet team and now an executive with ABC News, at Keen's Chop House just off Herald Square in Manhattan, not far from the statue of George M. Cohan. Both of us had been Marines in Vietnam and had survived the war and its bloody aftermath. Personally and professionally, we had also intersected with the other great issues that had transfixed and transformed America since that long-ago game against Rockaway. The assassinations of the Kennedys and Martin Luther King Jr. Watergate. The Civil Rights movement. The empowerment of women. The Sexual Revolution.

Yet after it all, what Eddie and I felt most poignantly that night was that the world we knew as Lynvets—that shaky state of grace—was gone, replaced by a world that was more than occasionally a mystery to us.

"He's the reason," said Eddie with a laugh. "Mike D'Amato is the reason the world is on its ass. With that catch he went from a Boy Scout to the single most hateful human being in the world."

I grinned and pumped my fist in agreement. By then, Eddie and I were a little drunk and having fun, and we both realized how ridiculous his remark sounded. As we knew, Mike was still a Boy Scout, at least as much as any of us still were.

Acknowledgments

I told Larry Kelly at the Lynvet reunion in 1995 that I was thinking of writing a book about the team and, if I did, I would need his help. At that point, Larry's throat cancer made verbal communication difficult, especially since my desire was to conduct a series of lengthy interviews with him. He was the team's institutional memory, not to mention an iconic figure to my generation of Lynvet players. Because it was hard for him to talk, we began a correspondence in which I posed questions and he replied in writing. His letters, in longhand, were detailed and vivid. Larry died after about five months and perhaps that many letters. We had gotten as far as his teenage years.

Larry's death was a blow to me and to his many other friends. It also stood to torpedo my bookwriting plans. I could not imagine trying to tell the story of the Lynvets without Larry's participation. At the same time, Larry's letters, and the effort I knew it took him to compose them, made my desire to write the book more compelling. I decided to do it anyhow. My old Lynvet teammates and coaches had come through for me before and I felt confident that they would do so again.

Many of them were still in the greater New York area, so in the summer of 1998, I took a leave of absence from my editing job at the *Baltimore Sun* Washington Bureau and moved to an apartment in the Bayside section of Queens. Over the course of the next year and a half I interviewed scores of old Lynvets, those I had played with and those I knew mostly by reputation. I also traveled to different parts of the country to speak to Lynvets no longer in the New York area.

I had a wonderful time. More to the point, I received the help that I needed, not just from Lynvets but from old rivals as well. Even from an unforgettable woman I will always think of as "the redoubtable Mrs. Wickers."

Every Lynvet I was able to find offered to help. As it turned out, I couldn't get to all of them. It's my loss. I'm sure this book would have profited from their recollections. I interviewed most of those on the list that follows at least once, in some instances numerous times. In some cases, the person mentioned provided kindnesses along the way. Barbara Bushman, Bob Bushman's wife, for example, found the Bayside apartment that spared me the daunting task of apartment hunting in New York. I know that some of those who took time to talk to me, mostly members of the great early Lynvet teams, may feel some disappointment because their part of the Lynvet story is not fully chronicled in this book. For that I apologize. The fact is, I could not have portrayed that time and place without the benefit of their reminiscences.

My thanks to the following members of the far-flung Lynvet family: Joe Aragona, Bob Bushman, Barbara Bushman, Peter Connor, Bobbi Connor, Robert (Chipper) Dombo, Kathy Dombo, Art Donelan, Richie Engert, Edie (Mueller) Engert, Mike Faulkner, Marti Faulkner, Bob Ferriola, Lee Ann Ferriola, Danny Gersbeck, Tom Giralomo, Kevin Glynn, Ronnie Grier, Eddie Keane, Lyn (Wheeler) Kutzelman, Bob Lulley, Tommy Marshall, Tom McCabe, Margie (Mueller) McCabe, Hank McCann, Frank Masella, Jackie Meyer, Mike Montore, Judi Montore, Kenny Mueller, Hugh Mulligan, Marlene Mulligan, Dick Petrarca, Tony Petrilli, Ken Rudzewick, John Schmauser, Bob Schmitt, Pat Schmitt, Al Schneeberg, Richie Schrage, George Sheeky, Larry Sifert, Jim Sims, Teddy Spiess, Eddie Steffens, Herb Tortolani, Tommy Vaughan, Tommy Wall, Kathleen Wall, and Bob Williams.

Larry Kelly's sister, Mary Michael, provided insights into Larry and his early years available nowhere else. Larry's half sister, Muriel Mahoney, and her husband, Tom, graciously took my son Craig to see the crypt in New Mexico where Larry's ashes reside. Bob Bushman, incredibly, had a copy of the letter he had written to me in the summer of 1960 that explained, in the kindest possible way, what a dork I had become.

My thanks as well to these old and worthy rivals: Torchy Smith (Garity Knights), Jimm Gantz (Garity Knights), Roger Smith (Garity Knights), John Hourican (Rockaway Knights), Richie Knott (Rockaway Knights), Clare Knott (Rockaway Knights), Don Moran (Rockaway Knights), Mike D'Amato (Baisley Park Bombers, Rockaway Knights), Woodie Wickers (Baisley Park Bombers, Rockaway Knights), Helen Wickers (Baisley Park Bombers, Rockaway Knights). Nick Mitsakos, a longtime official in the Brooklyn-Queens Pop Warner conference, also was helpful.

Daryl Plevy read and edited many drafts of this book. The chief of mental health in Montgomery County, Maryland, she helped an old reporter reclaim his youthful faith in public officials. And I'm always happy when she's around.

Some special people read drafts of the manuscript and offered invaluable criticism. Others cheered me on. Some made my life happier as I struggled with this book. Falling into one or all categories are Ernest B. (Pat) Furgurson, Minor Carter; Simon Avara; my sisters, Pat and Rosemarie; and the spouses of my three older children, Sara Scribner, Ruey Timberg, and Matt Horine. And, of course, my wonderful grandchildren, Cecilia and Andrew, the children of my son Craig and his wife, Ruey.

My boss at the *Baltimore Sun,* Washington Bureau Chief Paul West, generously agreed to my taking an eighteen-month leave of absence and has been supportive in every way even though my departure left the bureau shorthanded for much of that period. Fred Monyak, the bureau's news editor, so capably shouldered a daily burden that we normally share that I think Paul often forgot I was gone. The *Sun* had two editors during the time I was most intensively involved in reporting and writing this book. Their endorsement of my efforts was crucial and unstinting. My thanks to John Carroll, currently editor of the *Los Angeles Times,* and Bill Marimow, now managing editor for national news at National Public Radio.

Thanks to David Rosenthal, Executive Vice President and Publisher, for his confidence in me, and to Martha Levin, Executive Vice President and Publisher, for her direction and encouragement. I want to thank my editor at Free Press, Dominick Anfuso, for his guidance and for pointing me in the right direction when I strayed off course. Also, his assistant, Wylie O'Sullivan, who was there for me for so many things in the final months of this project. Jennifer Weidman, of the Simon & Schuster Free Press legal department, not only snake-checked the manuscript but offered some most welcome writing suggestions. Phil Metcalf and Janet Renard provided careful copy editing. And Eric Fuentecilla designed a fabulous cover.

When I was going through it, I doubted I would ever forget anything, good or bad, about Plebe Year. Now, as the great Class of 1964 prepares for its fortieth reunion this fall, much about those long-ago days has become blurred. But not the friendships, not the sense that these were men you could always count on, like the Lynvets. Special thanks to my Seventh Company classmates for helping me recall the craziness of Plebe Year. And thanks to Bernie Maguire, our class president, for providing information on classmates who hold a special place in our pantheon of heroes. Gary LaValley, the Naval Academy archivist, unearthed the film *Ring of Valor,* for which I'm most grateful.

Thanks to Jane Benson Timberg and Dr. Lynn Ketchum, without whom this book would never have been written.

My agent, Flip Brophy, became president of her company, Sterling Lord Literistic, during the course of my writing this book, but she still managed to read every draft, respond to every panicked phone call, and do all the things I needed her to do. Her able assistant, Cia Glover, cheerfully took care of many tasks for me as well.

My great friend Kelley Andrews is a fine writer and editor whose taste and judgment are impeccable. Her skills were invaluable to me. So was her willingness to give generously of her time when I fell into one of my book-related all-is-lost desponds. I can't thank her enough.

Mary Drake transcribed many of my interviews with speed and accuracy.

I found a special place when I was in Bayside, an Irish pub called Monahan and Fitzgerald, the preserve of John Monahan and Jim Fitzgerald. I spent many evenings at Monahan's, eating, drinking, and discovering the allure of a good neighborhood bar. The food was great, the beer was cold, and the company was incomparable. To all my friends, thanks for taking in an outsider and making him feel at home. Special thanks to Danny DeVoe, my choice for the best bartender in New York, and his youthful sidekick, Jeff Rhinehart.

I tried hard to get names right. I may have failed. John Hourican, aka John Hurricane, was only part of the problem. To this day, everyone remembers Peter Connor as Peter Connors. Tommy Vaughan was always Tommy Vaughn in newspaper sto-ries. In one of my best games, I was Art Timberg in the *Long Island Daily Press.*

This is an attempt to rectify an omission in the acknowledgments section of my first book, *The Nightingale's Song.* Jim Silberman, then a senior editor at Simon & Schuster, bought the book and, over the next two years, guided and encouraged me. He then moved to another publishing house and turned me over to Dominick An-fuso. So a much belated thank you to Jim.

I had an advantage in writing this book. Two of my sons, Scott and Craig, are professional journalists. My daughter, Amanda, edited her high school magazine for four years, though she has since gotten an honest job. My youngest child, Sam, a sophomore in college, is an outdoors kid, but he knows what he likes in books. All four helped me out. Amanda, against the recommendations of her older brothers, urged me not to kill a character out of the book. I took her advice and I'm glad I did. Sam, at a time when I was worried about a long scene that Scott and Craig were lukewarm about, said, "Don't even think of cutting that out." I didn't.

Scott, a feature writer for the *Los Angeles Times,* was a sharp, incisive critic. He offered ideas, pinpointed weaknesses, and urged on me cuts that saved me, I hope, from self-indulgence. He also helped me see the larger context in which this book needed to be set.

Craig, for a variety of reasons, was the most important contributor to this book. An important reason was that he was nearby. For virtually the entire time I was working on it he was covering politics for the *Baltimore Sun,* or politics and govern-ment in Virginia and the District of Columbia for the *Washington Post.* He was my confidant, my editor, my friend, and my most unsparing critic. Though under heavy daily deadline pressures himself, he was always available to read a chapter or a draft or meet me for coffee in the afternoon to help me puzzle through some book-related issue.

After two years of labor, most of it in Bayside, he told me the book wasn't work-ing. At that point I was keeping myself on the sidelines, an interested narrator of the tale, but not a character in it. Why did you want to write this book? he asked. I told him that I believed the team represented something important in America's past and that my own experience with the Lynvets had meant a great deal to me at a difficult time in my life. He drew me out on the second part, then said, that's what's missing; you need to tell your story, too. So, for better or worse, I did.

A couple of years after that, I gave him a draft to read. I thought I was finished and felt confident he would agree. What do you think? I asked. "I think there's a great book in here struggling to get out," he said. I wanted to murder him.

Sadly for me, Craig and his family are now in South Africa, where he is the *Post*'s Johannesburg bureau chief. He says he took the assignment because he's al-ways wanted to be a foreign correspondent and that southern Africa fascinated him. I think he just couldn't bear to endure any more hastily called afternoon coffee breaks at which I would agonize over still another element of the book.

A number of books were helpful to me, beginning with *Father Cyclone,* by Daisy Amoury. *The U.S. Naval Academy: An Illustrated History,* by Jack Sweetman, was a valuable resource. So was Richard A. Lupoff's *The Great American Paperback: An Il-lustrated Tribute to Legends of the Book,* where I found some favorite old paperback covers and had great fun along the way. Thanks to the Web, I secured a copy of *Ask for Linda.* The cover was the same as I remember it, maybe better. But the book itself, by Fan Nichols, was not wildly sexy. In fact, it was a good book, hard-boiled, gritty, well-written—not porn, but noire, an unacknowledged gem of the genre.

I know I've forgotten more than one person who helped me and I apologize for the oversight.

My favorite encounter during this process was my interview with Helen Wickers, mother of Lynvet tormentor Woodie Wickers. Somehow Mrs. Wickers, whom I had never met and never seen up close except for once on the football field, found out about this project when it was in its early stages and wrote me a long, detailed letter about sandlot football in Brooklyn and Queens and what it had meant to her family and her. I wrote back and one morning went to see her at her home on Long Island.

I got there about ten. We spent the better part of three hours together in her kitchen. She was fun, fiery, and had a colorful memory. She was also sweet and charming, as nice a person as I've ever met.

When we finished, she walked me to the door. I kissed her on the cheek and said, "Thank you, Mrs. Wickers." She said, with a lovely smile, "Please call me Helen." I said, also with a smile, "I don't think so, Mrs. Wickers." So she hit me with her handbag. No, I made up the last part.

Robert Timberg
June 2004

About the Author

Robert Timberg has been a newspaper reporter and editor for more than three decades. From 1973 to 1981, he worked for the *Baltimore Evening Sun*. In 1981, he joined the Washington bureau of the morning *Baltimore Sun*. From 1983 to 1988 he was the *Sun's* White House correspondent, covering the presidency of Ronald Reagan. He is currently deputy chief of the *Sun's* Washington bureau.

Timberg's first book, *The Nightingale's Song*, published in 1995 by Simon & Schuster, chronicled the lives of five well-known Naval Academy graduates to explore the impact of the Vietnam War on the nation. It was selected by *Time* magazine as one of the five best nonfiction books of the year and by the *New York Times* as one of the year's "notable" books. In 2000, Timberg's *John McCain: An American Odyssey,* was published by Touchstone, a Simon & Schuster imprint.

Timberg graduated from the U.S. Naval Academy in 1964 and was commissioned a second lieutenant in the Marine Corps. He holds a master's degree in journalism from Stanford. He was a Nieman Fellow at Harvard and a Fellow at the Woodrow Wilson International Center for Scholars in Washington, D.C. He lives in Bethesda, Maryland.

52721024R00167

Made in the USA
Columbia, SC
06 March 2019